North·South Center
UNIVERSITY OF MIAMI

The Reconstruction of Central America: The Role of the European Community

Joaquín Roy
Editor

AF738115

Iberian Studies Institute
European Community Research Institute

THE IBERIAN STUDIES/EUROPEAN COMMUNITY RESEARCH INSTITUTE is a scholarly unit dedicated to the study of the contemporary structure of Spain, with special emphasis on foreign relations, and to carry out research on the European Community, with special attention given to its relations with the Americas. The Institute is supported by grants from different branches of the Spanish Government through the Spain'92 Foundation and by the Commission of the European Community. Among the past and current activities and projects are the 'Letras de Oro' literary prizes, the journal *Ideas'92*, monographs, occasional papers, and informative newsletters (*InfoSpain* and *Euroforum*) series of lectures and guest speakers.

Joaquín Roy
Director
Iberian Studies Institute

THE NORTH-SOUTH CENTER promotes, through cultural and technical exchange, better relations among the United States, Canada, and the nations of Latin America and the Caribbean. The Center provides a disciplined, intellectual focus for improved relations, commerce, and understanding between North America and Latin America. The Center conducts programs of education, training, cooperative study, public outreach, and research and engages in an active program of publication and dissemination of information on the Americas. The North-South Center fosters linkages among academic and research institutions throughout the Americas and acts as an agent of change in the region.

Ambler H. Moss, Jr.
Director
North-South Center

© Copyright 1992 by the University of Miami Published by the University of Miami North-South Center. All rights reserved. No portion of the contents may be reproduced in any form without the written permission of the publisher.

ISBN-0-935501-46-0

THE RECONSTRUCTION OF CENTRAL AMERICA: THE ROLE OF THE EUROPEAN COMMUNITY

Joaquín Roy,
editor

Iberian Studies Institute and
European Community Research Institute
North-South Center
Graduate School of International Studies
University of Miami

Sponsored by the Commission of the European Communities

THE RECONSTRUCTION OF CENTRAL AMERICA: THE ROLE OF THE EUROPEAN COMMUNITY

Gabriel Aguilera Peralta
John A. Booth
Victor Bulmer-Thomas
Fernando Cardesa
Ford Cooper
Ricardo Córdova Macías
Rafael de Juan y Peñalosa
Cristina Eguizábal
JoAnn Fagot Aviel
Mark Falcoff
Albert Galinsoga Jordà
Roy H. Ginsberg
Wolf Grabendorff
René Herrera Zúñiga
Renato Iturriaga
Pierre-Henri Laurent
Abel Matutes
Rafael Menjívar Larín
James H. Michel
Guillermo Molina Chocano
Ambler H. Moss, Jr.
Mark B. Rosenberg
Joaquín Roy
Mitchell A. Seligson
Angel Viñas
Marko Voljc
Laurence Whitehead

Iberian Studies Institute
European Community Research Institute
North-South Center
Graduate School of International Studies
University of Miami

Sponsored by
The Commission of the European Communities

Introduction:

Abel Matutes
Latin America and the European Community 15

Joaquín Roy
Europe and Latin America: The Role of the European Community in the Reconstruction of Central America 23

Chapter I

An Overview of the European Community's Foreign Relations and Cooperation with Central America

Roy H. Ginsberg
Foreign Policy Actions of the European Community, 1986-1990: The Politics of Scale 45

Angel Viñas
The Role of Central America in the European Community's Foreign Policy 77

Fernando Cardesa
European Community's Regional Programs toward Central America 87

Wolf Grabendorff
The European Parliament and the Central American Parliament: The Parliamentary Dimension of the Relations between Central America and the European Community 95

Rafael Menjívar Larín
European Community-Central American Economic Relations: Possible Effects of the Single European Market 107

Chapter II

Evaluation of EC's Cooperation with Central America

Rafael de Juan y Peñalosa
Lessons from a Short History; Inferences from an Original Cooperation 125

Laurence Whitehead
The Identity of the New Europe and the San José Process 139

Pierre-Henri Laurent
To the Backburner: The European Community-Central American Relationship 155

Albert Galinsoga Jordà
The Central American Policy of the EC: Balance and Perspectives (A Spanish View) 166

Chapter III

Economic and Political Situation of Central America

Mitchell A. Seligson and Ricardo Córdova Macías
Integration and Disintegration of Regionalism in Central America: From 1950 to 1991 189

Gabriel Aguilera Peralta
The Post-Crisis Political Agenda: Central America Faces the 1990 Decade 213

Guillermo Molina Chocano
The Economic and Political Situation of Central America in the Present International Situation 227

René Herrera Zúñiga
Political Transition and Economic Recovery in Central America 239

Victor Bulmer-Thomas
Stabilization and Adjustment Programs in Central America–Why Are They Proving So Difficult? 253

Chapter IV

Interests of Other Actors in Central America

Cristina Eguizábal
The European Political Parties and the Reconstruction of Central America 269

JoAnn Fagot Aviel
The Role of Spain in the Pacification Process of Central America 289

Mark B. Rosenberg
The Changing Latin American Trade Environment: Opportunities and Challenges for Central America 305

John A. Booth
Toward Reconciliation and Democracy in Central America: Possible Roles for External Assistance 331

Mark Falcoff
Rethinking Spheres of Influence: The United States, Western Europe, and Central America 353

Ambler H. Moss, Jr.
United States Strategy After the Cold War: Central American Policy 365

James H. Michel
Democracy and Development in Central America: Opportunities for United States/ European Community Cooperation 381

Ford Cooper
Current Status and Issues 389

Renato Iturriaga
Mexican-Central American Cooperation Model 393

Marko Voljc
The World Bank's Role in Central America's Reconstruction and Recovery 399

Editor's Preface

The present volume includes the papers presented at a conference on the role of the European Community and other actors in the current political and economic process of Central America. The meeting took place at the Graduate School of International Studies of the University of Miami on March 14-15, 1991, under the sponsorship of the Commission of the European Commission. Dean Ambler H. Moss, Jr., opened the sessions and University of Miami President Edward T. Foote II addressed the participants during part of the debates. EC Commissioner Abel Matutes (who was presented a key of the City of Coral Gables by Vice-Mayor Robert Hildreth) delivered a keynote address at a dinner organized by the Spain-U.S. Chamber of Commerce in Florida (represented by its President Fernando Rodríguez Vila) and the University of Miami (represented by the President of the Board of Trustees R. Ray Goode). The EC Consular Corps in Miami participated in the event.

Besides the written presentations included in these proceedings, International Monetary Fund representative Joaquín Ferran and Inter-American Bank officer Joel Riley made oral presentations. Sessions were graciously and effectively chaired and moderated by University of Miami professors Bruce Bagley, Enrique Baloyra, Francisco García Amador, Robert Kirsner, Alexander McIntire, and Jaime Suchlicki, as well as Leon Hurwitz, Secretary-Treasurer of the European Community Studies Association.

I am especially grateful for the service rendered by the staff of the Iberian Studies Institute and the European Community Research Institute under the supervision of Maggie Hernández (Administrative Coordinator); Kathy Jones provided editing and managerial expertise in the early stages of the project; Susan Lacey edited and translated in the second stage, while Alberto Egea, Sylvia Lima, Mark A. Ludwig, and Heber Vellon contributed to the translation and late editing process. Alejandrino Jiménez provided research, translation, and supervision throughout the entire operation. David Mathis, Kathleen Hamman and Mary Mapes contributed to the final revision.

We would like to express our gratitude for the encouragement of Juan Prat, Director General of the European Commission DG-I and North-South Relations, and Angel Viñas, Director of the Latin American Area of the European Commission (without whose vision this project would have been impossible), and the financial and administrative guidance provided by Carmen Ortiz.

The content and spirit of the conference topic and the papers presented are an explicit vote of confidence in favor of the integration and development of Central America. During the final editing process of this volume the El Salvador Peace Treaty was signed in January 1992. Those members of the Commission of the European Community and its staff who supported this study, together with the European, U.S. and Latin American participants, have every reason to feel satisfied with this outcome.

Joaquín Roy
Editor

INTRODUCTION

LATIN AMERICA AND THE EUROPEAN COMMUNITY[1]

Abel Matutes

Commission of the European Communities

It is a great pleasure for me to join you at this dinner arranged by the University of Miami, the European Community, the Latin American Chambers of Commerce, and the consular representatives of the member states of the European Community.

I am always happy to come to Miami, a city bursting with energy, with a great future, and combining the best of U.S. daring and initiative with a warm Latin American welcome. It seems to me, as a European observer, that Miami has become the most important gateway between the powerful northern hemisphere and a vibrant Latin America, deep in the throes of change.

I think, therefore, that this is an ideal opportunity to share some thoughts with you, North American and Latin American businessmen, academics and researchers, about the current situation in Latin America, the general environment in which we move, the European Community's policy towards that continent and the European Community's attitude vis-à-vis new Latin American initiatives of the United States.

The Current Situation in Latin America

Latin America, a heterogeneous continent with more than 150 years of political independence and a wide ex-

[1]Keynote address at a dinner organized by the Spain-U.S. Chamber of Commerce in Florida in cooperation with the University of Miami, March 14, 1991.

perience in institutional, political, and economic development behind it, is going through a period of transformation. I would say that Latin America is on the very brink of a major challenge, its reactions to which will shape its role in the fast-approaching world of the twenty-first century. We must support the positive aspects that emerge from this great transformation. We must minimize the adverse aspects. What are the positive aspects? This evening I would like to mention three that I believe to be fundamental.

First, I would like to underline the enormous importance of the current process of democratization taking place throughout the continent. For the first time in history, all the Latin American governments, with one notable exception, have taken office as a result of democratic and free elections, in many cases bringing about a complete changeover in political power. The democratic model, closely bound up with the Latin American political process since independence but frequently obliterated by authoritarian, dictatorial, populist, or military systems, has now, more than ever, come into its own.

Second, I would like to say that although Latin America has gone through a bad ten years in economic terms, it has more behind it than just a "wasted decade," as it is so often termed. In these last few years, Latin America has learned many lessons which are vital if it is going to establish a better future. It has learned that the development strategies followed in the past are not the right way to achieve growth in what is now a totally different environment; it has learned to mistrust miracle, populist solutions, which do not attack the root of the problem; it has learned that it is only by pursuing rational economic policies that it will be able to ensure a stable future for forthcoming generations and, in a word, it has learned that economic success essentially depends on one's own efforts.

Third, I would like to stress the fact that Latin America now realizes that the development process gives rise to changes that can ease the way for economic, political, and social modernization. However this depends, in the last analysis, on what the collective response is to such changes. The organization, industrialization, communications, and literacy processes, for example, alter the social structure and the expectations of business and political circles. And in those countries where social and economic development has coincided with a greater opening-up, a greater permeability and fuller grassroots involvement, the results have been better and longerlasting.

I said too that the current changes in Latin America also have their adverse aspects. I would like to describe briefly the two that I consider most significant.

First, I must underline the unfortunate fact that the establishment of democracy and a more mature economic and political approach to the continent's problems have coincided with the most serious Latin American economic recession since the great depression. This means basically that the drop in economic and social standards casts doubts on the powers of endurance of democratic systems.

Second, I would like to mention the possibility that economically rational policies of modernization and change might once again be replaced by authoritarian solutions, or solutions that mask the need to keep one's own energies in play, by promising to transfer the harsh impact of adjustment. In this sense I think that the excellent ECLA report on changing production patterns with social equity is entirely correct in its approach.

In short, Latin America is on the brink of a major challenge. On the one hand, there are the short- and medium-term risks involved in following a stringent macroeconomic strategy aimed at cutting inflation, maintaining realistic exchange rates, sustaining financial discipline, keeping the growth in consumption below the increase in GDP, raising public investment to a level above that of current public expenditure, encouraging foreign investment and the return of capital that had been taken out of the country, and paving the way for Latin American production to be efficiently inserted into the international economy.

On the other hand, there are the apparent advantages to be gained from modifying the harsh economic reform policies followed in recent years and opting for a less stringent financial and macroeconomic approach in order to avoid, in the short-term, undesirable social consequences.

In my opinion, which is backed up by a whole series of prospective studies, the choice is clear: despite all the short- and medium-term risks, the only realistic, sound and promising option is the first one. Continued economic reform is essential, but it is not enough in itself. The international climate and the policies of the industrialized countries can push Latin America one way or the other in its response to the challenge now facing it. The high level of external debt is not an exclusively Latin American problem, and the fact that the continent has become a net exporter of capital has a lot to do with the situation of the international market.

The General Environment

In recent years there have been various highly significant developments that have affected the general environment in which Latin America operates. I shall cover just the three most important ones.

First, in Eastern Europe we have witnessed the final collapse of the alternative model to the democratic market economy system. There is now no other possible approach. Centrally planned economies in which scarce resources are managed on an authoritarian basis have failed the test of history—the ultimate test! I think that for Latin America this brings discredit on the far-fetched activities of Castro-Communism or the Sandinista movement, not to mention the terrorist, paleo-Communist approach of, for example, the Shining Path.

Second, the international climate has become more complex and unmanageable. The Cold War is over. The Warsaw Pact is disappearing and the East-West confrontation has been won by the West. But a period of enforced stability has been replaced by a period of instability in which regional and local crises can snowball and sometimes lead to major conflicts of the sort that we have seen in the Persian Gulf. The multipolarity of economic power is one factor—it inevitably results in a greater diversity of political interests. The handling of international politics and the international economy has become more complicated, and new actors, such as the European Community or new regional groupings, which want their share of the limelight, have appeared on the stage. This opens up new opportunities for Latin America, but it also generates new uncertainties.

Third, the process leading to a more global and international economy has gathered pace. The scientific and technological revolution not only increases our knowledge but also its applications in ever-shorter periods of time. The danger is that the East-West divide of the past—military, ideological, political, and social—may be replaced by a North-South divide of an essentially economic nature.

We, the industrialized countries, have a clear duty to keep control over the developments described above, not only for our own goal but also as part of our overall responsibilities. Latin America, a relatively advanced continent in international terms, is highly sensitive to such developments.

The Role of the European Community

The European Community, the main center of international trade, is on an unstoppable course toward the Single Market of the 1990s and in the midst of intense institutional discussions that will lead to economic and monetary union and a new structure of political coordination while it has diversified its international policies greatly in the last few years.

The European Community has put its faith in economic reform in the countries of Eastern Europe and in the Soviet Union itself. The Community is putting its faith in the eventual stability of the Middle East, that incredibly unstable region of the globe. The European Community is also putting its faith in Latin America.

Ever since I assumed responsibility for North-South relations in the European Commission, which involves not only North-South relations in general but also relations with Latin America, Asia, and the Mediterranean, I have tried to strengthen the European Community's economic and political role in all these areas. In doing so I have so far encountered no inconsistencies because throughout I have pursued a basic idea—the European Community cannot cut itself off from the South because if we, the North, were to do so, we would jeopardize our own future, something that we cannot afford to do.

In this respect, we have made considerable progress in recent years. In the specific case of Latin America the Community has structured its political and economic dialogue with the whole region; it has revised its cooperation policy, and it has stepped up its operational presence in the entire continent. Until a few years ago Latin America was virtually nonexistent in terms of the Community's external relations except as a passive recipient of generalized trade preferences and some modest development aid. Latin America is now a strong partner of the Community, and it has considerably stepped up its activities and presence vis-à-vis the Community.

For some time now our ministers have been meeting their Central American counterparts on a regular basis. From this year they will also be meeting the Rio Group ministers. We have completed (or shall be doing so this year) our network of cooperation agreements with all the Latin American countries except Cuba. We have renewed and revamped the longest-standing agreements. The agreement recently negotiated with Mexico is the most advanced that we have with any nonassociated country, either in Latin America or Asia.

The Dominican Republic and Haiti have acceded to the Lomé Convention, joining the network of preferential relations between the Community and the Caribbean. In Central America we have broken new ground in our approach to development cooperation. We have shifted our approach from managing projects with a microeconomic impact to projects of a clearly macroeconomic nature. And when no one else spoke out in favor of regional integration, the European Community consistently backed Central America as an economic area capable of being integrated.

The result of all this is that the European Community, which played no part in Latin America in the 1960s and 1970s, now has a definite policy for tackling the Latin American challenges of the 1990s. This policy is based on the institutional strengthening of mutual links, the improvement and expansion of cooperation activities, and the maintenance of high-level, formally enshrined political dialogue.

United States, Europe, and Latin America

Of course the European Community is not alone in revising its policy towards Latin America. This great country, the United States, is also doing so and sometimes to a spectacular degree. Within the limits of our real abilities to manage and promote individual interests there lies the fundamental question of the possible compatibility between the Community's innovative policy towards Latin America and that followed by the United States as part of Mr. Bush's initiative.

Allow me to explain, first and foremost, that the European Community does not see its role in Latin America as being the same as that of the individual member states or for that matter of the United States. The European Community is a new, young entity in the world arena whose outside influence owes as much to the action of our member states as to the multiple effect derived from the exercise of shared sovereignty in crucial areas of international relations, whether economic or political. By contrast, the United States has behind it a century of close relations with Latin America, relations that are far closer with Central America and the Caribbean than with the South American countries. It is a century in which interaction and conflict, attraction and rejection, hegemony and abandonment have combined. It is also a century that has witnessed the erosion of Europe's position in the continent, and this position was only re-established (less strongly than in the nineteenth century) during the 1970s.

Despite this, the United States and the European Community share strategic objectives in Latin America: both are interested in bolstering the process of democratization, both are interested in preventing anti-democratic responses to the crisis, both are interested in supporting policies of economic modernization and opening-up, both are interested in helping the Latin American economy to become more closely integrated into the international economy.

In fact in the last few years a certain similarity has emerged in both sides' objectives for Latin America. What separates us is our scope for action, the divergence of our starting positions, and our very different relative weight in the Latin American economic and political make-up. With regard to scope for action, for example, the Community as such does not yet have the instruments with which to respond to the major Latin American problem of excessive external debt. Our member states have taken measures both bilaterally and in the multilateral financing bodies, but none of this has involved the application of Community rules and discipline. The move towards economic and monetary union, however, is bound to enhance the scope for action.

The Community has a highly sophisticated common external trade policy, which is the nerve center of European integration. It cannot, however, gear this to Latin America except via the multilateral negotiations in the GATT. We are therefore examining Mr. Bush's initiative with interest, but we are not seeking to imitate it, and we trust that it will take due account of the United States international obligations and those of our Latin American partners.

EUROPE AND LATIN AMERICA: THE ROLE OF THE EUROPEAN COMMUNITY IN THE RECONSTRUCTION OF CENTRAL AMERICA[1]

Joaquín Roy

University of Miami

A Very Special Year

Nineteen ninety-two appears destined to mark numerous unprecedented historic opportunities. What barely a decade ago was simply a year commemorating yet another Hispanic anniversary (frequently without economic or political content) was suddenly converted into a year of magical dimensions when the European Community decided in 1987 to set the last day of 1992 as the end of a stage in the slow process of economic integration. It was implied at

---

[1]Introduction to the presentations and debates of the international conference organized by the Institute of Iberian Studies of the Graduate School of International Studies at the University of Miami sponsored by the European Commission, March 14-15, 1991. In addition to the participants, whose compensation will never equal their efforts, I would like to thank Juan José Santos, cultural attaché at the Spanish Embassy in Brussels, for his invitation to enjoyable meetings in Brugge and at the headquarters of the Commission of the European Community, the vision of Angel Viñas on this theme, and the systematic labors of Ambler H. Moss, Jr., dean of the Graduate School of International Studies, and Associate Dean Enrique Baloyra for providing the proper atmosphere for developing undertakings such as this one. From a distance I remember the teachings of Manuel Díez de Velasco and Manuel Jiménez de Parga on international topics during their classes at the Law School at the University of Barcelona. I am also especially grateful to Alejandrino Jiménez, Kathy Jones, Susan J. Lacey, Mark Ludwig, Eduardo Soren Triff, and Heber Vellon for translating and/or editing the conference documents.

the same time that the clock would not stop with the commercial dimension but would move to a second and more definitive era of political integration which, in turn, could lead to federation or confederation before the year 2000 (another number full of symbolism, this time positive in contrast to the bad omen associated with the year 1000). This process would also require a change from the classical name, "European Community," to "European Union."

Although in the mid-1980s some of the signs of change in the Soviet Union and Central and Eastern Europe were only barely perceptible, in 1989 they reached revolutionary proportions. The European Community, having gone through the phases of "eurosclerosis" and "europessimism," pushed by "europhoria," and recovering from the indigestion caused by German unification and the start of the Persian Gulf crisis, was contemplating how its external borders had ceased to coincide exactly with Europe's natural geographical demarcations of mountain ridges, lakes, rivers, and seas. The European Community was forced to heed the call of destiny to become one of the protagonists in the new post-Cold War world order. Paradoxically, Europe could no longer be the limited theatre of operations for the new actors in the unfolding international drama.

For this reason, the Community's institutions (Parliament, Commission, and Council of Ministers, in addition to the different agencies of each of the member states) reshaped their programs in different parts of the world where the presence of the Community was expected to increase (Eastern Europe), be consolidated (Arab countries, sub-Saharan Africa, Asia-Pacific rim) or be substantially redesigned (Latin America and the Caribbean).

Two principal objectives were urgently set forth. The first was to correct the serious developmental deficiencies in the most destitute areas of the globe (sources of instability leading to conflicts with potential international repercussions). This mission was encouraged both by a certain guilt complex generated by sudden prosperity and as an exculpatory act for domestic racism. All of these sentiments showed obvious Christian Democratic roots, a mix of Protestantism, vestiges of traditional charity from Catholic agencies, and the social justice policies prescribed by Social Democratic organizations. The second objective was solidifying the relationship between Europe and the Americas, a region that had been colonized by Europeans since 1492.

These objectives represent some of the motives of Community leaders for their concerted action in the reconstruction and pacification of Central America. This process will allow economic and social development and, subsequently, the consolidation of a democratic basis necessary for future coexistence. In this sense the European Community has inherited the missions of individual countries of promoting development of democratic habits, such as the work by the foundations affiliated with the Federal Republic of Germany's two major political parties or coalitions. These entities had (and still have) a significant impact on the development of political and labor organizations in different Latin American countries.[2] Another form of joint cooperation is the conversion of Spain's modest cultural, social, and economic programs once its political transition period had matured.[3]

Two Unequal and Distant Regions

The relationship between the European Community and Central America,[4] which at the least has to be con-

[2]For a critical view, see paper by Eguizábal.

[3]Viñas, "La comunidad europea," *Información Comercial Española*; however, Galinsoga has a different view in his paper.

[4]While the expression European Community represents a supranational alliance formed by the 12 actual members, the entity called Central America, in international forums, often does not coincide with the geographical boundaries of the isthmus: Panama is considered separately

sidered atypical and asymmetric, is dominated by the international cooperation models concerning aid from the industrialized world to the less developed countries. The difficulty in comparing these two entities is not only due to their different political structures.

The European Community has had problems with self-definition and outside perception from the beginning. By restrictive analysis it was intended to be limited to a purely intergovernmental organization (along the lines of the Arab League or the Organization of American States). Its founding treaties were the standard for external development pointing to a supranational entity (an unprecedented category in International Law now put into practice), with the ensuing independence of the sovereign member states that have several of the governing entities, as is the case of the Commission and the Parliament after its election by universal suffrage.[5] From its beginnings, the Community has provoked confusion and debate among specialists in International Law who attempt to fit it into the exact structures of federalism, functionalism, or neofunctionalism. Nevertheless, it has been seen, especially in Latin America, as an international organization somewhere between a cooperation agency and a federation of strong states that is situated, specifically in our study, before a group of five Central American countries, underdeveloped but politically sovereign with a tradition of limited cooperation. Hence the tone of the EC's discourse in praise of integration. While the member states of the European Community have enjoyed an impeccable democratic status since its found-

---

(for a combination of reasons, both historical and political), and Belize is excluded because of its British heritage and because it has not been subject to the dictatorial regimes nor to the bloody confrontations of most of the other Central American countries.

[5]See the statements of Juan Prat in "Supranacionalidad y nacionalismos en la integración europea," *Le Monde Diplomatique*, Latin American special edition (May 1990): xii; and speech by Abel Matutes in the introduction of this volume.

ing—or since the special accession of Spain, Portugal, and Greece—most Central American states have frequently been governed by regimes not up to the standards of representative democracy. In addition, contrasts have been made of the economic conditions in both regions, which also demonstrates differences in social status. The European Community of the 1990s has a disproportionate internal product and per capita income with that of the Central American countries. Beyond the differences in political structure, these two regions differ in the peculiar projected "federal" system of the Community as opposed to the traditional state sovereignty found in the isthmus.[6]

As an additional concern, Europe's historical legacy does not appear at first glance to be a viable model for Latin American countries. Continental wars, continuing conflicts among neighbors (Germany and France were at war three times in one century), civil strife, the elimination of historical nationalities absorbed by unified states, and the repression of religious and political minorities cannot be positive ingredients for an entity that can easily be emulated. In the second place, the precedents for European integration include (along with the theoretical dreams set forth by Briand and Coundenhove-Kalergi, Churchill, Marshall, and Truman, and more recently Gorbachev and his "common European home") events as disparate as Charlemagne's designs for the Germanic Holy Roman Empire, the ambitions of the Spanish crown under the Hapsburg dynasty, the Napoleonic Empire, and the disastrous experiments of the Third Reich allied with Mussolini's Italy.[7] Furthermore, the long journey toward the Single Act is sown with the corpses and mummified remains of modest inter-European undertakings, such as the European Community for Defense, the Western European

---

[6]Hence the potential of emulation of the EC Parliament, as Grabendorff describes in his contribution.

[7]See paper by Laurent.

Union, the Organization for European Economic Cooperation, the Organization for Economic Cooperation and Development, and the Council of Europe. But precisely this internal tragedy faced by most of the European Community countries and their cooperation toward a common goal could provide Central America with an opportunity to learn how to deal with its own seemingly impossible integration process. From another's punishment there can be benefit. The long road extending from the Holocaust of 1939-1945 to the modest European Coal and Steel Community and later to the approval of the Single Act should at least be an object of serious study for the writers of the constitution for the Central American Parliament (to be headquartered in the symbolic city of Esquipulas[8]) as a way to encourage regional cooperation.

From a cultural standpoint, history shows that the European Community has several different historical and linguistic characteristics from Central America. Reconciliation between France and Germany was the cornerstone to what is frequently called the Common Market. Meanwhile, Spain, the European country with the closest cultural ties with Central America, was still a pariah in Europe, its middle of the road regime fluctuating between a pure dictatorship and authoritarian paternalism although already stripped of the disturbing totalitarianism remaining from Hitler and Mussolini's influence. The result was that the external policy of the European Community developed slowly and unequally in Latin America. In previous decades it focused on areas that had been part of the colonial empires of the major European powers, principally France and later Great Britain.[9] For this reason the European Community's foreign aid programs developed around the ACP (Africa, Caribbean, Pacific) countries.

---

[8]Papers by Grabendorff and Whitehead.

[9]Consult paper by Whitehead.

The Inter-American Scene

An examination of alternatives shows that several international systems seem to be destined for obsolescence. In the first place is direct intervention to control the natural resources of various Latin American countries by European powers. Although it is tragicomical, the world economic interdependence and the virtual evaporation of the Soviet Union as an interventionist power have eroded the bases that originally (before the threat of the Holy Alliance) gave rise to first the Monroe Doctrine and then to all of its corollaries, later bringing about the doctrines of national security and counterinsurgency. The elimination of this ideological threat means that Washington will no longer be able to wield national security arguments to encourage repression in certain circumstances, as it happened during the dictatorial military regimes in the Southern Cone or with the support of the personal or family autocracies in Central America and the Caribbean.

It is precisely in these two complementary scenarios, dominated since the 1960s by confrontation stemming from the nature of the Cuban regime and its foreign interventions, does cooperation between Europe and the United States seem necessary. New pragmatism and new ideas coming from Brussels or Strasbourg can yield even greater results.

However, in the second half of the 1980s there occurred several crucial events that facilitated decision-making by policymakers in the United States. While the transformation of the Soviet regime was beginning and the first signs of Eastern Europe's liberation could be seen, the European Community decided to accelerate integration by implementing the Single Act. This action was immediately perceived in financial power centers in the United States as construction of a "Fortress Europe." On the U.S.'s southern border the ideological and even military confrontations worsened between the United States or its allied regimes and hostile governments and guerrillas. In the beginning it seemed risky to attempt cooperation in an area where U.S.-

European interests collided. While some European governments argued for pacification and compromise, Washington (during Ronald Reagan's term) seemed inclined to simply eliminate the political contestants (for example, the Sandinistas).

With the unfolding of German unification and irrevocable changes in Eastern Europe, attention has turned to an area that remained a possible scene of confrontation between world powers, especially since the Sandinistas' electoral defeat and the virtual disappearance of the Cuban threat. The Persian Gulf crisis and war, the precarious state of the United States economy, and the European Community's need to aid the Eastern European economies all point to the advisability of abandoning competitive and wasteful monopolistic policies in these zones.

To avoid evasion and feuds, it is important to study those systems most suitable for promoting collaboration among the various cooperation organizations of the United States and the European Community. In fact, similar systems involving various international and inter-American entities had been founded precisely to accomplish this purpose, although not always with very satisfactory results: the Organization of American States, the Inter-American Development Bank, the World Bank, and the International Monetary Fund.

Ignorance and Myth

While in 1988 plans for European integration accelerated, events in the fall and winter of the following year proceeded at a dizzying speed. In spite of the Western intelligence services generally shared among the various powers that are part of the international framework (France, Great Britain, the United States), no one in the decision-making centers of the European Community (not even in West Germany) could have foreseen the drastic November 1989 "revolution."

Advancing the structure envisioned for 1992 became

a priority in 1990. Examples of this effort are the June agreement among five countries meeting in Schengen, Luxembourg, to enact this year what they had scheduled for 1990 and the decisions reached at the Dublin summit. In the background there was uncertainty about the situation in the Soviet Union, the corruption in some of the former satellites (such as Romania), and Gorbachev's deteriorating power base (always a protagonist because of constant speculation about the ideological direction of his policies and the dimensions of his acts). In addition, many were impatient to help with the Soviet Union's potential transition. This evolution proceeded so rapidly at first (until mid-1990) that it raised suspicions among both Europeans who were afraid to pay for the dismantling of a centralized economy (without an ideological change) and those in the United States who believed their country had exclusive domain in these developments.

Changes in the East are precisely the major obstacle to moderating the guidelines governing the relationship between the European Community and Latin America. Most of the Latin American countries, like those in Eastern Europe, are developing societies with nascent middle classes. This characteristic differentiates them from most of Africa and Asia. But from a point of view somewhere between sarcastic and realistic, it is suspected that in reality the November 1989 "revolution" was a welcome excuse to ease away from a relationship (mostly economic) with a continent for which those in Europe felt (often justifiably) a sense of reticence.

Relations and Ties

Until 1980 it could be said that Latin America was one world area the European Community ignored, although its member states maintained limited bilateral commercial ties. With growth in the 1960s and 1970s, its external relations concentrated primarily around developmental aid to former European colonies (principally France, on a much smaller scale the Netherlands and Belgium, and after its entrance, Great Britain). The result was the so-called Lomé Convention for the ACP (Africa, Caribbean, and Pacific) regions.

According to Angel Viñas, EC Latin America area director (a personal view does not *necessarily* correspond with that of the Commission),[10] since the 1980s a series of factors have served to revitalize dormant relations with a region that historically and culturally was the most closely tied to Europe. In the first place, the Malvinas (Falklands) War forced the European Community to align itself with Great Britain, although this action left some members with a slightly uncomfortable sensation. And while military regimes were slowly retreating from presidential palaces, Spain solidified its democracy and entered the European Community. This new member had morally supported Argentina, mainly because it also is victim of the only remaining case of colonialism in Europe: Gibraltar.

At the same time several European banks were affected by Latin America's alarming inability to repay its external debt. Although the European Community does not have a special external debt policy, events affecting the financial systems of its members have obvious repercussions. The first plan of action was for the Community to intervene, with understandable limitations, in contributing to resolve the serious political and social crisis in Central America. Here European political and commercial interests (first German, and later Spanish) had already been established through ties with various political parties.

Finally, the "rediscovery" of Latin America accelerated with the entrance of Spain (and, in a lesser way, Portugal) to the European Community precisely when Spain's political transition to democracy was being solidified. The mother country could offer itself as a viable model, a fact that earlier had been impossible.

Changes in the East also affected this slow evolution.

---

[10]See bibliography.

Realistic observers argue that what happens in Panama has some significance for Brussels; any variation in the economic or political contours of Poland is crucially important for the European Community. The geographic factor is a strong point; although the Soviet armored divisions were a threat earlier, now in a few days one can drive on the super highways to the borders of any European country. Pessimists say that Latin America has ceased to be a priority or even interesting; others say it is only a myth that once existed. Now, with the events of 1989 as well as the crisis and war in the Persian Gulf, attitudes return to normal: disdain.

Images and Perceptions

A measure of the European Community's perception of Latin America is how those who are responsible for Latin American relations express themselves. How this relation is actually perceived by Latin American as well as European and U.S. scholars, is the central theme of the conference and its product, the present volume.

The high-ranking dignitaries most directly involved with activities in Latin America propagate in various forums and publications their programs and changes, cataloging what has actually been done. Those who are responsible for global regions express their disappointment that Latin America does not have anyone who speaks for it since it is not an integrated whole.[11] Most important in this regard are the statements of Abel Matutes, a member of the Commission of the European Community and a Spanish entrepreneur who is responsible for ties with the developing countries.[12] He frequently offers[13] a comprehensive plan

---

[11]By way of example, see bibliography of documents generated by the Commission of the European Community.

[12]See speeches in London, Sao Paulo, Montevideo, and Buenos Aires.

[13]See bibliography.

that is hopeful about growth possibilities while offering a cautious diagnosis: if Latin America is not unified, at least regionally, Europe will do no more than listen.

Latin America's mythical perception of the European Community suffers from a lack of understanding about the ideological origins of the idea of a new Europe, buried by the image of a "Common Market," a pragmatic formality (of which Margaret Thatcher was the primary proponent), which not a few European leaders now regret. It is important that foreign observers and Latin American diplomats do not forget that the European Community was founded to defend certain values which were considered a vital part of European life (threatened by nazism, fascism, and later Marxism) by becoming not only a leader and definer of the rules of the game but, most importantly, a society based on the concept of a free market. As an anecdotal illustration, perhaps there is no better example of this message than the one received by the Sandinistas. Although the European Commission cannot hold to a particular ideology, its attitude toward Nicaraguan President Daniel Ortega, who visited President of the Commission Jacques Delors dressed in a military uniform, was obvious. He received understanding but also certain demands: first, he should hold elections and then his request for reconstruction aid would be considered. It would not be done any other way, since it would then be interpreted as support by the European Community for the Sandinista Front's ambiguous economic and ideological policies. This attitude also explains the cooling of relations with the Chilean regime of Augusto Pinochet and the practically nonexistent ties with the Cuban regime, which at the end of the 1980s remained the only exception to democracy in the hemisphere.

The crumbling Soviet empire in Eastern Europe has resulted in the establishment of triangular relations in which inevitably the United States is a part. While in the Pacific basin the protagonist is Japan (inheritor of the influence that first Great Britain and then the United States wielded in the Western hemisphere), Latin America finds itself unavoidably an angle in an unequal polygon shared with Europe and the United States. But the circumstances are somewhat different from the time when all external ties inescapably passed through Washington.

Latin America and the United States share, in the first place, the common symptom of a different outlook toward Europe. While the United States finds itself obsessed with the image of a European fortress that threatens to exclude its products, Latin Americans, since the integration project (not just economic but also political) has become a reality, have been especially wary of a new unknown Europe.

Today, as did intellectuals from the end of the nineteenth century until the middle of the present one, Latin American leaders are looking toward Europe for a solution to their economic problems. Disillusioned with the United States, they are freely modifying a phrase attributed to Porfirio Díaz: "Poor Latin America, so far from Europe and so close to the United States." From this idea, it is possible to see the signs of competition between Europe and the United States in a region that was (and still is, although not with the same exclusivity of the 1960s) a priority interest. Washington never encouraged Latin American integration; instead it favored bilateral relations, often choosing its spokesmen from countries which, for different reasons (political or economic), were most suitable as agents or intermediaries.

In this sense there exist two schools of thought. The first (best known as "hyper-realist") considers it possible to divide zones of influence among Europe, Japan, and the United States. Latin America would remain under the "protection" of the United States, especially since the disintegration of the Marxist utopia, while Asia would come under Japanese influence, and the European Community would be responsible for Africa and now the East. The second line of thinking resists such simplification: the European Community has many more complex interests. In the first place, it cannot abandon its interests in the Pacific, in part because it is a region of historical influence for the

European powers (France, Holland, Great Britain), nor can it forget Latin America (economically or culturally).

Coordination or Digression

To cooperate, the most sensible action is a policy of collaboration and maximization of functions that takes advantage of the different member states' unique relationships with Latin America—as in the obvious case of Spain.

The efforts of various Spanish delegations in the commissions of the European Parliament should not pass unnoticed. Conservatives (Carlos Robles Piquer, Fernando Suárez) and Socialists (Manuel Medina, Xavier Rubert de Ventós), in addition to *autonómicos* (Carlos Garaikoetxea, a Basque, and Concepció Ferrer, a Catalan), Centrists (Guadalupe Ruiz Jiménez), and Communists (Antoni Gutiérrez), have been appointed to work at mediating peace in Central America and in reforming (a utopian dream for many) the Cuban regime. It is not by chance that Medina was selected to head the subcommittee for South America and Suárez the one for Central America.[14] While perhaps there is not the ability (or the desire) to work through Washington, Strasbourg and Brussels can perform the same functions using the arm of the Parliament[15] that speaks the same language. In the same way, a European connection should be established as an extension of the activities of the Ibero-American Cooperation Institute (Instituto de Cooperación Iberoamericana), designed after the Spanish Agency for International Cooperation (Agencia Española de Cooperación Internacional), and other minor entities such as CEDEAL, along with the projected Instituto

[14]See Viñas, "La Comunidad Europea ante América Latina."

[15]Enrique Barón, former minister of transport, communication, and tourism in Felipe González's first cabinet, is president of the EC's legislative branch. See his book, *Europa 92. El rapto del futuro* (Barcelona: Plaza y Janés, 1989).

Cervantes that should be the Spanish "loyal" response to the Alliance Française and the German Goethe Institute. It would be the finishing touch to a Community plan that began under the inspiration of a Frenchman, Claude Cheysson, and a German, Hans Dieter Gensher.

Finally, it is not advisable to underestimate the efforts of private entities or exclude individuals of Spanish descent with ties in thc arca: from businessmen to missionaries, all have worked productively as intermediaries between the initiatives of the Community and the needs of Central America.

Prospects for the Immediate Future

In Latin American circles there is fear that changes in European interests will lead to concentration solely on internal affairs and especially on the domestic economies of member states since they are more attractive and the results are virtually guaranteed. Secondly, Europe logically will expand into the EFTA countries and then cautiously perhaps into peripheral countries along the southern Mediterranean. According to decision makers in the Community, Latin America must compete for more European investment especially since Eastern Europe is so attractive because of its proximity and destiny. In addition to consolidating its requests, Latin America should change its import substitution strategy. Latin America's balance of trade in the 1980s was discouraging. Although 22 percent of exports went to EC countries, only 4 percent of imports were from Europe.

A solution to this problem, perhaps, would be to follow Mexico's example, joining the common market between the United States and Canada to produce a new common market of the North. The unsuspected triumph of European influence over American will occur, although this time not by imperialistic political motives or economic domination. Even if the unification experience is not imitated in other regions, the mechanisms through which it was accomplished are indeed adaptable.

The unification of Europe began over its own ashes, produced by the third European war in less than a century. Latin America is slowly emerging from a long century of civil wars, both internal and occasionally inter-American. The European model of integration, moderated by national sovereignty, can be imitated effectively by Latin America, suspicious since the construction of a national identity by its individual states. Jacques Delors (with ambitions never officially denied of being democratically elected president by popular election) stresses that the European process of integration is the first in the history of mankind, one which respects the national identity of each member, who then agrees on the management of joint sovereignty. To dissipate the fears of Great Britain and Spain in particular, it is made clear that each constitutional monarch will continue to be the guarantor of his own sovereignty. In addition, it has rejected the expression the "United States of Europe" because it is both confusing and inexact.

It is possible to offer as an excuse the fact that the elites of Latin America have never been inclined toward integration. One can respond with the arguments of Alberto Van Klaveren.[16] However, the process of European integration was the work of a few inspired political visionaries (Shuman, De Gasperi, Monnet) and other technocrats who did not have an impact on European popular opinion, which was then preoccupied with survival. Latin America's interior isolation—frequently mitigated paradoxically by North American airlines—its (apparent) economic self-sufficiency, financial chaos, and changes are the factors that in reality have the most impact on the absence of integration processes.

For Latin America, cooperation with the European Community represents its admission (although modestly) into the context of international relations. It has always either been absent, or worse, in the hands of the world

---

[16] "La integración latinoamericana entre la utopía y la realidad," *Le Monde Diplomatique*, Latin American special edition, (May 1990): vii.

powers—often for strategic motives, as Cuba is now. The twenty-first century will be (and should be, considering the enormous human and energy potential of the continent) very different. It will be important for all. Or, in the diplomatic style of the Community's publications, the interests of the European Community and of Latin America do coincide.[17]

Bibliography

Commission of the European Communities. "Trece años de cooperación al desarrollo con los PVD de Asia y de América Latina: Datos y resultados de la experiencia." *Informe decenal.* (May 10, 1989).

_____."Evaluation of the European Community Development Cooperation with the Developing Countries of Latin America and Asia: Experiences and Lessons Learned." (August 1, 1989).

_____."Relaciones Comunidad Europea\Latinoamérica." *Relaciones Exteriores*, Europa Información. 2\89, December 1989.

_____."The European Community's Relations with Latin America." *External Relations*, Europe Information, 2\89, December 1989.

_____."Análisis de las exportaciones latinoamericanas a la Comunidad Europea." Brussels 1990. English text: "Analysis of the Performance of Latin American Exports to the European Community."

_____."Conclusiones del Consejo y de los Representantes de los Gobiernos de los Estados Miembros sobre las relaciones entre la Comunidad Europea y América Latina." Anexo a Informe No. 7216/87.

_____."Rome Declaration on Relations Between the European Community and the Rio Group." Rome, 20 December 1990.

_____."Propuesta de decisión del Consejo relativa a las orientaciones generales de la cooperación financiera y técnica en favor de los países en vías de desarrollo de América Latina y de Asia para el periodo 1991-1995." Brussels, December 17, 1990.

_____."Proposal for a Council Decision concerning General Guidelines for Financial and Technical Cooperation with the Developing Countries in Latin America and Asia during the Period of 1991-86." Brussels, December 17, 1990.

Matutes, Abel. "La Comunidad y América Latina en un tiempo de desafíos." *Le Monde Diplomatique* (in Spanish), special edition,

---

[17]*Europe Information*, December 1989.

May 1990, i and vi.
_____."The European Community and Latin America: Are We Shaping a Common Future?" Address at Canning House, London, October 23, 1989.
_____."Cooperación e integración en el Cono Sur: Adecuación a un nuevo contexto internacional." Intervención al Seminario sobre Cooperación e Integración. Buenos Aires, July 6, 1990.
_____.Discurso ante la ALADI. Montevideo, July 1990.
_____.Discurso en el Primer Foro Euro-Latinoamericano. Sao Paulo, July 1990.
Viñas, Angel. "Community Relations with Latin America: Past, Present, and Future," presented at a conference concerning "The European Community after 1992: A New Role in World Politics.", held in Luxembourg, May 28-31, 1990.
_____."Exposición al Vigésimo Tercer Periodo de Sesiones de la Comisión Económica para América Latina y el Caribe (CEPAL)." Caracas, May 1990.
_____."La Comunidad Europea ante América Latina: Olvido, transición y cambio." *Información Comercial Española*, February 1991.

CHAPTER I

AN OVERVIEW OF THE EUROPEAN COMMUNITY'S FOREIGN RELATIONS AND COOPERATION WITH CENTRAL AMERICA

FOREIGN POLICY ACTIONS OF THE EUROPEAN COMMUNITY, 1986-1990: THE POLITICS OF SCALE

Roy H. Ginsberg

Skidmore College

The purpose of this paper is to show through empirical data the widening scope of European Community (EC) foreign policy actions and to explain the causes of those actions. The premium here is placed on development and interpretation of macropolitical data. These data show that the EC is a very active foreign policy actor. The growth of EC foreign policy actions provides a critical backdrop to the study of EC-Central American relations. This paper draws heavily on, and expands upon, the author's work in *Foreign Policy Actions of the European Community: The Politics of Scale.*[1]

An EC foreign policy action is a specific, conscious, goal-oriented undertaking putting forth a unified membership position toward nonmembers, international bodies, and international events and issues (Ginsberg, 1989, p. 2). Joint foreign policy activity refers to the process by which the EC and its members coordinate and implement joint civilian foreign policy actions to reap benefits from politics of scale.

Politics of scale refers to the benefits of collective over individual action in the conduct of foreign policy. Politics of scale enables members to conduct joint foreign policy actions at lower costs and risks than when they act on their own. Members—large and small—generally perceive that they carry more weight in certain areas when they act together as a bloc than when they act separately (Ginsberg,

---

[1]Boulder: Lynne Rienner Publishers, 1989. All future references to this book are stated directly in the text by the page number.

1989, p. 3). Politics of scale is a driving force behind EC foreign policy actions.

This study inventories, classifies, and attempts to explain the 189 foreign policy actions taken from 1986-90. For the sake of comparison, the 1986-90 period is compared to two previous five-year periods: 1981-85 when 121 actions were taken and 1976-80 when 108 actions were taken (p. 106). A total of 418 foreign policy actions were taken over the three periods: 45 percent of these were taken in 1986-90, 30 percent in 1981-85, and 25 percent in 1976-80.

How do we explain this growth? Three explanatory logics are at work: integration logic, interdependence logic, and self-styled logic (Ginsberg, 1989).

The logic of integration emphasizes the negative effects of internal EC policies on outsiders, who in turn press the EC for compensation, forcing members to pull together to develop joint defensive responses. The existence of the customs union affects outsiders who press the EC for tariff preferences, development and technical assistance, humanitarian aid, loans, grants, association, membership, and diplomatic recognition.

The logic of interdependence suggests that the current of global politics influences the EC to respond with actions rooted not in the internal market but in the international system. The EC does not operate in an international power vacuum; it is, like a state actor, captive to the vicissitudes of global interdependence and must respond to survive even though it is just a "common market."

The self-styled logic underscores the EC's own sense of mission and independence in the world, whereby foreign policy actions not taken in response to outside pressures are products of the EC's own internal negotiations, decision making, and political dynamics. Self-styled actions are initiated by the EC, reflect EC interests, are implemented within the context of the EC's own style of diplomacy, and are driven by politics of scale.

How To Interpret the Data Base

How were the data generated? Foreign policy actions were chronicled from a wide variety of sources, including the EC's *General Report on the Activities of the EC*, the EC's *Official Journal*, other EC publications, such as the *Monthly Bulletins* and *Europe*, *Agence Europe*, *The Financial Times*, *The Economist*, elite interviews, scholarly articles, and case studies.

In understanding what data were included and excluded in the inventory, there are six words of caution. First, rather than closely study year-to-year fluctuations in EC foreign policy activity, it is more productive to view overall trends, as they tend to mitigate the effect of peculiar events and reflect a more normal pattern of behavior over time. Second, for the sake of parsimony, the data base only includes actions as earlier defined and thus excludes demarches, declarations, and resolutions of the EC institutions if they are not activated. Third, the premium here is on the final outcomes of negotiations—actions—rather than on the negotiations themselves. Fourth, the inventory provides a comprehensive, not exhaustive, list of EC actions—a floor rather than a ceiling. Fifth, foreign policy actions are merely identified in this inventory; no examination is made of the extent to which each action achieved its intended purpose. The emphasis is on quantifying the scope of actions. Sixth, routine agreements with third countries regulating trade in a single product area are generally excluded as they are strictly commercial and too numerous to quantify. There are, however, two exceptions. Single-product trade agreements with the Eastern European states during the Cold War are included because they helped to give body to the EC's adoption of *ostpolitik*. Actions pertaining to the EC becoming a signatory to an international commodity agreement are included, as they indicate a significant amount of prior consultation both on an international scale and within the EC. Antidumping and countervailing duties, routine food aid without evidence of political intent, and high-level bilateral and multilateral meetings subsequent to their inauguration are also excluded.

Tables 2-6 inventory foreign policy actions from 1986-90 and Tables 7-8 tabulate the results, classify the actions by type and explanatory logic, and compare the data for 1986-90 with the data for the two previous five-year periods drawn from earlier work.

Types of actions include multilateral, bilateral, security-related, unilateral, and interregional. Some actions may appear to fit more than one of these categories: parsimony calls for careful selection of the type that primarily categorizes the action. Bilateral actions are those in which the EC deals as a unit with a nonmember state or a group of states. Multilateral actions are those in which the EC deals as a unit with international conferences, issues, and organizations. Security-related actions are those in which the EC deals as a unit with questions that affect its own physical and material security, the security of a closely associated state or group of states, or the security of the international system. Even as a civilian actor, the EC has a stake in promoting its own security and in responding to threats to international peace and security outside Europe. Interregional actions are those the EC takes as a unit when it deals with other regions of the world. A cornerstone of EC foreign policy activity is the promotion of regional cooperation elsewhere; the EC operates on the assumption that it is the world's leading example of what can be accomplished by interstate regional collaboration. Unilateral actions are those the EC takes that do not fit into the other categories, such as development of EPC (European Political Cooperation), or when the EC takes an action that is not interactive but willed solely by the EC, such as imposing punitive sanctions.

Actions are also categorized by legal mandate. Table 1 lists the various articles in the ECSC (European Coal and Steel Community), the EEC (European Economic Community), and EUROATOM (European Atomic Energy Community) Treaties that give the EC the legal basis for operating in the international system. Establishment of EPC in the early 1970s and its codification in the 1987 Single European Act has provided the EC foreign ministers and their political directors and experts with a critical forum through which to coordinate foreign policy. A handful of actions are directly linked to EPC. However, since EPC outcomes to date have been more declaratory than action-oriented, the vast majority of EC foreign policy actions are still directly rooted in the treaties and thus form the bulk of the data base.

Explanations of actions, as mentioned, are drawn from three logics. The logic of integration is the primary explanation of EC foreign policy actions. It shows that actions are based on the very existence of the EC as an emerging common market and explains its effects on countries outside the exclusive club. These outsiders press the EC to act in response to their needs, resulting in EC foreign policy action. During the EC's early years, from 1958-72, the logic of integration explained nearly all foreign policy actions (Ginsberg, 1989). Only after 1972, with the admission of the UK and the sea changes internationally, did the EC begin to take foreign policy actions beyond the confines of the European project. The EC had become more attuned to its place in the international system; as a result, it took actions in response to international stimuli or to influence international events. The interdependent international system of the 1970s-1990s placed demands on the EC to act in ways that went beyond the confines of foreign policy traditions earlier established. An interdependent global system, unlike the preceding bipolar configuration, gave greater weight to EC presence in the world; power was no longer conceived in purely military terms but in economic and diplomatic terms as well. The two logics, however, do not capture explanations of all actions. A growing number of actions, rooted in the EC's own internal dynamic, provide evidence of a unique (unprecedented) style of regional diplomacy. These actions are not dependent on the need to respond to external stimuli but are the products of habits of working together, EC and member state initiatives, a sense of what Europeans want in foreign policy questions, and politics of scale.

In many instances, a single action may be explained by more than one logic. Parsimony and clarity call for careful selection of the logic that primarily explains the cause of the initial action, even though subsequent development of that action may be explained by another logic.

Review of Foreign Policy Actions by Year and Type

Table 2 shows that the accession of Spain and Portugal; sanctions against Libya, Syria, South Africa, and countries backing terrorism; the lifting of sanctions against Turkey; and special measures to help ease development of Israeli occupied territories and exports from those territories to the EC dominated foreign policy activity in 1986.

EC enlargement to include the two Iberian states was categorized as security-related. Given the previous political instability in the Iberian states and the military importance to the EC of its "soft underbelly," the geostrategic importance of bringing Spain and Portugal into the democratic EC fold cannot be given short shrift. Indeed the most powerful foreign policy action the EC can take is the one that decides which countries may join the EC, which may become associated with the EC, which may develop other contractual relations with the EC, and which will remain far removed from the EC.

Use of EC diplomatic or economic sanctions to punish countries involved in terrorist activity (Libya, Syria) or suppressing the human rights of its own people (South Africa) shows how the EC has been affected by participation in an interdependent world order often demanding the EC to take action. The decision by the European Parliament to hold up an accord with Israel over Israeli policy in the West Bank and Gaza and the EC's efforts to forge direct development links with these territories showed the resolve of the EC to register its dissatisfaction with Israeli policy. An accord with the Southern African Development Cooperation Council (SADCC) reflected the EC's interests in Southern Africa and in helping another regional group to develop.

As with previous and subsequent years, the EC participated actively in the annual Western Economic Summit and addressed the United Nations General Assembly on the EC's U.N. policies and positions. The EC continued its annual program of fixing import quotas for the State Trading Countries (STCs) and making adjustments for the purpose of *ostpolitik*, and proving preferential tariff rates for the world's poorest states through its Generalized System of Preferences (GSP).

EC activity was spread somewhat evenly over all types of actions with the exception of interregional actions. Interregional actions, along with security-related actions, tend to be more sporadic. In the case of interregional actions, they appear periodically depending on when the EC negotiates accords with groups of states or states within a region that is supported by the EC. Security-related actions depend on the state of war and peace in the international system in any one given year.

Table 3 shows that the EC was involved across a wide mix of bilateral, multilateral, and interregional activities in 1987. Morocco's interest in becoming an EC member was not realized because the EC only accepts European states. It was a year of an unusually high number of interregional activities. This was in large part due to the need for the EC and the Mediterranean states to renegotiate existing cooperation and association accords given the accession of Spain and Portugal to the EC in 1986. The EC also concluded accords with the Central American states and the Andean Pact—evidence again of the EC's interest in working with other regional groupings. Entry into force of the Single European Act put EPC under the EC's legal rubric and codified EPC procedures that had developed by custom into practice since the early 1970s.

Table 4 shows the early effects of the opening up of Eastern Europe in 1988 on the EC. The EC adopted the policy of *ostpolitik* in the 1970s and continued to nurture political and commercial relations with the individual member states of the Council for Mutual Economic Assistance (CMEA). The EC intentionally would not recognize CMEA itself because of the Soviet dominance of that organization. However, all of this changed in 1988 with the establishment of diplomatic relations with CMEA due in large part to the "new thinking" of Mikhail Gorbachev. The EC and Cuba, Hungary, the U.S.S.R., Czechoslovakia, East Germany, Bulgaria, and Poland also established diplomatic relations. Accords with Hungary and Czechoslovakia were historically unprecedented and began to pave the way for a much expanded EC role in the development of Eastern Europe.

Israel was again signalled out for punitive action. First, the European Parliament held back approval for the upgrading of the EC's 1975 trade accord with and loan package for Israel to protest the country's policies in the occupied territories. Second, the European Parliament in a report on the issue called on the EC Commission to suspend Israel's preferential treatment on the EC market as a means to force the Israelis to stop setting up alleged barriers to trade between the occupied territories and the EC. Israel complied with the EC demand to permit direct shipments of Arab produce from the occupied territories to the EC.

Finally, the EC was occupied with a number of international negotiations and agreements ranging from saving the African elephant to protecting the Indian Ocean environment to protecting the ozone layer to combatting drug abuse to relations with the Inter-American Bank.

Table 5 further chronicles the rapid expansion in 1989 of EC relations with the U.S.S.R. and former Soviet bloc states and the use of diplomatic and economic sanctions against targeted countries for behavior the EC deemed worthy of condemnation and punitive action. The EC normalized relations with Mongolia and concluded cooperation accords with Poland and the U.S.S.R. Most-favored-nation treatment (MFN) was extended to the Soviet Union, and European Investment Bank (EIB) loans were granted to Poland and Hungary. The EC banned ivory imports, politely but negatively responded to Turkey's membership bid (for the time being), tied development aid to Central America to the establishment of political pluralism, banned exports of chemicals to belligerent states, and imposed a wide variety of political, economic, and/or diplomatic sanctions.

China was the recipient of political, economic, military, and diplomatic sanctions for using force to suppress the pro-democracy student demonstrations. The EC banned all military trade and cooperation, suspended all bilateral ministerial and high-level contacts, postponed all other cooperation projects, diminished cultural, scientific, and technical cooperation programs, and raised the issue of human rights violations in appropriate international fora. The EC also decided to prolong the visas of Chinese students wishing to remain longer in the members states and announced that it would advocate the postponement of consideration of new credits to China from the World Bank. Romania was the recipient of diplomatic and economic sanctions for the violations of human rights by the Ceausescu regime. The EC condemned Romania for refusing to disclose details of the welfare of 24 dissidents, claiming the Romanian Government was in violation of CSCE (Conference on Security and Cooperation in Europe) accords. In retaliation, the EC ended negotiations with Romania to upgrade the 1980 EC-Romanian trade accord and suspended GSP benefits. The EC cancelled a planned high-ranking mission to Israel to again register displeasure with Israeli occupation policies

The most significant action in 1989 in terms of the long-term development of EC foreign policy was when the EC became the coordinator/leader of aid for Eastern Europe on behalf of 24 advanced industrialized states (Group-24). The decision to put the EC in charge of this large international operation was made at the Paris Western Economic Summit. The EC was ideally situated in terms of geography, financial resources, experience, and example to lead the western effort to help Eastern Europe develop and liberalize.

Table 6 shows the explosion of foreign policy actions taken in response to the collapse of Soviet power in Eastern Europe, the urgent development needs of the liberalizing Eastern European states, the charge of the Group-24 to coordinate western financial and development aid to Eastern Europe, German reunification, and the Iraqi invasion, occupation, and annexation of Kuwait.

The EC opened delegations in four countries, expanded and upgraded institutional ties with the United States, restored diplomatic relations with Vietnam, expanded development assistance, loans, and trade accords with all Eastern European states (except Albania), participated as a single and recognized negotiating unit in the Conference on Security and Cooperation in Europe (CSCE) Summit, signed the CSCE Paris Charter for a New Europe, and became a signatory to the new European Bank for Reconstruction and Development (EBRD). The EC concluded the Lomé Convention IV, the most far reaching North-South political, economic, and trade accord in the international system. Much to Israel's chagrin, the EC Council directed the commission to appoint an EC representative to the occupied territories.

The EC imposed full-scale sanctions against Iraq and occupied Kuwait (in advance of the U.N. sanctions) and provided emergency aid to the front line states—Egypt, Jordan, and Turkey. Immediately following the Iraqi invasion, the EC banned oil imports from Iraq and occupied Kuwait, banned military equipment and arms exports to Iraq and occupied Kuwait, suspended trade and military cooperation agreements, took measures to protect all Kuwaiti assets in the EC, and froze Iraqi assets in the EC. Other sanctions followed during fall 1990. The EC expelled all military staff from Iraqi embassies in the member states and restricted the movement of remaining Iraqi diplomats in the EC in response to the forced entry of Iraqi troops into the embassies of EC member states in Kuwait City.

The EC widened the embargo of Iraq and Kuwait by banning trade in services.

The EC imposed sanctions against Iran over the Iranian death threat against author Salman Rushdie by recalling its ambassadors from Tehran and banning all high-level EC visits to Iran. The EC also imposed sanctions on Romania—over the use of force in suppressing protest demonstrations in Bucharest by the Iliescu government—by withholding economic assistance and a new cooperation accord (both granted to other Eastern European states).

By year's end, the EC lifted sanctions against China, Iran, Vietnam, and Romania. The EC lifted sanctions against China imposed in 1989, although it continued to ban arms sales and military cooperation. The lifting of EC sanctions against China was likely linked to China's support for the anti-Iraq coalition of states. EC members began to return their ambassadors to Teheran but continued to ban all high-level visits to Iran. The EC and Vietnam resumed diplomatic relations and the EC and Romania finally concluded their long-delayed cooperation accord after the EC determined that the new government was acting with more restraint against protest demonstrators.

Numerical Trends in EC Foreign Policy Actions

Table 7 totals the number of EC foreign policy actions from 1986-90 and then compares the aggregate data from that period with data from two previous five-year periods, 1981-85 and 1976-80, derived from earlier work (Ginsberg, 1989). The aggregate data show a huge jump in the number of foreign policy actions from 30 in 1986 to 62 in 1990, although 1990 was an exceptional year given the changes in Europe and the war in the Persian Gulf. At most, 1990 may be a precursor of what is to follow; a vastly increased volume of actions in the 1990s over the 1980s because of the:

* Continuing demands of the EFTA (European Free Trade Association) and Eastern European states for closer association with or membership in the EC;

* Outcome of the intergovernmental conference on political union, which began in December 1990 and could lead to an expansion of EC foreign policy powers and the adoption of a security policy by 1993;

* Impact of the "1992 project" on the EC's many trading partners outside Europe;

* Pressures on the EC from Central and South America and South Asia for more equal attention in the distribution of tariff preferences and development aid; and

* Changing distribution of power in the international system, which will continue to give greater weight to the EC's peculiar strengths; financial resources, market accessibility, development assistance, diplomatic involvement, and leadership by example for the emerging democracies of Eastern Europe.

At a minimum, the EC has sustained a high level of foreign policy activity during the last half of the 1980s even if 1990 was an exceptional year. The number of actions during 1986-90 increased over two earlier five-year periods. Table 7 shows that there were 189 actions taken in 1986-90, up from 121 in 1981-85, and 108 in 1976-80 (Ginsberg, 1989).

Numerical Trends in Types of EC Foreign Policy Actions

Table 7 depicts just how active the EC was during 1986-90 in multilateral and bilateral foreign policy actions. It took 55 multilateral and 63 bilateral actions, which together accounted for 62 percent of all actions as shown in Table 8. Multilateral and bilateral actions have always grabbed the lion's share of total EC actions because they are the main areas of international politics and economics. The number of multilateral actions more than tripled and the number of bilateral actions more than doubled between 1986 and 1990. The increase in multilateral actions suggests that the EC is very active in international issues and organizations and the increase in bilateral actions suggests how much the EC continues to work with individual states and how much nonmember states value their relationship with the EC.

Table 8 shows that multilateral actions as a percentage of total actions actually dropped from 44 percent in 1976-80 to 29 percent in 1986-90, suggesting the expansion of EC foreign policy actions to other types, especially bilateral and unilateral actions. Table 8 also depicts the jump in bilateral actions, which represented 24 percent of total actions in 1976-80 but grew to 34 percent in 1986-90. The jump in bilateral actions again suggests that nonmember states continue to pressure the EC to make trade-and-aid agreements given the importance of the EC market to their exports.

During the 1986-90 period, the EC took 13 security-related, 33 unilateral, and 25 interregional actions, which together accounted for 38 percent of all actions. It is still rather remarkable that the EC takes actions that are related to security given the EC's traditional preoccupation with trade. The accession of the Iberian states was designed in large part to stabilize the EC's southern flank. Sanctions against states supporting international terrorism was the EC's response to another kind of security problem. The EC sanctions against Iraqi aggression, peace initiatives in the Israeli-Palestinian dispute, and ban on chemical exports to belligerent states also helped define the EC as an actor involved with security-related actions, even though the EC itself is not a military power. The trend in security-related actions as a percentage of total actions is depicted in Table 8. No clear trend emerges from the data, which suggests that security-related actions tend to be ad hoc depending on the state of international peace and security and the willingness of the EC members to act in unison in any given year.

Unilateral actions are those that most clearly show the ability of the EC to act decisively and independently. When the EC takes unilateral actions, it is not being pressed by an outsider to act; instead it is acting on its own volition to alter the behavior of another actor or to influence the outcome of an international issue. Codification of the EPC was a unilateral internal action that had major implications for the conduct of EC foreign policy actions. Unilateral actions were taken to influence Israeli policy in the occupied lands, South Africa's policy of apartheid, and Romania's human rights record. The EC acted unilaterally to reward the behavior of states who changed their policy (and thus met EC expectations) by lifting previous sanctions (e.g., Turkey and Vietnam). Unilateral actions as a percentage of total actions are depicted in Table 8. Whereas in 1976-80, unilateral actions accounted for just 11 percent of total EC actions, that percentage increased to 17 in the 1986-90 period, suggesting that the EC has gained more confidence in its ability to act independently.

Interregional actions were taken to offer support to other regions and regional groupings from the Mediterranean to the Persian Gulf to Central America to Southern Africa. The EC treats the Mediterranean Basin as a region strategically and commercially vital to its interests and offers tariff preferences, industrial free trade, and development assistance in exchange for market access, good will, and regional stability (or the hopes thereof). The EC offers economic and commercial incentives to other regional integration movements because of its own experience in regional cooperation. Table 8 shows that interregional actions as a percentage of total actions has remained at 13 percent for the 1976-80 and 1986-90 periods. During the 1981-85 period, interregional actions accounted for just 7 percent of total actions.

Trends in Explanations of EC Foreign Policy Actions

During the 1986-90 period, the number of foreign policy actions explained by the logic of integration doubled from 16 to 33 as shown in Table 7. This suggests that the effects of the customs union on outsiders continued to prompt the latter to press the former to make accommodation. However, that observation must be made against the data depicted in Table 8. Table 8 shows that actions explained by the integration logic as a percentage of total actions during 1986-90 fluctuated between a low of 47 percent and a high of 72 percent with no clear trend or direction. Indeed the rise in the number of actions explained by the integration logic was not reflected in the number of actions explained by the integration logic as a percentage of total actions. This suggests that other logics have expanded their explanatory power.

Despite the rise in the number of actions explained by the integration logic between 1986-90, the integration logic as an explanation of total actions over time shows a somewhat different picture. Table 8 shows that the integration logic as an explanation of total actions in 1986-90 was 58 percent, down from 73 percent in 1976-80. This suggests that the integration logic has declined in its explanatory power as the EC strikes out in new foreign policy directions. As it expands into international activities rooted in the international interdependent system and develops its own style of foreign policy actions, the integration logic explains fewer actions. The net effect is a more internationally active EC whose foreign policy personality is less influenced by the effect of the customs union on the outside world than by other factors.

During the 1986-90 period, the number of foreign policy actions explained by the interdependence logic increased from 7 to 13, as shown in Table 7. However, that growth also mirrored the growth in total number of actions. Actions explained by the interdependence logic grew from 18 in 1976-80 to 25 in 1981-85 to 37 in 1986-90. Table 8 shows that the interdependence logic as an explanation of foreign policy actions changed little from 1986 to 1990. The longer-term trend is more revealing. The interdependence logic as an explanation of total actions rose from 17 percent in 1976-80 to 20 percent in 1986-90, which suggests a small but meaningful increase in EC actions in response to pressures from participation in the international system.

Certainly the decline of the integration logic as an explanation of total actions from 1976-1990 is partially attributed to the rise in the explanatory power of the interdependence logic. What is perhaps more telling is the jump in actions explained by the self-styled logic in numerical terms and as a percentage of the total.

During the 1986-90 period, the number of foreign policy actions explained by the self-styled logic jumped from 7 to 16. There were 42 foreign policy actions explained by the self-styled logic during 1986-90, up substantially from 19 in 1981-85 and 11 in 1976-80. The expansion of actions accounted for by this logic is perhaps the most stunning finding of this analysis. If the EC is to become an influential and permanent actor in international affairs it must develop its own style and content of foreign policy. By taking actions rooted neither in the existence and effect of the customs union nor in response to pressures of participation in the international system but in the EC's own sense of self-interest and internal political dynamic, the EC is likely to play a more independent and influential role in international relations in the years ahead. The test of the expansion of the self-styled logic as an explanation of actions is depicted in Table 8.

Table 8 shows that the self-styled logic as an explanation of action rose from just 10 percent in the 1976-80 period to 15 percent in 1981-85 and then to 22 percent in 1986-90. As the integration logic decreased in explanatory power during the 1976-90 years, the power of the self-styled logic to explain action increased.

EC Foreign Policy Actions and Central America

Trends in EC foreign policy actions show that the frequency of action has been increasing for some time. Yet this does not mean that the EC has developed or is going to develop common foreign policy likened to that of a single nation-state. Member states pursue their own foreign policy actions and will continue to do so. They are still free agents in many areas of international relations not regulated by the EC or subject to consultation under EPC.

What is clear is that EC and individual member state foreign policy actions now coexist. It may be that—given the benefits reaped by politics of scale—members will continue to find it in their own interests to coordinate joint responses to external stimuli because the weight of the EC is heavier, more cost-effective, and more influential than that of their own individual weight. The outcome of EC foreign policy activity is still uncertain in terms of where it will eventually lead. Since that is too conjectural for the social scientist to grasp, it seems reasonable to conclude that the EC will continue to take foreign policy actions with more frequency and across wider areas of international relations given 1) historical trends revealed in this study; and 2) the momentum for further political union that now exists. It also seems judicious to conclude that over time the members will use the EC as a conduit for their particular foreign policy interests. At times, members will succeed in funneling their particular foreign policy interest into EC action or will be forced to compromise with other members to reach a consensus. There will be other times when member governments fail to persuade the EC to adopt their foreign policy interests. At that time, the individual member government is free to pursue its own action independently of the EC (so long as there is no violation of EC law or custom) or accept the defeat and take no further action. Membership entails a series of trade-offs.Thus far no members have permanently left the EC because of differences concerning foreign policy actions.

As shown in this study, three logics are at work in explaining what triggers foreign policy actions. The majority of foreign policy actions can be explained by the integration logic. However, the explanatory power of the logic of integration has declined substantially as the EC has taken actions in response to the current of international interdependence and to its own internal dynamic and sense of mission in the world. It seems reasonable to predict that as EC foreign policy activity continues to mature, the integration logic as an explanation of action will continue to decline as a percentage of total actions. This is not to say that the customs union will no longer spur outsiders to pressure the EC for action but that the EC will take actions that mange the effects of global interdependence and those that take into account European interests. What will continue to make the integration logic quite relevant is the expansion of the EC itself. As the EC expands in membership and into new policy areas, new external pressures will emerge from adversely affected outsiders. The integration logic will continue to remain an important explanation of what catalyzes action.

The global interdependence logic has helped us to explain EC actions designed to respond to outside pressures that bear on European and international peace and security. When one examines foreign policy actions charged neither by the customs union's existence nor by participation in an interdependent global order, a view of the future course of foreign policy activity may be surmised. Self-styled actions substantiate one of the original intents of European unification—that, although the destroyed powers of Europe in 1945 might not alone regain the influence they had before World War II, they could together regain some of this influence. To the extent that politics of scale are at work in the making of EC foreign policy activity, self-styled actions can be expected to increase in number as the EC states gain confidence in the benefits of foreign policy cooperation. As the EC reaches beyond the confines of the original treaty into the Single European Act, EPC, and monetary/economic and political union, self-styled actions provide a basis for growth of independent foreign policy.

For students of EC-Central American relations, this chapter shows the potential of the EC to act decisively in various parts of the world far away from the borders of Europe. It shows that the EC has the capability of acting in the defense of its own foreign policy interests and that it is actively involved in nearly all areas of civilian international relations. The EC is interested in providing assistance to other regions and regional groups because this pattern of development mirrors the EC's own approach to stability and growth. This assistance takes various forms ranging from seed money to help new regional institutions get started to tariff preferences to technological and development aid to diplomatic and political recognition, support, and encouragement. The Central American region is of immense interest to the EC for obvious historical, commercial, and cultural reasons, but also because the EC has adopted a policy toward the region—independently of the United States. Indeed, EC involvement in the region is seen as more objective and less interventionist by the Central Americans when compared to United States involvement. To abdicate its unique policy in Central America to the United States—given U.S.-EC policy differences over the region—would throw into question the EC's international reputation and stature as an independent foreign policy power.

Of course, the EC is heavily occupied by the development needs of the newly free and liberalizing regimes of Eastern Europe, the incorporation of the former East Germany into the EC, and the negotiations with EFTA for a "European economic space." However, the EC is too dependent on international trade and too extensively involved in the international system to turn its back on the non-European world. Surely a period of internal European consolidation will be needed. However, the EC has the staying power, the financial resources, and the potential political will to become a leading force in the international system, if this has not already happened. If the EC looks to the United States for support in the reconstruction of Eastern Europe, then it is not unreasonable for the United States to continue to ask for and receive EC support for the reconstruction of Central America.

This study provided the empirical evidence and theoretical explanation of EC foreign policy actions that reach across the globe to many nation-states and regions and touch upon many international issues. As an economic superpower with undeniable political ambitions in international relations, the EC will not be able to shirk its global responsibilities. The reconstruction of Central America cannot be given short shrift in favor of the reconstruction of Poland or Romania. Such a scenario would be out of line with the EC's emerging sense of global responsibilities and interests given commitments of involvement to the Central American region that predate the collapse of the Soviet empire.

Table 1: The Law of EC Foreign Policy Actions

Treaty/Articles	Abstract
ECSC Treaty	
Article 6	Gives ECSC the legal capacity to act in diplomatic relations and international organizations
EEC Treaty	
Article 110	Provides for participation in the GATT and other international trade organizations
Article 113	Gives the EC power to conduct relations and make agreements with third countries on all questions pertaining to import/export trade; implements the CET
Article 131	Permits members to associate with non-European states
Article 228	Provides for EC accords with third states and international organizations where the treaty provides for their conclusion
Article 229	Empowers the commission to ensure maintenance of all relations with all appropriate international bodies, e.g., the United Nations, GATT
Article 230	Authorizes the EC to establish relations with the Council of Europe
Article 231	Authorizes the EC to establish relations with the OECD
Article 237	Provides for the enlargement of the EC to include new members
Article 238	Provides for association agreements with nonmembers involving reciprocal rights, obligations, common action, and special procedures
EURATOM Treaty	
Article 101	Empowers the EC to conclude accords or contracts with third states and international bodies

Table 2: Inventory of EC Foreign Policy Actions, 1986

Joint Action	Type	Treaty Basis	Logic
Scientific Cooperation Accords with EFTA States	Bilateral x5	113,228,238	Integration x5
Diplomatic Relations Established with Kuwait	Bilateral	113,228	Integration
Accord with U.S. on Controlled Thermonuclear Fusion	Bilateral	EURATOM 101	Integration
First Quadripartite Meeting of EC, U.S., Japan, Canada	Multilateral	113,228,229	Interdependence
Lomé Convention III	Multilateral	113,131,228,238	Integration
U.N. General Assembly Address on EC Positions	Multilateral	229, EPC	Interdependence
Signatory to International Cocoa Pact	Multilateral	113,228,229	Integration
Became Negotiating Partner in U.N. Olive Oil Conference	Multilateral	113,228,229	Integration
First Meeting of the ACP-EEC Joint Assembly	Multilateral	113,131,228,238	Integration
Tokyo Economic Summit	Multilateral	229	Interdependence
Annual GSP Program	Multilateral	113,228	Integration
Accord with SADCC on Regional Resource Planning	Interregional	113,229	Self-styled
Accession of Spain	Security-related	237	Integration
Accession of Portugal	Security-related	237	Integration
Diplomatic Sanctions Against Libya	Security-related	EPC	Interdependence
Arms Embargo Against Countries Backing Terrorism	Security-related	EPC	Interdependence
Diplomatic and Economic Sanctions Against Syria	Security-related	EPC,113	Interdependence
Tariff Preferences on Exports from Gaza, West Bank	Unilateral	113	Self-styled
Development Scheme for West Bank, Gaza	Unilateral	113	Self-styled
Relief Measures for Victims of Apartheid	Unilateral	EPC,113	Self-styled
Approval for Accord with Israel Held Up by Parliament	Unilateral	Parliament action	Self-styled
Increase in EC Commission Powers to Raise Food Aid	Unilateral	113,228	Integration
Fixation of Import Quotas for STCs	Unilateral	113,228	Integration
Drought Plan for Rehabilitation of Affected African States	Unilateral	113,228	Self-styled
Trade Sanctions Against South Africa	Unilateral	113,228,ECSC 6	Interdependence
Economic Sanctions Against Turkey Lifted	Unilateral	EPC,113,228	Self-styled

Table 3 (cont.)

Joint Action	Type	Treaty Basis	Logic
Fixation of Import Quotas for STCs	Unilateral	113,228	Integration
Entry Into Force of the Single European Act Codifying EPC	Unilateral	EPC	Self-styled
Set up Working Group on Human Rights	Unilateral	EPC	Self-styled

Table 3: Inventory of EC Foreign Policy Actions, 1987

Joint Action	Type	Treaty Basis	Logic
Conventions with EFTA States on Flow of Goods	Bilateral x5	113,228,238	Integration x5
Accord with Canada on Research, Environment	Bilateral	113,228	Integration
Accord with China on Biotechnology Research Center	Bilateral	113,228	Integration
Industrial Cooperation Program With India	Bilateral	113,228	Integration
Rejection of Morrocco's Bid for Membership	Bilateral	237	Integration
Annual GSP Program	Multilateral	113,228	Integration
Adoption of IAEA Accord on Early Notification of Accident	Multilateral	EURATOM 101	Integration
U.N. General Assembly Address on EC Positions	Multilateral	229,EPC	Interdependence
Vienna Economic Summit	Multilateral	229	Interdependence
Participation in Council of Europe Accord/Disaster Relief	Multilateral	113,228	Interdependence
Signatory to Animal Protection Convention	Multilateral	229	Self-styled
Participant/U.N. Conference on Disarmament/Development	Multilateral	113,228,229	Interdependence
Signatory to the Multi-Fiber Agreement	Multilateral	113,228,229	Integration
Adoption of Harmonized System of Customs Classification	Multilateral	113,228,229	Integration
Cooperation Accord with Central America States and Contadora Group	Interregional	113,228	Integration
Mediterranean Policy Updated	Interregional	113,228,238	Integration
Association Accord with Cyprus Revised	Interregional	113,228	Integration
Association Accord with Turkey Revised	Interregional	113,228	Integration
Aid for South Asian Association for Regional Cooperation	Interregional	113,228	Self-styled
Cooperation Accord with Andean Pact (Cartegena Pact)	Interregional	113,228	Integration
Adoption of Strategy for Relations with Latin America	Interregional	113,228	Self-styled
Backing for Contadora Peace Process	Interregional	113,228	Self-styled
EC-Rio Group Ministerial Dialogue	Interregional	113,228	Integration
Cooperation Accord with Algeria, Tunisia, Egypt, Jordan, Lebanon, and Israel Revised	Interregional x6	113,228	Integration x6

Table 4: Inventory of EC Foreign Policy Actions, 1988

Joint Action	Type	Treaty Basis	Logic
Cooperation Accord with Hungary	Bilateral	113,228	Integration
Trade Accord with Czechoslovakia	Bilateral	113,228	Integration
Adoption of Annual Ministerial Dialogue with Canada	Bilateral	113,228	Integration
Amendment of Trade Accord with Romania	Bilateral	113,228	Integration
Accord with Canada on Controlled Thermonuclear Fusion	Bilateral	EURATOM 101	Integration
Diplomatic Relations with Cuba, Hungary, CMEA, U.S.S.R., Czechoslovakia, East Germany, Bulgaria and Poland	Bilateral x8	113,228	Integration x8
Ratification of Vienna Convention to Protect Ozone Layer	Multilateral	113,228,229	Interdependence
Accord with Indian Ocean Commission	Multilateral	113,228,229	Interdependence
U.N. General Assembly Address on EC Positions	Multilateral	229,EPC	Interdependence
Toronto Economic Summit	Multilateral	229	Interdependence
Agreement to Cooperate with Inter-American Bank	Multilateral	113,228,229	Integration
Annual GSP Program	Multilateral	113,228	Integration
Became Member in U.N. Fund for Drug Abuse Control	Multilateral	113,228,229	Interdependence
Member of Elephant Conservation Coordinating Group	Multilateral	113,228,229	Interdependence
Participation in European Convention on Transfrontier Television under the Council of Europe	Multilateral	113,228,229	Integration
Aid Program for Central America	Interregional	113,228	Integration
Cooperation Accord with Gulf Cooperation Council	Interregional	113,228	Integration
Trade Accord with Yugoslavia	Interregional	113,228	Integration
Peace Initiative on Israel-Palestinian Dispute	Security-related	EPC	Self-styled
Threat of Economic Sanctions Against Israel	Unilateral	EPC,113,228	Self-styled
Update on Trade Accord with Loans to Israel Held Up	Unilateral	Parliament action	Self-styled
Fixation of Import Quotas for STCs	Unilateral	113,228	Integration

Table 5: Inventory of EC Foreign Policy Actions, 1989

Joint Action	Type	Treaty Basis	Logic
Diplomatic Relations with Mongolia	Bilateral	113,228	Integration
Cooperation Accord with Poland	Bilateral	113,228	Integration
Accord with United States on Standards Setting Procedure	Bilateral	113,228	Integration
EIB Loans for Poland, Hungary	Bilateral x2	EIB	Integration x2
Cooperation Accord with U.S.S.R.	Bilateral	113,228,EURATOM	Integration
MFN Granted to U.S.S.R.	Bilateral	113,228	Integration
Signatory to International Convention Against Illicit Traffic in Narcotic Drugs	Multilateral	229	Integration
Euro-Arab Dialogue Revived	Multilateral	113,228,EPC	Interdependence
First-time Participation in Human Rights Debate at U.N.	Multilateral	229,EPC	Interdependence
U.N. General Assembly Address on EC Positions	Multilateral	229,EPC	Interdependence
Paris Economic Summit	Multilateral	229	Interdependence
Support of Peace Movement in Angola, Mozambique	Multilateral	EPC	Interdependence
Annual GSP Program	Multilateral	113,228	Integration
Ivory Imports Banned to Save Elephant under U.N. Accord	Multilateral	113,228,229	Self-styled
Decision to End Chlorofluorocarbon Production	Multilateral	113	Self-styled
EC Accepted Request of the Paris Economic Summit Participants to Coordinate Aid to Eastern Europe	Multilateral	229	Self-styled
Response to Turkish Membership Bid	Interregional	237	Integration
EC Accord with EFTA on Product Standards Consultations	Interregional	113,228	Integration
Aid to Central America Tied to Political Pluralism	Interregional	113,228,EPC	Self-styled
Association Accords with Cyprus and Malta Updated	Interregional x2	113,131	Integration x2
Ban on Chemical Exports to Belligerents, Tension Areas	Security-related	113,EPC	Interdependence
Political/Economic/Diplomatic Sanctions against China	Unilateral	113,228,EPC	Self-styled
Diplomatic Sanctions Against Romania	Unilateral	EPC	Self-styled

Table 5 (cont.)

Joint Action	Type	Treaty Basis	Logic
Economic Sanctions Against Romania	Unilateral	113,228,EPC	Self-styled
Emergency Medical/Food Aid to Romania	Unilateral	113,228,EPC	Self-styled
Cancellation of High-Ranking EC Mission to Israel	Unilateral	113,228,EPC	Self-styled
Emergency Food Aid to Poland	Unilateral	113,228,EPC	Self-styled
Fixation of Import Quotas for STCs	Unilateral	113,228	Integration
Emergency Aid to Lebanon/Fact-Finding Team Dispatched	Unilateral	113,228EPC	Interdependence
Common Strategy for Easing Restriction on Hi-Tech Exports to Eastern Europe	Unilateral	113,EPC	Integration

Table 6: Inventory of EC Foreign Policy Actions, 1990

Joint Action	Type	Treaty Basis	Logic
EC Delegation Opened in Warsaw, Budapest, Nicosia, Manila	Bilateral x4	113,228	Integration x4
Expanded/Upgraded Institutional Ties with United States	Bilateral	113,EPC	Integration
Trade Accord with Argentina	Bilateral	113,228	Integration
Cooperation Accord with Chile	Bilateral	113,228	Integration
Diplomatic Relations with Vietnam Restored	Bilateral	113,EPC	Self-Styled
GSP Granted to Poland, Hungary, Czechoslovakia	Bilateral x3	113,228	Integration x3
Loans to Poland, Hungary, Bulgaria, Czechoslovakia	Bilateral x4	EIB	Integration x4
Approval of Financial Aid Package to U.S.S.R.	Bilateral	113,228	Interdependence
MFN Treatment Granted to Bulgaria	Bilateral	113,228	Integration
Emergency Food Aid Granted to U.S.S.R., Bulgaria, Romania	Bilateral x3	113,228	Integration x3
Elimination of QRs on Polish and Hungarian Imports	Bilateral x2	113,228	Integration x2
Admission of East Germany into EC	Bilateral	237	Integration
Cooperation Accords with Bulgaria, East Germany, Romania, and Czechoslovakia	Bilateral x4	113,228,EURATOM	Integration x4
Expansion of PHARE Assistance to Czechoslovakia, Bulgaria, Yugoslavia, and East Germany x4	Multilateral x4	228,229	Interdependence
Participation as a Single Unit in the CSCE Paris Summit	Multilateral	228,229,EPC	Interdependence
Signatory to the Paris Charter	Multilateral	228,229,EPC	Interdependence
Signatory to the EBRD	Multilateral	228,229,EIB	Interdependence
EC Sought/Received Single Entity Status at CSCE	Multilateral	228,229	Self-styled
EC Signed CSCE's Charter of Paris for a New Europe	Multilateral	228,229	Interdependence
Lomé Convention IV Enacted	Multilateral	113,131,228,229	Integration
Imposition of United Nations Sanctions Against Iraq	Multilateral	113,EPC	Interdependence
U.N. General Assembly Address on EC Positions	Multilateral	229,EPC	Interdependence
Houston Economic Summit	Multilateral	229	Interdependence
Annual GSP Program	Multilateral	113,228	Integration
Participation in Gulf Crisis Financial Coordination Group	Multilateral	228,229	Interdependence
Signatory to International Jute Agreement	Multilateral	113,228,229	Integration

Table 6 (cont.)

Joint Action	Type	Treaty Basis	Logic
Diplomatic Sanctions Against Iran	Unilateral	EPC	Self-styled
Fixation of Import Quotas for STCs	Unilateral	113,228	Integration
Accession of Namibia, Haiti, and Dominican Republic to Lomé Convention	Multilateral x3	113,131,228,229	Integration x3
Cooperation Accord with Gulf Cooperation Council	Interregional	113,228	Integration
Agreement to Protect Nationals whose Embassies were Forcibly Closed in Kuwait City by the Iraqis	Security-related	EPC	Self-styled
Economic Sanctions Against Iraq	Security-related	113,228,EPC	Self-styled
Diplomatic Sanctions Against Iraq	Security-related	113,EPC	Self-styled
Emergency Aid to Frontline States (Egypt, Jordan, and Turkey) in Conflict with Iraq	Security-related x3	113,228,EPC	Self-styled x3
Economic Sanctions Against Israel	Unilateral	113,228,EPC	Self-styled
Withholding of PHARE Assistance to Romania	Unilateral	113,228	Self-styled
Denial of GSP for Romania	Unilateral	113,228	Self-styled
Withholding of Trade/Economic Accord with Romania	Unilateral	113,228	Self-styled
Resumption of Diplomatic Relations with Romania	Unilateral	113,228	Self-styled
Economic Sanctions on China Lifted	Unilateral	113,228	Self-styled
Appointment of EC Representative to Occupied Territories	Unilateral	113,EPC	Self-styled

Table 7: Summary of EC Foreign Policy Actions by Type and Explanation, 1986-90, 1981-85, 1976-80

Year	Total	Multi	Bilat	Secur	Unil	Interreg	Integ	Inter	Self-styled
1986	30	8	7	5	9	1	16	7	7
1987	36	9	9	0	3	15	26	4	6
1988	29	9	13	1	3	3	20	6	3
1989	32	10	7	1	9	5	15	7	10
1990	62	19	27	6	9	1	33	13	16
Total, 86-90	189	55	63	13	33	25	110	37	42
Total, 81-85	121	53	30	14	15	9	77	25	19
Total, 76-80	108	48	26	8	12	14	79	18	11

Table 8: Summary of EC Foreign Policy Actions by Type and Explanation, 1986-90, 1981-85, 1976-80 As a Percentage of Total

Year	Total	Multi	Bilat	Secur	Unil	Interreg	Integ	Inter	Self-styled
1986	30	27	23	17	30	3	53	23	23
1987	36	25	25	0	8	42	72	11	17
1988	29	31	45	3	10	10	69	21	10
1989	32	31	22	3	28	16	47	22	31
1990	62	31	44	10	14	1	53	21	26
Total, 86-90	189	29	34	7	17	13	58	20	22
Total, 81-85	121	43	25	12	12	7	64	21	15
Total, 76-80	108	44	24	7	11	13	73	17	10

THE ROLE OF CENTRAL AMERICA IN THE EUROPEAN COMMUNITY'S FOREIGN POLICY

Angel Viñas

Commission of the European Community

Several years ago, the distinguished conservative author Irving Kristol started a brilliant essay by stating:

> American policy toward Central America is certainly an important and perplexing issue for the United States. It is also clearly an issue of overriding importance for the nations of Central America and of Latin America as a whole. But why is it an issue for the nations of Western Europe? To an American the answer to that question is not at all self-evident.[1]

Professor Kristol had his own answer: Western European countries tended to be "frivolous, distancing themselves publicly from American policy in order to appease anti-American political opinion at home."[2]

Kristol's conclusion was evident: Western Europe had no role in Central America. The Europeans ought to take the important security concerns of the United States seriously. Nothing was gained by frivolity or lack of rigor.

These remarks were published in 1985. Needless to say European involvement in Central America went on unabated, leading to annual endorsements of the Contadora

---

[1]Irving Kristol, "Should Europe Be Concerned about Central America?," in *Third World Instability. Central America as an European-American Issue*, Andrew J. Pierre, ed. (New York: Council on Foreign Relations, 1985), p. 45.

[2]Ibid., p. 69.

peace process. These actions, says Ginsberg, run counter to U.S. policies.[3]

European Community interest towards Central America dates back to the declaration of the European Council of March 30, 1982. According to this declaration, the conflicts and tensions in that region frequently originated in serious economic problems and social inequalities that were aggravated by the international economic environment.

A year later, the European Council forcefully stated: "...The problems of Central America cannot be solved by military means but only by a political solution springing from the region itself and respecting the principles of non-interference and inviolability of frontiers." The Heads of State and Government of the European Community underlined that there was a "need for the establishment of democratic conditions and for the strict observance of human rights throughout the region" and manifested their readiness to contribute "to the further development in the area, in order to promote progress towards stability."

This declaration was well received in the region. Intensive contacts at both official and ministerial levels followed. The troika of the European Community ministers met with their counterparts of the Contadora Group countries at the U.N. General Assembly in September 1983. This paved the way for the formal opening of the political dialogue between the European Community, the Contadora Group, and the Central American countries. The first meeting was held in San José, Costa Rica, September 28-29, 1984.

The participants assessed their meeting as the inauguration of "a new structure of a political and economic dialogue between Europe and Central America" and agreed to continue their contacts on a regular basis. Portugal and Spain participated fully in this exercise although negotia-

---

[3]Roy H. Ginsberg, *Foreign Policy Actions of the European Community. The Politics of Scale* (Boulder: Lynne Rienne Publishers, 1988), pp. 134 and 147-148.

tions on their entry into the European Community were not yet concluded.

At their second meeting in Luxembourg, November 11-12, 1985, the ministers signed a final act, which provides for the institutionalization of the political dialogue (annual meetings at a ministerial level). The signatories confirmed their full support for the Contadora Group and its initiatives for a negotiated solution to the Central American crisis.

Simultaneously the Central American states, including Panama, signed a cooperation agreement with the European Community underscored the political symbolism of the new relationship. In retrospect, it seems strange that the European Community entered this political relationship with a group of countries in which the European presence was very limited. At the time of the San José and Luxembourg ministerial meetings, the only group of countries with which this kind of relationship was sustained was ASEAN. Furthermore, the formula of full representation of the European interests by the foreign ministers of the member states and the commission was highly unusual at that time. The Europeans tended to prefer the troika formula or use the presidency as a channel for high-level contacts with other countries.

From the beginning, therefore, the political dialogue offered by the Europeans to the Central Americans had a very high profile. The German Foreign Minister Hans-Dieter Genscher stated in the Bundestag:

> Exactly because it is a matter of securing and maintaining–by peaceful means–economic stabilization, social justice, national sovereignty, and social pluralism in a geostrategically important region ridden by crises and conflicts, our friends in Central America need the partnership of the European Community. If we refuse this partnership, or if we are too fainthearted or even only too indecisive in our political and economic involvement, we will be abandoning the

peoples of this region to growing destabilization and the burden of severe social problems.[4]

There are different reasons why the Europeans entered into the new political relationship with the Central Americans in the backyard of the U.S. The former socialist Spanish Foreign Minister Fernando Morán listed three:

*Europe, as a part of the West, could not allow the United States alone to arrogate to itself the sole representation of Western interests.

*Europe might be affected by the military deployment carried out by the United States in Central America.

*Europe was worried that the logic of U.S. policy in Central America might lead to a military intervention in the region.[5]

On the Christian-Democratic side of the European political spectrum the then German minister of state for foreign affairs, Alois Mertes, stated that the "West must prove to Latin America that it does not primarily support the traditional power elites but rather is prepared to stand up in the region for Western values such as democracy, the constitutional state, and social justice." A common Western position on Central America, Mertes went on to say, "based on free choice and mutual consultation and discussion would contribute to the strengthening of the West's credibility throughout the world."[6] It is fair to say that in its ideological overtones and in its stated aims the San José dialogue between the European Community and Central America was at odds with the line actually pursued by the Reagan Administration in a part of the world had

---

[4]Quoted in Pierre, op. cit., p. 108.

[5]Ibid. pp. 29-30.

[6]Alois Mertes, "Europe's Role in Central America: A West German Christian Democratic View," in Pierre, pp. 128-129.

traditionally been regarded as the safe backyard of the United States.

There were, however, other reasons for the awakening of European interest in Central America. I shall mention only three:

*In 1982 the Argentine military government occupied the Falkland Islands. In response the United Kingdom resorted to military action against Argentina. European Community solidarity was put to a severe test in helping one of the member states. Latin America countries professed support for Argentina. The conflict left resentment throughout the continent. Its consequences needed to be counteracted. The deepening crisis in Central America brought together the European Community and Latin American needs.

*The spread of the democratization process in Latin America also helped awaken interest in European Community circles. Central America became a test case where European inputs, be they ideological, economic, or political might push the balance.

*Finally, the third enlargement made the European Community more heterogeneous and more open towards economic and social realities far removed from those of Northern or Central Europe. The new member states, Spain and Portugal, brought with them long-standing relations with Latin America and in the case of Spain at least it is safe to say that interest in the continent had been a mainstay of foreign policy for many decades.

The political dialogue and the economic cooperation activities in Central America developed by the European Community and its member states weathered all the difficulties and became an entrenched feature in Community foreign policy. Such contacts fulfilled three important tasks:

*They contributed to enhancing the effectiveness and the influence of the Europeans in foreign policy.

*They contributed to reinforcing the European identity in international politics.

*They led the European Community to formally obtain information from its partners on important current issues.

That the European-Central American dialogue gained strength since 1985 was a remarkable achievement. In the 1980s Central America had become a center for ideological conflict. Polarization in Nicaragua and El Salvador, for example, seemed to be self-reinforcing. The United States sought by a vast array of means to overthrow the Sandinista regime. Nicaraguans and Cubans went to great lengths to try to prevent a defeat of the guerrillas in El Salvador.

Throughout this period the Community and its member states continued to attach utmost importance to the relationship with Central America. It was primarily through political and economic means that they wished to reduce the tensions in the region. Through numerous declarations within the framework of the European Political Cooperation and regular contacts with the parties concerned, it was hoped that progress towards a peaceful settlement of the conflict would be made. Economic cooperation was intensified and became a permanent feature of the relationship.

All through these years the approach consistently followed by the Europeans was at odds with the line actually followed by the Reagan Administration. The Europeans never publicly expressed disagreement with the United States. Nevertheless the definition of the European positions necessitated a lot of internal bargaining before a consensus could be achieved. Some member states wanted to establish a direct link between economic assistance and the political situation in Nicaragua and El Salvador. Others accepted a less restrictive course. However, in order to avoid further tensions with the United States about the situation in Central America, steps were taken to improve consultations with Washington in 1987 and 1988.

European Community relations with Central America took a turn for the better after the signing of the Esquipulas agreement in August 1987, following the initiatives launched by the Costa Rican president, Dr. Oscar Arias. As stated by Professor Pastor, "by constructing a framework that would require each Central American nation to comply with each principle at the same time, Arias placed the burden on the country that refused to comply."[7]

This was exactly what the European Community needed. The step taken by the Central Americans was a leap beyond Contadora. The Sandinista Government could not accept an imposition emanating directly from Washington. However, it could reconcile itself to accept a new dialogue proposed by the Central Americans themselves in a regional framework.

Since 1987 the annuality of the ministerial conferences within the San José dialogue became firmly established. In February of that year the meeting took place in Guatemala; in February-March of 1988 in Hamburg; in February 1990 in San Pedro Sula, Honduras; and in April 1990 in Dublin. The 1991 meeting was scheduled for March in Managua.

Some negative comments on the course of the San José dialogue have been made on the basis of the actual participation of European foreign ministers at the meetings. It is true that in 1984 and 1985 the European side was represented almost entirely by the foreign ministers themselves. Later, from 1987 onwards, about half of the twelve governments were represented only at a lower level (minister of state), while the dialogue partners continued to be present at the foreign minister level.

From this fact some observers have concluded that the European interest towards Central America had lessened. A more complete picture emerges, however, when the actual content of the decisions made at the meetings is considered. Were this to be done, it could be concluded that direct economic and financial commitments by the European Community towards Central America have become more complex and ambitious. In 1989 lengthy consideration was given to the establishment, with Community funds, of a Central American regional payments

---

[7]Robert A. Pastor, *Condemned to Repetition. The United States and Nicaragua* (Princeton: Princeton University Press, 1987), p. 335.

system, which was formally approved the following year at the Dublin ministerial meeting. It will commit up to 140 million ECUs within the next three years.

The type of dialogue established by the European side with Central America became a permanent feature of European Political Cooperation in the late 1980s. During all this period the market share of the Central American states in the European Community remained minimal. The continuation of the dialogue was therefore not primarily based on economic considerations by the Community but on political ones.

The ratio of a low economic relevance on the one hand and the high quality of the political dialogue on the other supports the view that political motives were the driving force of the European approach. It is precisely through the means the European Community has at its disposal like diplomatic and political solidarity, underpinned by economic cooperation measures, that the Europeans wish to make their own contribution to fostering the Central American peace process.

The experience so far shows that, whatever the individual assessments by the Community member states of the Central American situation and of United States policies towards the area, each party within the European Community considers the benefits to be drawn from collective policy-making in the San José dialogue to be greater than the cost of investing in it. The member states have not sustained any loss of national sovereignty or any higher degree of exposure to pressures from the outside in conducting this exercise. Neither have they been constrained in their traditional diplomacy for the sake of the San José dialogue. On the contrary, the multilateral, European level adds a new dimension to the external position of the participants without replacing national ones.

It is therefore not surprising that the San José dialogue has been maintained without difficulty. The dialogue has combined the European Community's desire to help stabilize the forces and countries engaged in the search for peace and the Central Americans' interest in obtaining economic assistance and political support from Europe.

Has the San José dialogue been effective?

The San José dialogue has performed some important roles, both from the European and the Central American point of view. For the Community, this dialogue, which was developed in the face of some opposition from the United States, helped enhance the European Community's role in the international scene. It was instrumental in shaping perceptions and actions in a common direction towards a faraway region where many of the member states had nothing to gain or to lose. It led to a willingness to allocate highly scarce budgetary Community resources to countries where the European presence, with a few exceptions, was and is very small. It generated dynamics whereby common denominators were found to establish diagnoses of the actions to follow and of the causes of instability in the region.

For the Central Americans, the San José dialogue opened a second window of opportunity. It created some pressure to establish a common front to negotiate political statements with the Europeans concerning the strategy and tactics to find Central American solutions to Central American problems. It gave a helping hand to governments such as the Sandinista, which became very embattled as a result of U.S. animosity.

On the other hand, the European Community was well aware of the limits of the exercise. The dialogue was conducted as a flanking maneuver for the benefit of Central American responses to the crisis. Whenever the Intra-Central American pace slackened, the Community showed a little red flag. Whenever the pace quickened, the Community became more willing to contemplate further co-operative action.

Never did the European Community intend to substitute itself for other actors more directly interested in the Central American crisis, be they the Central Americans, Contadora nations, or the United States. However, the joining of efforts with the Contadora countries meant for the Community the possibility of developing new group-to-group contacts, once Contadora and the Contadora support group developed into the Rio Group. To that extent the San José dialogue was a necessary, although not a sufficient condition for the institutionalization of the current political dialogue between the European Community and the enlarged Rio Group.

The political situation has changed in Central America, because of external and internal factors. On the external side, the crumbling of the Communist regimes in Eastern Europe and reforms within the Soviet Union have drastically reduced Eastern European involvement in the region. Cuba has become isolated. The rigid, confrontational strategy of the Reagan Administration was replaced by more flexible tactics. All this has contributed to lessening outside interference in the region. On the internal side, the 1990 elections in Nicaragua and the launching of the domestic peace process have lessened pressures and led to a renewed effort in the search for Central American solutions. Only in El Salvador and Guatemala do factors of instability remain active.

The reasons which were operational at the outset of the San José dialogue no longer apply. However, the political capital created by the European Community both in Central America and in Latin America at large remains intact. Now that peace in the region is a distinct possibility, it would be inconsistent with stated Community policy if the political and economic efforts were to slacken. The next ministerial meetings of the San José dialogue will point the way forward.

EUROPEAN COMMUNITY'S REGIONAL PROGRAMS TOWARD CENTRAL AMERICA

Fernando Cardesa

Commission of the European Community

European Community cooperation with the region of Central America began in 1976, from which time various funds have been designated in the Community budget for cooperation with developing countries in Asia and Latin America. It is since this date that the European Community, as a supranational entity, has opened itself up for cooperation toward other areas apart from the traditional countries of Africa, the Caribbean, and the Pacific (ACP), former colonies associated with the European Economic Community through the Lomé Conventions.

Between 1976 and 1984 EC cooperation with Central America was negligible due to the little political interest it inspired. Before 1976, the region, which was not yet overwhelmed by the ordeals of the crisis, enjoyed levels of well-being comparable to some member states of the European Economic Community. In addition, the military regimes that had proliferated in the region did not arouse a spirit of *animus cooperandi* on the part of the EC.

Since this date, the Community has begun a new role as a moderator in the international scene and since 1983 has devoted its presence in the world to its foreign relations as a supranational entity, establishing diplomatic relations, and accrediting representatives to the posts of ambassadors to third countries.

During the period from 1976-1984, Community cooperation with the region of Central America amounted to 197.66 million ECUs. In 1984 there began a period of growing changes in Community cooperation with the region. This landmark was determined by the first ministerial meeting between the foreign ministers of the Community and of Central America, a meeting which formed the basis for the annual San José Conferences. The name comes from the capital of Costa Rica, San José, where the first conference was held.

The Community objectives of the conference were, in the first phase, to contribute to the relaxation of tensions in the region; reduce the conflict; to mitigate the effects of an East-West confrontation, which was gaining attention as well as overtones of escalation; and definitively to support regional attempts at an internal solution to the conflicts of the Isthmus.

The European Community in this way asserted its presence in the international scene as a benevolent power. The new phase of cooperation began with more substantive budgetary designations:

YEAR	*ECUs*[1]
1984	38.88[2]
1985	73.87
1986	56.91
1987	77.77
1988	109.97
1989	92.65
1990	116.72
Total 1984 - 1990	565.97

The primary philosophy of this cooperation is that of giving support and content to the economic and political dialogue started between the EC and Central America, based on two cardinal points:

---

[1]One ECU = U.S. $1.20 (November 1991)

[2]In millions

1) Support a triangulation of *Peace - Democracy - Development*

2) Support the regional forces in economic and political integration

The two points complement each other, and the cooperation is primarily destined to benefit the sectors of the population less favored by rural development programs with the goal of eliminating the centers of societal margination, conflict and subversion on one hand, and to the economic integration of growing social sectors with an objective of increasing dialogue between political and economic agents which particularly contribute to the relaxation of tensions and to the creation of areas of common interest in order to help in the search for regional solutions to the conflicts.

The cooperation programs that have been approved and financed with technical and financial assistance funds to the countries of the region are the following:

COUNTRY	*TITLE*	*ECUs (mill.)*
GUATEMALA	Aid to the small farmer in the Pacific Region (Arisco)	12.0
	Support to agrarian transformation of the Pacific region (Montellano, San Carlos Málaga)	5.5
	Development program in the Lake Atitlán region	3.5

EL SALVADOR	Rehabilitation program for the University of El Salvador	3.3
	Construction of a Zacamil hospital	12.0
	Program for the development of craftsmanship in lesser developed zones	6.0
HONDURAS	Road construction in coffee farming regions	2.1
	Construction of storage bins for basic grains	3.5
	Development project for indigenous communities	1.4
	Strengthening of agrarian reform and rural development integration	16.9
	Consolidation of agrarian reform groups in the southern zone	9.0
	Rehabilitating and maintaining penetrating roads	2.75
	Supplying water and basic sanitation in the rural sector of health region #1	14.5

NICARAGUA	Development program for basic food products	7.4
	Regional integration development of Waslala	3.5
	Program to improve the trade patterns and diminish losses of the basic grains harvests	2.5
COSTA RICA	Program for rural integration development for the region of Osa and Golfito	9.95
	Support to agrarian reform and rural development	23.0
	Program for productive micro-projects in favor of Costa Rican refugees	3.6
PANAMA	Rehabilitation of St. Thomas Hospital	4.0

Regional Cooperation in Favor of Integration

Actions of a regional character have taken into consideration the social sectors most deprived: infants, fishing, and health, the economic sectors with the most social impact such as the small and medium-sized businesses and cooperatives. The latter absorbs 10 percent of the active population of the region.

The Central American small and medium-sized businesses with a great capacity for strengthening and expanding have been discriminated against by the financial system due to the inflexibility of the credit mechanisms whose methods and guarantees were badly adapted to the particularities of this sector.

There has been an effort, as well as with this program with the small and medium-sized businesses, to strengthen the institutional and financial capacity of the Central American Bank of Economic Integration (BCIE), putting at its disposal resources of approximately 22 million ECUs.

In the cooperative sector there has been a desire to obtain for this sector the protective assistance of the state in order to put it in the atmosphere of business activity corresponding to the Central American economic situation. There have been efforts to convert the cooperative sector into a dynamic sector that is exclusively business oriented under the rules of the market.

CENTRAL AMERICA

PROGRAM	*ECUs (mill.)*
Program to eradicate rabies	2.9
Program of aid to small and medium-sized industry	20
Regional program of nutritional security	4.82
Regional program of infant survival	16.5
Development of the fishing sector	14.1
Regional program to encourage cooperatives	22
Regional program of strengthening agricultural investigation of grains	10.8
Radar control for civil air traffic	18.5
Regional system of payments	120
Pilot development project in the Trifinio region	7.5
TOTAL Central America	237

THE EUROPEAN PARLIAMENT AND THE CENTRAL AMERICAN PARLIAMENT: THE PARLIAMENTARY DIMENSION OF RELATIONS BETWEEN CENTRAL AMERICA AND THE EUROPEAN COMMUNITY

Wolf Grabendorff

IRELA

The European Community (EC) and, particularly, the European Parliament (EP) have shown a special interest in the establishment of the Central American Parliament (PARLACEN). This new Central American entity could be established by the end of 1991 with at least three countries (Guatemala, El Salvador, and Honduras) based on the September 1989 Protocol of the PARLACEN Constitutive Treaty, which permits its partial application.

In this context, it is relevant to analyze the motives have driven both regions to pay greater attention to this theme in the framework of relations developed over recent years—principally that which concerns the political dialogue driven by the Cooperation Agreement signed in Luxembourg on November 12, 1985, and the six inter-ministerial conferences of the San José process held between 1984 and 1990. It can be foreseen that in the upcoming San José VII conference to be held in Managua March 18-19, 1991, the PARLACEN theme will once again be considered. It is probable the EC will assign a cooperation line for the operations of the PARLACEN.

It is impossible to establish a parallel between the EP and the PARLACEN; however, it is interesting to present some comparative elements, above all, with relation to other regional parliaments such as the Latin American Parliament (PARLATINO) and the Andean Pact Parliament (PARLANDINO). On the other hand, it is necessary to identify the relationship exists between the processes of economic integration and the emergence of regional parliamentarianism. Also it is necessary to indicate the political function of these and the extent of the diversification and broadening of parliamentary activity at the regional level, as well as the inter-parliamentary contacts in the international sphere, considering the possibilities and obstacles for influencing the regional political, economic, and social processes, internationally and in the respective member countries.

Regional Parliamentarianism

One of the political expressions of regional integration processes of the interdependence and internationalization of the coexistence of the countries of the world is the creation of regional parliaments. Undoubtedly the existence of a climate of peace, the development of representative democracy and historic, political, economic, and cultural links in the different regions of the planet form the fundamental base for the appearance and functioning of regional parliamentarianism.

Nevertheless, the different parliamentary bodies in Asia, the Arab world, Africa, Europe, and Latin America face limits on their functions. In the majority of cases it has to do with forums that meet for a short time in relatively relaxed periods and whose functions cover the deliberation over regional themes such as integration. Likewise, the range and impact of resolutions can only be considered short. On the other hand, the degree of legitimacy is reduced because they have to deal with the delegates of the national parliaments, which means that their regional role is not recognized by the people of their countries, with the exception of the EP and possibly of the PARLACEN in the near future as well as the PARLANDINO at the end of the century, given their character as directly elected parliaments.

In the case of Latin America, in addition to the three parliaments already mentioned (PARLACEN, PARLATINO, and PARLANDINO) initiatives have been proposed under the framework of the Amazonian and River Plate Basin Pact. Elsewhere, active Latin American participation in the World Interparliamentary Union (WIU) and in interparliamentary meetings between the European Parliament and Latin America is an indicator of a certain boom in regional parliamentary action.

The historical antecedents of regional parliamentarianism in Latin America go back to Simón Bolívar's ideas and the experiences of the political unions between various countries in South America and Central America at the beginning of the last century. Until the end of the nineteenth century the idea of political union between states was privileged, while in the last 50 years economic integration has had support.

Economic integration and the emergence of regional parliaments can be considered parallel processes. The origins of PARLATINO go back to 1964 when it was founded by 13 countries in a context of support for integration. It can be pointed out that the Latin American Free Trade Association (LAFTA), created in 1960, and the Central American Common Market (CACM), constituted in 1962, were important points of reference for this subcontinental parliamentary entity, which at the present time groups 19 countries.

The presidents of the member countries of the Andean Pact created PARLANDINO in 1979. This parliament is considered in its Constitutive Treaty to be the common organ for deliberation of the subregional integration process, and in 1987 it was designated as the principal organ of the Cartagena Treaty. The Amazonian Parliament is constituted under the Amazonian Pact and made up of the five countries of the Andean Pact, Brazil, Suriname, and Guyana.

The Context and Motives of the Relationship Between the EP and PARLACEN

The initiative for creation of PARLACEN was expressed in the Esquipulas I declaration by the five Central American presidents on May 25, 1985, and retaken in the Esquipulas II declaration of August 8, 1987. The EP demonstrated its support for the PARLACEN initiative on September 17, 1987, and in the San José III Political Communiqué in 1987 offered its support to PARLACEN. In 1988 the EP assigned 20 million ECUs for the electoral processes of PARLACEN. Subsequently, this matter was presented in the next meetings of the San José process, in various resolutions of the EP, and at the eighth and ninth interparliamentary meetings between the EP and the PARLATINO. Likewise, a vigorous EP delegation travelled in 1988 through the five countries to promote ratification of the PARLACEN Treaty by the national parliaments. All this is an indicator of an intense bi-regional exchange on this idea.

This European identification with the shaping of PARLACEN and the particular Central American orientation toward the European example of political and economic integration, and especially, the functioning of its regional parliament, coincide with various favorable factors for this interregional rapprochement:

1) The first phase of the San José process stresses peace, democracy, and regional integration. This feeds a political perception of biregional relations. To this must be added the fact that the economic interests of the EC and its member countries in Central America are insignificant,

although it is not considered opportune to be absent from the region, given the European intention of supporting Latin American alternatives of seeking solutions to the crisis through the Contadora and Esquipulas processes.

2) The parliamentary dimension of relations is stimulated by the boom in development cooperation. In the period between 1979 and 1985 the EC assigned for this area an annual average of 40 million ECUs, while in the last five years it grew to an annual average of around 100 million ECUs, which represents more than 50 percent of total aid for all Latin America. With the creation of PARLACEN a new kind of direct political cooperation between the EP and PARLACEN could be opened.

3) The European perception is that PARLACEN could be a factor that propels integration and could transform itself into a permanent forum for dialogue, which institutionalizes the Esquipulas process and contributes to democratization and pluralism. This coincides with the EC's conception regarding group to group relations and European democratic traditions.

4) On the other hand, PARLACEN will be the only regional parliament, besides the EP, which will be elected directly. The EP considers this precedent important in the search for legitimization similar to other regional parliaments integrated by delegates of the national parliaments because the electoral route strengthens the position of regional and international parliamentarianism.

5) We cannot lose sight of the degree of affinity between the different political forces of both regions grouped in the Christian Democrat, Social

Democrat, Liberal, and International Democratic Union international parties. In the past ten years the Central American governments have been led by political group members of or close to one of these parties. This has facilitated dialogue between their leaders and the playing of a regional political role by the parliamentarians.

6) The EP has assumed a direct role with regard to the organization of observer missions in the recent electoral processes in Panama, Nicaragua, and El Salvador. Its members have participated in numerous events relevant to the region and the PARLACEN in Central America and Europe. Central American officials have long been trained in Brussels, Luxembourg, and Strasbourg in branches of the EC and EP for their activities related to the creation and functioning of the PARLACEN. This has led to an intensification of contacts between politicians, deputies, and specialists from both regions with direct relation to the issue of the emergence of PARLACEN, which has generated an important exchange of experiences and expectations on both sides, which also exercise the informal function of a feed back mechanism.

Similarities and Differences between the EP and PARLACEN

The common aspects between these two regional parliaments are based on the fact that both emerge as a product of the experience in their respective armed conflicts, the search for alternatives for a lasting peace, and in the framework of the necessity of pushing integration. On the other hand, its deputies will be elected in a direct manner. Obviously, the degree and dimension of progress in integration of the European Community are much wider and profound than in the Central American case.

In 1962 the parliamentary body of the old continent, in existence since 1952, assumes the name of European Parliament and becomes an integral part of the EC institutions, along with the Council, the Commission, and the Court of Justice. At the present time it is made up of 518 deputies elected in direct form and practically simultaneously in the 12 member countries, based on a proportional distribution by country. This is why countries with a larger population have between 60 and 81 seats and those with a smaller population between six and 25 deputies. Its functions include parliamentary control organ over the EC and aspects related to its budget.

Its political influence grew after the first direct elections in 1979 and due to its prior position in favor of economic and political integration, above all, concerning pushing the implementation of the Single European Act, the Single European Market, and European Political Union, as well as its role as a European forum in which multiple international political issues, environmental protection, citizens' rights, and others are discussed, perhaps, in other cases, with greater audacity than in the national parliaments.

One of the principal roles of the EP is developing a regional parliamentary dimension, pluralism, and the generation of political consensus beyond national frontiers. It must be balanced between national positions; the interests of certain regions such as Catalonia, Northern Ireland, etc., and the postures adopted by political groups organized by multinational factions. In any case, the EP has been gaining space and political weight within the EC.

According to the critics of the EP this frankness is due to the fact that its resolutions are not binding and do not necessarily have a real impact on community-wide legislation, a function that is primordially assumed by the Council made up of governments, just as they do not have an effect on the promulgation of national laws. In addition, its high operating cost, with an elevated number of parliamentarians and employees, is criticized.

PARLACEN will be made up of 20 deputies from each member country. This signifies that, in contrast to the EP, it will not have proportional representation. In addition, PARLACEN will incorporate former presidents and vice-presidents, something not contemplated in the EP. Its functions are deliberative and give impetus to regional integration, peace, and democracy. This, and its possible organization by multinational political factions, constitutes an element similar to the EP.

Although PARLACEN will elect, now that it has been formed by the five Central American Common Market (CACM) countries, the executives of integration institutions (such as the permanent secretariat of the Central American Integration Treaty (SIECA) and others) and the Meeting of Vice-Presidents will assume other functions for pushing regional integration, this initial PARLACEN treaty does not form an integral part of the existing economic integration treaties—which also happens with the EP. Nevertheless, there exists no juridical contradiction between both types of treaties. Moreover, parliamentary ratification of the PARLACEN Treaty gives legal force to integration, which presently has only partial force in the four countries that have already ratified it—Costa Rica being the exception.

PARLACEN's critics consider its functions very limited; it is a relatively expensive entity and will not be joined by all the countries. Still, the elections in Nicaragua, according to the protocol and ratification of the PARLACEN Treaty in Costa Rica's Legislative Assembly, are pending.

The Role of Regional Elections

Elections imply a greater degree of legitimacy and moral and political force, as well as being an important advancement among the population through electoral campaigns. (This is related to the way regional parliaments develop their potential and fulfill their functions.) Likewise, decisions made under an electoral process have greater social and political presence in their respective regions and at the international level. On the other hand, one may assume that its possibilities of gaining more space and extending its funcions will increase with direct elections.

The electoral process of the EP is founded on twelve national legislatures and a text common to the twelve member countries. This text establishes that elections shall be simultaneous and that results cannot be known until the elections are finished in all the different countries. Similarly, in the case of PARLACEN elections are also realized in accordance with the national legislative texts and based on what is established in the Protocol and the parts in force of the Constitutive Treaty. This means that a period of 18 months is granted for the holding of elections in the countries which have ratified the Protocol. In Honduras, the 20 active deputies and their substitutes were elected in November 1989; in Guatemala in November 1990; in El Salvador in March 1991 (all of them within the framework of general elections); while Nicaragua must hold elections before November 1991.

A fundamental difference between the electoral processes in both regions is that the democratic system and the electoral system in the EC can rely on a high degree of development and consolidation, and to a great extent, are sustained by a long historic tradition and popular culture. The degree of acceptance of the EP role is established by a reasonable level of participation in the elections (although it does not reach the percentages of the general elections for the governments or the national parliaments).

In Central America, with the exception of Costa Rica, the national electoral processes bring together the formal legal requisites necessary to comply with the principles of democracy, representation, and liberty. Nevertheless, those are various problems related to the internal political situation present themselves: in some cases violence and armed conflict, administrative weaknesses of the electoral system due to a lack of qualified human resources and financial means, and difficulties in the electoral register. Moreover, in some countries a consistent electoral tradition has not yet been generated.

Nevertheless, it can be assumed that the fulfillment and continuity of the national electoral processes and the future realization of true regional elections for PARLACEN could mean substantial advances in overcoming these problems—the strengthening of valid democratic systems, as well as the generation of substantive changes in favor of the development of a political culture that gradually overcomes the use of violence as an attitude in the political process. Concrete European cooperation could take into account elements which aid the consolidation of a process of this nature.

The Role of Parties, Factions, and Internationals

In the EC a reconciliation has been produced between the electorate and the objectives of economic and political integration through the political parties and the electoral campaigns, especially for the EP elections. A similar phenomenon could take place in Central America in the five countries, close to 50 parties of different political currents could participate. This could imply a greater familiarity and identification with PARLACEN and the Central American integration process.

Similar to the EP, in PARLACEN an internal dynamic shaping political groups could take place and specialized commissions and a rapprochement with the integration organs. This same dynamic, along with partisan activity and legitimization through direct elections, could translate itself into important political capital for PAR-

LACEN. On the other hand, the birth of regional political bodies with links to the political groups of the EP and the party internationals could contribute to the diversification, regionalization, and internationalization of parliamentary activity, and transform PARLACEN into a platform to push for a greater Latin American presence in the international community.

In short, the cooperation of the EP and the party internationals could contribute to modernizing regional parliamentary activity and widening the political-partisan vision of regional integration.

EUROPEAN COMMUNITY - CENTRAL AMERICAN ECONOMIC RELATIONS: POSSIBLE EFFECTS OF THE SINGLE EUROPEAN MARKET

Rafael Menjívar Larín

FLACSO - Costa Rica

Since the signing of the Single Act in 1987, steps have been accelerated towards the construction in January 1993 of the Single European Market (SEM) and towards the consolidation of the European Economic Community as one of the most important economic blocs in the world. This process explains the action that other blocs and countries have developed during this period in order to take advantage of the benefits or in order to avoid the possible negative effects that such a process will certainly bring about.

Central America, despite its weaknesses, potentials and in terms of its relative importance, is not exempt from the effects of the process of constitution of the SEM. The implications, however, have other dimensions and a different framework compared with other countries. This is particularly so, first because of the profoundly political profile of the relations established with the EEC in 1984 and cemented by means of the Luxembourg Agreement, and, secondly, due to the features of its productive apparatus, deteriorated after ten years of crisis. Such a productive system must face the significant restructuring of the world.

According to the definition in the Single European Act, the single market is considered as "an area without internal frontiers, in which the free movement of goods, persons, services and capital is ensured in accordance with the provisions of the Treaty." From this, it is clear that in a strict sense the 1992 process refers to the removal, within the Community, of non-tariff barriers through a series of legal measures established in the White Paper. Derived effects of such a process will affect, in different ways, third countries, among them the Central American States.

In this paper, in a general approach and based on the results of the Cecchini paper, some considerations will be made about the benefits that the SEM could bring about to Central American-EEC relations in the future. However, the main purpose of this paper is to address the aspects that, despite the fact that in the above definition they are not in themselves a part of the 1992 process and could remarkably neutralize the advantages of 1992. To make such considerations, we are convinced that the framework of the exceptional relations between the EEC and Central America established in the San José meetings and in the Luxembourg Agreement is the only basis that could allow the Central American countries not only to take advantage of the benefits, but to have a more structural effect on the reactivation and economic and social development of the region.

To the extent that it is the result of a series of research papers concerning the matter, is presented schematically and in the form of conclusions with regard to the economic and financial relations among the two regions. We think that such a presentation will provide some elements to take into account in the discussion. In any case, the exposition and discussion could conduce to develop, based on data, the arguments advanced here.

Central American-European Economic Community Relations

Trade between Central America and the EEC

The Central American countries as a whole are gradually returning to a market concentration, a former trend that was reduced in the past by means of the economic integration; broader relations with Europe; and partial agreements with the rest of the Latin American countries. This change in the geographical structure of the markets is partially the result of the economic policy applied since the mid-1980s. Although this is a strong trend, after the crisis the Central American countries are modestly returning to the path of intra-regional trade, in the framework of a policy of support of the solution of the financial problems derived from the intra-regional commercial debt generated during the crisis of the 1980s and with the financial support of the EEC.

In the case that it proves to be difficult to go beyond this only element of support to the payment system in Central America, the Central American countries (except in the case of a new and serious crisis) will continue to increase their imports. This secular trend will tend to be more dynamic according to the consolidation of external trade liberalization. The EC is the second most important supplier to the Central American region, but despite its increasing trend in absolute terms, purchases from the EC by Central America have maintained a relatively stable level (15 percent of the total), and despite the geographical changes presented in trade we cannot see any dynamism in import related transactions.

The EC market is very important for banana, coffee, and cotton. In a certain manner is also important for non-processed and semi-elaborated wood (the main purchasers are other countries). It has no significance for meat, crustaceans, mollusks, and sugar. Over time, it appears that changes in European purchases for coffee tend to stagnate and only shows a positive trend in the case of bananas. As a consequence, the EC has been reducing its emphasis on traditional exports, except for the case of bananas.

The European market is still an important market for other traditional goods, but this importance tends to be downplayed. For plants, cacao and industrial parts, its participation is very low compared to the United States and other markets; in the case of plants that are used particularly for the pharmaceutical and beauty industries, the markets have virtually disappeared. In tobacco, exports to Europe are minimal and still decreasing. Just in the case of oleaginous seeds and fruits there is a significant increment, both for total exports and for exports to the European market. It is also worth mentioning that in the case of traditional goods with reduced trade significance, such as natural honey, cardamom and other seeds, molasses, minerals, and leather, the European market had an important presence by the end of the 1970s.

By the end of the 1980s, however, it was only in the group of minerals that the proportion of total exports to Europe remained important. The European market is constant for the case of natural bee honey.

In summary, it can be concluded that, for Central America, in the case of traditional goods: 1) these types of products continue to constitute a high proportion of total Central American exports to the rest of the world—this proportion has even increased from 73 percent to 78 percent; 2) trade between EC and Central America consists basically of these kinds of goods (96 percent) and remains steady. On the other hand, concerning trade with the U.S. and other markets, while the proportion is still high, it is decreasing; 3) all these considerations show that while access to the European market continues to consist of traditional products and the tendency is toward concentration of a few of them, trade possibilities among the two regions are restricted.

In general terms, trade on nontraditional products with third countries is dynamic. The main source of dynamism is sales to the U.S. market; this dynamism has been propagated to other markets, including the European one, supported by the internal productive base as well as the multiplier effect of exports to the U.S. growth rates on trade with Europe, in recent years, are still far below the ones observed with other markets, except for the case of agricultural-based nontraditional products (flowers, plants, vegetables, tuberculous). There is no trade on sea goods, despite the fact that after 1986 this became an export in Central America; trade on extractive industries has been declining; trade on manufactured goods is still insignificant.

With respect to Central American nontraditional exports of industrial origin, there exists a remarkable export potential which does not seem to be utilized with due intensity; that is the case even in the institutional framework established from 1984 and reinforced by the economic agreement signed in Luxembourg. One of the explanations for this situation is the fact that the conditions of access are not broad enough; studies have been carried out in order to determine the degree to which this kind of trade is linked to the Generalized System of Preferences (GSP) applied to developing countries. It is not possible to assure that for manufactured Central American goods there exists a substantive treatment and broad access to the European market that, as related data shows, are originated in industries established and developed by the Central American Common Market itself.

Technological Dependence

In Central America, there is a clear technological dependence on the rest of the world, as its import structures show. In the past, import controls were a main aspect of the development policy, but this aspect has been abandoned by the new policy.

There is a trend towards "specialization" in the markets of origin of imports, which in the case of Central America has resulted in an interesting process of "diversification" of suppliers. As a consequence, there exists a high level of competitiveness in import structure in the industrialized countries in the West that supply Central America. This competition is brought about by means of participation—with certain degrees of specialization—in some kind of goods or in a more open participation with others.

The EC is an important supplier for Central American imports because of its apparent "specialization" chemical goods), but also because of the important presence of manufactured and capital goods in total imports. But from the specialization in its import structure it cannot be concluded that there is necessarily a broad participation in Central American demand, at least in all cases; hence, in a certain manner the permanent strong presence of the U.S. reduces the relative significance of the EC, particularly in chemical and connected industries, in capital goods, and in industrial inputs. The same is true about the participation of other countries in Latin America and the Caribbean; with respect to Japan the case is referred to United States goods mainly in transport materials.

As a consequence, in all those goods so important for development and according to import total and structure, it should not be said that there is a strong consistency in European supply for Central American countries compared with other regions in the world. All figures confirm the traditional relations and strong reliance on U.S. imports, and this dependence seems to be increasing by means of the significant neo-liberal policies in these Central American countries.

Central American Financial Situation

In these difficult times for international financial issues, all financing through credits, investment and unilateral transfers, is very much needed for Central American countries. Under these types of urgent circumstances, there is usually pressure for the acceptance of conditions—not necessarily favorable—in the short-or long-term. It is this historical circumstance that gives force and power to the conditionality of creditors, besides capital scarcity from other sources.

Year by year, particularly in recent times, the Central American countries have observed how their expectations for a coherent and sustained development have fallen. A significant proportion of domestic resources should be transferred abroad in payments. Part of this is sent abroad, with all connotations implied in the so-called "capital flight."

If external financial support is not assured, there are no possibilities of investment and infrastructure development.

Today in most of the countries of this region, net transfers of resources from credits yield negative results and, consequently, due payments have been accumulated, even with EC countries. Other countries have gone beyond that and have re-financed their obligations with the Paris Club and with private international creditors. It is obvious that the most convenient situation is that, at least, the present conditions do not worsen and, preferably, that actions are taken in order to meet the obligations and improve financial flows.

Financial cooperation from the EC and its member states is important for Central America. Such financing is estimated at least $2.5 billion by December 31, 1988. Financial relations with the EC and its member states are advantageous in terms of private investment and credits. The former, as peace in the region consolidates, can accelerate its already observed dynamism in countries where political conditions are more favorable. Credits tend to continue the support of the acute balance of payment problem as well as development needs. All these features make this cooperation essentially different from others.

The European finance "structure" is quite aware of the needs and requirements of Central American development, in contrast with other experiences. To quote just one example, from total financial cooperation (with the exception of credits), an average of 33 percent between 1985 and 1987 was addressed to food aid, and this concentrated in several countries (El Salvador and Honduras). Support for a broad scope of problems related with refugees and displaced persons is another relatively important part of this financial cooperation—a solution to Central American needs that is shared in great manner with the United Nations Organization.

Also evident, with respect to other sources, is European interest in rescuing and giving impulse to Central American regional integration, in respect to the legitimate aspiration of these countries but also on the basis of a clear historical conception from the EC. Financial support recently approved in order to stimulate intra-regional trade is a major signal of this new approach.

The geographical distribution of cooperation—an approach that does not seem to exist in other cases—shows on the part of the EC a high level of sensibility and flexibility, in order to respond to the sometimes profound and large-scale requirements of the Central American people.

Finally, in the case of financial relations between the EC and Central America, a new "style" of financial cooperation has been witnessed. At the same time, this is carried out both bilaterally and regional on a regional basis—based on previous consultations and negotiations in different forums established specifically for that purpose. This modality of a new style offers very positive opportunities for the future.

General Conclusions

From the development point of view, economic relations with the EEC are of great importance for Central American countries but of small significance for European countries. From the perspective of supply for consumption it has particular significance—in some specific goods—for the European countries; this significance in consumption translates, for Central American countries, into an important element in the performance of economic activity mainly related to: 1) the maintenance of an external demand in traditional goods; 2) the impulse of banana exports; and 3) the possibility of increasing, in a constant and progressive manner, nontraditional exports. Hence, these relations are particularly significant for development.

From the point of view of supply of goods for Central American countries, European exports are a very small percentage of total exports; from the Central American point of view, such purchases from Europe are an essential element of its supply of inputs, capital goods, and transport material and equipment—that is to say that they are significant in terms of productive development.

For Europe, financial relations with Central America have a very low profile with respect to total international financial support, but they have a political significance; for Central Americans they are of vital importance if we take into account that they represent from 13 percent to 15 percent of all external financial cooperation in the last ten years. Its impact on development is very broad, given the nature of the financing, its favorable conditions, and its specific destination. Furthermore, its conditionality is weaker than other sources and its intention is more related to the support of the integration than in other cases.

There is no substantial relationship (neither positive nor conflictive) between Europe and Central America with respect to the external debt of the Central American countries; the proportion of the external debt owed to Europe is very small.

It is the only case in Latin America and the Caribbean in which, since 1984, such political-economic relations have been truly institutionalized in terms of a group of countries independent one from the other.

The economic cooperation carried out by the EC has a high political significance for the Central American countries and for the European countries; European support is very significant from both the economic and social points of view in Central America.

Possible Effects of the SEM and Factors That Could Neutralize its Positive Effects

Possible Effects of the SEM

There is no doubt that the economic consequences of Europe after 1992 will constitute an important turning point in international economic relations—the way we observe them now. To a greater or lesser extent to different countries and regions, the Single European Market can have a positive effect according to various elements, among which should be the ability of the countries to develop, compete and negotiate, as well as the way the process itself provided in the Single Act will affect the way the EC behaves.

Independent of the critical observations that necessarily are made of the Cecchini Paper (1988)[3] to evaluate the concrete impact in each region or group of countries, this is still a valid framework to estimate the positive effects that the SEM will have in third countries. Hence, in this paper, the Cecchini Paper will be used as a guide to measure the possible positive effects in the case of Central America.

In macroeconomic terms, what has been evaluated are the effects of the reduction of obstacles and customs procedures in governmental purchases and financial services. These elements would have effects on prices, demand and production, as well as an appreciable increase in investment. Cecchini estimated an increase of 4.5 percent in GDP, 1.8 millon in new employment, a reduction of 6.1 percent in consumer prices and an improvement of 2.2 percent in the global balance of the public sector.

From those main issues, in the case of Central America because of its present level of development, it can be predicted that, for the time being, the impact of public biddings will be small, since definitive incorporation into GATT is still pending, and there are no enterprises established in the EEC; in the future there can be considered the establishment of joint ventures in some cases. By the same token, important effects derived from the new provisions can be dismissed in the areas of high technology industries, telecommunications, and intellectual property rights. The same conditions would apply to financial

---

[3]See CEPAL *Europa 1992 y sus consecuencias económicas para América Latina* (Europe 1992 and its Economic Consequences for Latin America). LC/R.918 (sem. 59/3), Santiago, October 1990.

services—given the small capacity of these countries to offer such services in the SEM.

Conversely, and with respect to what is considered 1992 itself, there will be positive effects in cost reductions of financial services used by Central America, as well as in other services such as telecommunications. The same will occur with price reductions in imports of capital and manufactured goods realized by Central America from the EEC, in which there is estimated a savings equivalent up to 1.6 percent of the total value of such imports.

The foreseeable income effect in macroeconomic terms (estimated by Cecchini in the range of 4.3 percent to 6.4 percent of GDP) could, without considering product elasticities, signify an increase in Central American exports to the SEM, not only consisting of the goods mentioned above but of other goods with a higher industrial component and a stronger impact on the productive structure of the region. This phenomenon could be related to, and actually is already, an increment in European investment in Central America in activities related to exports to the SEM—as in the case of bananas—and in the area of transport between the two regions.

In this respect, however, tariff and non-tariff barriers could affect this perspective. In the case of the Generalized System of Preferences (GSP) for the Central American region, it is important to point out some general aspects:

> *Exclusion of goods of interest to Central America;
>
> *GSP discrimination in favor of least developed countries, to which have been added recently other Latin American countries;
>
> *Incomplete utilization of GSP by Central America, due mainly to the complexity and lack of transparency of the system.

In this global observation of the direct effects of the SEM, it can be assured that, in summary, in terms of 1992 trade relations, the dimensions of transport and investment have the greatest relevance.

Elements That Can Potentially Neutralize Its Effects

Favorable effects of the European Single Market for the Central American region can be neutralized by a series of factors which do not constitute in and of themselves part of the '92 process, but which affect the existing relations and their potential broadening. Among these factors could be considered the GSP special treatment given in such a framework to other Latin American countries, the common agricultural policy (CAP) final results of the GATT Uruguay Round (particularly in the case of tropical goods), preferences given in the framework of Lomé Agreement, and the transition of Spain and Portugal into the EC.

In addition, the terms already established in the commercial and financial relations between the EC and Central America cannot be forgotten. In fact, there is a clear political decision of support of the region, not only in the scope and spirit of the Luxembourg Agreement, but also during the meetings originated in this agreement. Such attitudes have been ratified in the last meeting, San José VI (recently celebrated in Dublin), and in the aftermath of the changes in Eastern Europe. From this Luxembourg spirit there is derived as well the comprehension by the EC that development in Central America—and the still unconsolidated peace—does not only depend on trade levels and access to the European market, but also on financial cooperation in its multiple forms.

This context of the relations is evidence to the fact that treatment of Central American countries, as in the case of ACP countries and territories, is not necessarily linked to the size and weight of the real or potential small markets, but that they are based on factors different from the strictly commercial markets. Central American countries are increasingly given importance in economic relations with the EC, not only because of the fact that the EC is the major supplier of financial support, but also because of the fact that the EC represents an important alternative in terms of geographical diversification of external supply, and in addition, it offers the opportunity of limiting the increasing reliance on the U.S. market. From the side of exports this market has a high potential if the present trade treatment is overhauled.

Some Prospective Considerations About EC-Central American Relations

From the above considerations it can be concluded first that the EC and the Central American countries should intensify the use of negotiation mechanisms already established in order to deepen and model their relations in broader terms in the new international context. This task could be carried out taking into account the following aspects.

In the case of trade, Central America should be granted commercial treatment that reflects an intention to facilitate mutual trade. In this sense, in the short term, there is proposed a profound revision of GSP mechanisms to avoid discrimination against Central American countries, and a broadening of a more favorable treatment in the context of GSP—in terms of tariffs and administrative aspects—for goods of interest to Central American countries. In particular, those linked to the regional policy of export promotion.

Member states of the EC that have a more or less stable trade with Central America are Germany, Italy, Holland. and United Kingdom, as well as Spain and France. These are the countries with which there has been a higher level of trade during the last 12 years. Hence, it is recommended that relations with the EC should be mediated, when it proves necessary, for a closer contact between Central American countries and those of the Community with whom trade is more intense. It would be very useful, therefore, that in the future and in terms of trade relations with the EC—which would appear in the near future to be seriously affected due to different reasons—more intense bilateral talks be carried out with those member states of the EC. All this can be attained by the establishment of subcommissions that could later facilitate multilateral agreements in the context of the Luxembourg Agreement.

In the case of traditional goods, and independently of the accords of the GATT Uruguay Round, it is necessary for the EC and Central America to achieve in the shortest possible time at least three kinds of commitments. One in the specific case of bananas, because as it has already been stated it is here where we encounter a real sense of relations between the two regions. It is important to take into account the following: 1) real participation in the market should not be reduced; 2) non-tariff barriers, particularly administrative or regulatory ones, should not be added, as this would be an additional discrimination against trade of this product; and 3) support should be granted in order to allow Central American marketing enterprises to develop.

Secondly, in the case of coffee, the first aspect to consider is that in order to reorganize the relations and commercial treatment of this product, Central American producers should be granted the same treatment that has been granted to four South American countries. Moreover, the terms and agreements in this case should be negotiated with respect to the treatment that the EC member states will grant to coffee in terms of internal taxes.

Third, on minor traditional goods included in the studies on which this paper is based, it is necessary to revise the GSP system—as in previous cases—and to eliminate the discrimination established since November 1990 in addition to undertaking research in order to determine dispositions can ease exports, distribution, and sales in the European countries so that exports can be revitalized. With respect to industrial origin goods, it is necessary that through the mechanisms of the Luxembourg Agreement, a program established that allows Central American countries to increase exportable supply and exports to the EC. This project has the purpose of supporting and significantly changing the productive structure of Central America on a completely regional basis, beginning with efforts that CACM has already realized in the integration program. In this manner, the EC would support directly the regional integration efforts according to the word and spirit of 1984 ministerial agreements and the Luxembourg agreement. It is recommended therefore that this new program include at least the following aspects: 1) the promotion of European joint ventures in Central America; 2) the development of specific support for a technological program for those industries; and 3) the favorable access of these industrial goods to the European market. For these purposes a mechanism could be established with the participation of three parties: the EC, Central American countries, and entrepreneurs in order to follow up the program. In addition related finance could be channelled through the Central American Bank for Economic Integration (CABEI).

As a complement of the above, we think that it is necessary to intensify relations between the EC and Central America in order to achieve a consolidation of a broad range of technological agreements to establish an important and realistic net of cooperation in this matter. This effort could begin with a pilot program utilizing European technology on the basis of the intensive use of capital goods and linked to a program of purchases of capital goods from European countries.

With respect to financing productive investment, it is necessary not only to support but to intensify these kinds of relations between the EC and Central America. Our studies show that in some way there is an appropriate area for negotiations on development aid. Here we can distinguish two mainstreams: negotiations on external debt and financial support for regional and national development projects.

With regard to the external debt, the ministerial meeting in San José in 1984 indicated that Community ministers declared their disposition to support the Central American countries in specific forums in order to find policies that could contribute to the solution of debt problems. It is necessary to take a firmer step in this matter in order to arrive at an agreement that allows a substantive reallocation of the Central American external debt with the EC and its member states.

With respect to finance for development, important steps have been made such as the support to the financing of Central American regional trade. With the same criteria regional efforts should be supported independently of the financial cooperation granted to CABEI and Central American Parliament. It is necessary to establish important financial lines for integration projects. For such objectives, it is recommended that a special commission on the context of the Luxembourg agreement be constituted in order to determine the integration projects that, in the short-term, should be covered for the next years with this type of financing.

CHAPTER II

EVALUATION OF EUROPEAN COMMUNITY'S COOPERATION WITH CENTRAL AMERICA

LESSONS FROM A SHORT HISTORY;

INFERENCES FROM AN ORIGINAL COOPERATION

Rafael de Juan y Peñalosa

University of the Basque Country

The European Community's relations with Latin America have seen, like love between relatives, times of prohibition, of decriminalization, of liberation, and of rapprochement. It continues without being a true marriage. Could now be a good time to loosen the demands of this demanding love, even though the human family is in an uproar? Some events, such as the *Guidelines for Cooperation with the Latin American and Asian Developing Countries* (June 11, 1990) and the *Rome Declaration on Relations between the Rio Group and the European Community* (December 20, 1990) appear to endorse the present goodwill; others, such as Eastern Europe's growing demands for assistance and the dizzying situation that the Mediterranean creates for the Community (now and much more in the foreseeable future) cause us to consider any optimism cautiously.

Genetics also operate in social organisms. When the Community was created, none of the European personalities who participated thought about Latin America when they made their commitments, attentions, priorities, favorable agreements...; and the Community they brought into being turned its back on that America with which we are now concerned and preoccupied.

Even more, Latin America did not enter into their dreams of the future, not even as a fantasy. I will only now reiterate a quote of Jean Monnet, the Community's true father, because in reality it has confirmed his worth as a prophet. When in his memoirs he lets his imagination run toward the future (something that went against his natural working method, as he himself said several times), he confessed his illusions of power "to reach as soon as possible the time when the Community would be able to enlarge itself and share its prosperity with other European and African countries. With them the time of political construction will also accelerate." Latin America was not even on the horizon; it was the farthest continent in the Community's preoccupation despite its being, with many differences, the most Europeanized.

I leave to establish so distant a history; and I do it because I believe that history continues tying like a bundle the Community's bundles with our America.

Central American Alibi

Despite what has been said, the first Community trade agreements with some Latin American countries were very early (Argentina, 1971; Uruguay, 1973...), above all if we note that the Lomé I Convention, which regulates relations between the Community and the ACP countries, was signed February 28, 1975. Only agreements with some Mediterranean Basin countries (including Spain) preceded the one with Argentina, and those signed with EFTA countries are contemporary with those already mentioned. This relative dawning in the signing of trade accords with some Latin American countries were neither in sync with the Community's best interests, nor followed its criteria for relations with developing countries.

One must wait until the political crisis in Central America for the Community to stop ignoring Latin American countries. This convergence was achieved through politics and not by economics. It could not have been any other way. Latin America counted for little significance in the Community's trade statistics while Central America was even more insignificant. Not so in politics, the Central American volcano, poorly understood and managed even worse by United States diplomacy, became the alibi to ease the distention. Central Europe's prolonged and costly efforts to reach an understanding with Eastern Europe could be eased by a mistaken short cut occurring behind its back: Central America.

If in October 1962, during the Cuban missile crisis, the European Community had no other option but to wait and see, the Central American crisis did not repeat this, which progressively unrolled after the triumph of the Sandinista revolution (July 19, 1979). The Community's political credit with Latin American democratic (or semi-democratic) countries was very high, completely in contrast to what transpired with the United States. Democratic Europe's intervention was requested, and Europe went to the site. The time was propitious and the credit exaggerated. The Central American crisis was the revulsion, the catalyst, the energizer for relations between the Community and Latin America. At the European Council in Stuttgart (June 1983), the Community demonstrated for the first time its full support for the Central American peace initiatives (the Contadora Group had been established January 5 of the same year), at the same time recognizing the importance of increased cooperation for Central America's socioeconomic development. In December of the same year the Economic Cooperation Accord was signed with the Andean Pact member countries, which included many new features and a radical change of focus from previous accords; and November 12, 1985, (in Luxembourg, and coinciding with San José II) a similar accord was signed with Central America but with singular and significant characteristics. They are now the so-called second generation accords.

The Central American crisis, besides acting as a catalyst, was an alibi justifying the Community's intervention in Latin America. Intervention, which neither interfered nor intruded because it happened at the request of the countries involved in the conflict. It is still too early to gain a perspective adequate for a consistent interpretation; but I believe it is not totally risky to suggest some motivations for the intervention, while remembering that political habits are slow to change, which is to say they are stable for a long time. We can think that 1980 will go down in world economic history as the year in which the volume of the U.S.'s trade with Pacific area countries exceeded, for the first time, its exchanges with Atlantic countries. Finally, Marx and Engels had partially responded, after so many prophetic failures, and Jung's warnings made in 1930 were going to be fulfilled: Europe's significance was merely as a hyphen between America and Asia. We also can think that the Community, conscious of its success as a project and, consequently, of its power, found that it had sufficient power to intervene more actively and effectively in those marginal world scenarios that now were assessable and interesting, Latin America among others. Another view is that the Community had learned from its own experience that intervening in other little-explored markets was the best way to slow U.S. and Japanese penetration of its own market. Reflecting on the still emerging motives for the Community's partial change of strategy toward Latin American countries, but let us not forget that the survival instinct always supplants re-election. And we are still at the instinct stage.

The Central American crisis acted simultaneously to awaken the other Latin American countries. In this case, too, it was politics, not economics, which activated the alarm. The peace process begun by the formation of the Contadora Group (January 5, 1983) had much greater extraction power and greater cohesive power with the grave foreign debt problem, which was then in full strength and threatening all Latin American countries without exception. Before a problem such as the debt, which since 1982 had imposed a negative net capital flow from Latin American countries toward the industrialized countries, had blocked all development possibilities, the reply was a disconcerted cry to save yourself, beginning with the most powerful countries that had the most leadership capabilities. And yet before a problem such as the Central American one, for many far away and for all an old one, Latin American countries reacted unanimously, as if they had rediscovered Bolívar's dreams of unity.

Why did it happen like this? Why is solidarity toward political problems easier than toward economic ones? Why had democratization in the American countries begun an unstoppable path? Why did the Reagan administration's policies toward the region have too many similarities with other times that were thought happy in the past? The answers to these questions are not easy, perhaps because it is still too early to determine the correct terms in which to formulate these questions.

But what interests us now is to remember another singular act that had important repercussions: the Rio Group's appearance. Also named the Group of Eight and, even more pompous, Permanent Consultative and Political Reconciliation Mechanism, it was born of the fusion of two other groups, created during the heat of the Central American political crisis: Contadora and the Support Group. The fusion took place in Rio de Janeiro in December 1986 at a meeting of the foreign affairs ministers for the eight member countries. The *sine qua non* condition to belong to the group is to be a democratic country to the bone. This is important for two reasons (which at the moment represents 80 percent of Latin America's population, the greatest part of its GNP as well as the intra and extra-community trade): for its much-vaunted independent action and its desire to be Latin America's incarnate mouthpiece.

The testimony of former Peruvian President Alan García, given during an address in Punta del Este at the group's second presidential meeting, attests to this independence: "For the first time [he was referring to the group's first head of state meeting in Acapulco November 29, 1987], Latin American presidents are meeting without having been convoked by the president of the United States." In this explicit expression, too, is the group's desire to be the valid spokesperson for Latin America.

The Community, embarked on the Central American crisis, immediately perceived the significance the group could have: on the one hand it could act as a third party in the concord, thereby avoiding whatever misstep it could have in a confrontation with the United States over Central

America; and, on the other hand, it could become the much hoped for valid spokesperson for Latin America. The political reasons that led to the group's formation (the Central American conflict) made it the ideal candidate. We find a good example of the Community's rapid perception of this in the fact that two months before the first Rio Group head of states meeting, the Community took advantage of the forty-second United Nations General Assembly meeting (although marginally) to celebrate the first informal ministerial meeting in the same city of New York (September 23, 1987). Even more this political dialogue was in agreement with the conclusions of the Community's Council of Ministers, approved three months before (June 22, 1987), and in which the Rio Group was named explicitly.

In sum, the Central American crisis brought forth a double phenomena that are key to interpreting the Community's present role in Central America's reconstruction (and which must be considered within the broader context of Latin America): the Community's intervention (embodied in San José I), and Latin America's extroversion (represented by the Rio Group)—-mutual phenomena, which in its later development, will implicate and strengthen themselves.

Brief History

Thus, in the mid-1980s we see a Latin America standing up by itself, decisively motivated by a desire for unity, while it seeks, in itself and with renewed oaths, old and new forms and formulas of integration. We also see a Community committing itself more and more to a largely forgotten America. And although we now are to concern ourselves with Central American relations, it behooves us to insist, for better understanding, that these relations only become meaningful when they are considered within the larger picture of the Community's relations with the region's countries or groups of countries.

The least we may say about the Community's relations with Central America is that they are peculiar as well as original. For the first time in the Community's relations with third countries, economic collaboration is linked, in good part, to determined political efforts. Since these relations began, political events, in the broadest sense, precede promises of economic collaboration. Even more, at all times and in all joint declarations, the political conditions (especially peace, democracy, and respect for human rights) have become the basis for constructing new projects for exchanges, assistance, and economic collaboration.

Concerning the first, it quickly presented serious dangers of changing from meddling to intrusion. Economic generosity is applauded or silenced. Political action, in the best of cases, is contemplated fearfully, frequently it is only endured and when the moment comes, it is denied. In this sense, I do not believe it is exaggerated to confirm the exquisite way in which the Community was headed. Without a doubt, the active presence of various groups of Latin American countries (Contadora Group, Support Group, and, above all, the Rio Group) in the resolution of the conflict and their frequent encounters with the Community was a determinate factor in the outcome.

Although the history of these relations is brief (six and a half years since the celebration of San José I), they are surprising because of their intensity (and, at times accelerated). In the political imbrication (Community and Latin American operations) one finds in economics the reason for this speedy development. At first glance one sees that it is the peace initiatives and institutions of the Central American countries, as well as of other groups and Latin American countries, which have been heading in that direction and on which have been built the successive replies to the Community. Contadora preceded the ministerial conference in Costa Rica (San José I); Nicaragua's situation and elections were before Luxembourg (San José II); Esquipulas I preceded the third conference in Guatemala (San José III); the Arias plan and Esquipulas II were conditions for the Hamburg conference (San José IV); the meeting of Central American presidents in El Salvador was the avenue for the joint communiqués of the San Pedro de

Sula conference (San José V); the Central American presidential summits in Tela and San Isidro de Coronado preceded the Dublin conference (San José VI). Negative aspects worsen if we add other political events with minor repercussions and, above all, if we include the Rio Group summits (in whose communiques Central America always has preferential attention) and the Group's informal meetings with the Community.

This initial political commitment of the Community with Central America will lead to greater attention being given to the rest of Latin America (with the following implication). The commitment has led, for the time being, to the Rome Conference (December 20, 1990) in which, on the one hand the political discussions with all of Latin America were institutionalized through the Rio Group, and on the other hand, a new type of assistance and cooperation agreements were inaugurated, the so-called third generation accords, broader and more ambitious than the former ones (and which the Community and the Republic of Chile signed at the same time).

This brief history has another perspective—economics. It is not now my intention (others at the conference are more able to do so) to consider assistance levels, their percentages of distribution, the significance of these sums in relations to broader standards, evolution of the sums during this time, etc.; I will only do so in moderation and with the goal of saving annoying explanations. But, yes, I will give my judgment on the broad topic they delineate, keeping in mind that together they form a tapestry as yet unfinished.

Total Community aid has increased slowly from year to year with rapid decreases from 1986 to 1989 because of, in the first place, a sharp decrease in regional aid, and in the second place, exceptional food aid the previous year. More significant is that, in this regard, regional aid was increased more than bilateral aid (except in 1986).

In fact, for all of the 1980s the combined food aid and financial and technical aid (AFT) was a high percentage of total aid with a tendency toward sharp declines in the last three years. If until 1986 both types of aid were more than 85 percent of the total, in the following years it has decreased to approximately 75 percent. Of the two, in the last years the percentage of financial and technical aid has grown to 60 percent in 1989.

The other two parts of Community aid in descending levels of importance have been humanitarian aid for refugees and displaced persons and co-financing of the nongovernmental organizations (ONGs); in 1989, both types reached about 8 percent of total aid.

This picture, already veering from its scheme, will lose all its color if we do not include aid diversification and more ambitious projects since San José V and San José VI. In San José V (San Pedro de Sula), the Project for Reactivating the Central American Common Market was proposed with its main points confirmed at San José VI (Dublin). In San José VI itself a strategy of regional aid for the immediate future was outlined, which had a triple goal: 1) repatriation of persons; 2) support for regional integration; and 3) relaunching Central America's economy. For the first goal there have to be actions to resettle refugees and displaced persons; in the second, to begin an interesting regional fisheries development project; in the third, a regional payment system.

A few examples will illustrate the designs of San José VI. It suffices to add, for example, that in 1989 trade promotion assistance tripled from the levels of the previous year; cooperation in the energy sector is intensifying; the Fisheries and Small Business Support Program (PAPIC II) second phase has begun. We have export creation projects (ASOEXPO), tourism development (Maya World), professional training to utilize better the Generalized System of Preferences (only some 66 percent of eligible Central America's exports to the Community benefit), in the first steps taken toward scientific and technical collaboration, etc.

In a few words, I believe that because of the scarcity of quantitative and percentages in relation to the others, the Community's economic aid had sought to adapt, not always easily, to rigidities of large organizations, to a Central

America beaten and punished by war and by its own structure of small countries and with difficulties for a good reconciliation (remember the adventures and misadventures of the projects and efforts to regional integration). Aid and cooperation that continues faddish for reasons of urgency, to food and humanitarian aid, but which has made notable efforts to diversify since, and with the legal support of the conclusions of the Council, June 2, 1987. Aid and cooperation, in sum, to the extent possible tries to transform structures with what remains after resolving urgent needs.

To this point, one of the possible sketches of the brief history of these relations has been characterized and individualized by marriage, in an unpublished form, of political premises with economic promises. And, as with any other history, from this one we can infer some lessons.

The Inferences

As I have written in another place, it is difficult to pinpoint why, in the Latin American mosaic, Central America has become the apple of the European Community's eye. Nevertheless, one can suggest some reasons:

> It is a midway zone in the possibilities and generosities of Europe. It is a zone punished by the Reagan administration's incomprehension and all that it came to signify. A zone excessively fragmented and divided by the circumstances of decolonization and following counterfeit interests, and which fights for its common market and common parliament, known and experienced tasks for the Community. A zone whose member countries have not become the Associated States of North America thanks to Mexico, which interposes itself like obstructing buffer state. A zone, in sum, meshed by political blocs and indefensible because of its small size.

I wrote this in 1987 when the Berlin Wall continued to be holy and sound as the recognized division of the world and the West. It then continued to distract us with its pirouettes on the slack wire.

Today Central America continues offering us a supply of proofs for the effectiveness of international aid, as much for the region's intrinsic difficulties as for the smaller dimensions (relative and real ones) of aid needed to launch the Central American countries' economies on the right track.

It is no less true that Central America has lost in part the "catalytic power" we spoke of at the beginning. And it has lost it not because its problems have changed appreciably despite some advances in the political systems and realities of demilitarization, but because the rest of the world wants to show that history has not ended with the fall of the Berlin Wall. Central America has stopped being a dangerous dividing alibi by becoming but another denunciation of the International Economic Disorder.

However, during the critical years, it left an impression, an international network of compromises. It is in this network too (I hope) that the European Community is entwined. This brief history shows us the role the Community should play and the responsibility it should assume in the beautiful Central American reconstruction project. A role and responsibility which, in line with what has transpired until now, presents a double course: political and economic. Of the two, I consider the first to be the most important, although only because it is irreplaceable.

In effect, the Community's political responsibility is, for now, not transferrable. A recent example more than suffices to confirm this. On July 27, 1990, United States President George Bush launched with fanfare his "Initiative for the Americas" proposal; an initiative to improve trade between the two hemispheres as well as to increase investments (North-South direction) to improve debt payment prospects (the Southern hemisphere's, of course). During the Rio Group's heads of state meeting months later in Caracas, and for the fourth time since the group was established, in their final declaration they responded positively, without enthusiasm or expectant energy, to the initiative, noting that "for the first time the themes of debt, trade, and investment were linked." But what is interesting is the subtle and formal finesse with which they affirmed that the initiative should not "exclude our indispensable efforts to other world regions in search of increased economic, financial, and technical cooperation." As if this were not enough to show that Latin America does not want to be left alone before the northern giant, they added later "their interest in the possibility that the EEC formulate initiatives designed to assure the development of its economic relations and cooperation with Latin America as was expressed in New York during the Community and group's foreign ministers' discussions."

The testimony is eloquent. Latin America and Central America are making demands on Europe. The powerful northern neighbor continues to be an object of suspicion, more so the closer one is, because of its very well-known colonialist and interventionist history. The Community is an equalizing factor. It is the security valve that gives assurances that the time of "America for the Americans" and the powerful neighbor's twisted mess will not return. It is the living example of what countries' integration can achieve, who had, moreover, spent centuries warring and had been the origin of two world wars in our century. The Community, is after all, Europe, which is the source in large measure of Latin America's culture; and if the colonial ties were the earliest governing factors in an important Treaty of Rome chapter, it is foreseeable that the cultural ties, so boasted about in accords and declarations, will in the end be what leads Europe to seek a new treaty. The Rome Conference and its declaration institutionalizing the political dialogue with the Rio Group, allows one to hope so.

It appears clear that regarding the economic course referred to, the Community will not change substantially toward Central America in the foreseeable future. Spending is inelastic and the allotment variation margins are narrow. The *New Cooperation Orientations with the Developing Countries of Latin America and Asia* give testimony that the Community does not want to remain boxed into its traditional regions and seeks, by other ways, "to expand the budget" to the maximum of its possibilities. It is not foolish to remember now, as Annex II of those *Orientations* reminds us, that in 1988 the Community dedicated to Public Development Assistance (APD) more than double what the United States allocated (in real terms as well as in percentages per capita) and that despite the distances, interests, and other histories, 13.4 percent of the Community's APD was for Latin America (versus 19 percent of the United States aid).

The desirability of a mini-Marshall Plan for Central America has been spoken and written about. Unfortunately or fortunately, according to how one sees it, Central America has stopped being a priority focal point of instability for the international community, and this has quieted those speakers and writers. In any case Central America's existence today explains the lack of capital investment. There is no capability, neither human nor productive, to reply. I do not want to say that additional aid would be unnecessary, that if it were (the conditional verb form is the result of my thinking), only that it would not be sufficient.

Consequently, and assuming the relative inelasticity of aid volumes, there is no other way to improve their profitability while seeking a rational allotment. We keep bumping against the inescapable drainage of urgently needed food and humanitarian aid. However, what there may be is precarious but not sterile. And that, according to my loyal knowledge and understanding, should be directed in two directions: 1) toward projects to transform internal structures, train human resources, and integrate Central American countries, such as through aid to the universities or the recent System of Payments, to give only two examples; and 2) toward projects which take advantage of the power and multiplying abilities of nongovernmental organizations.

The Community has understood it thus, or so it seems to me. V. Guiliarovschki's words about Russia can apply *secundum quid* to Central America: "Below, the power of the darkness, above, the darkness of power."

Central America is the waistband of the American hemisphere. A fragile waist because of its geographic dimensions and because it is punctured by the canal, which is clasped by the Carter-Torrijos Accord, about whose approaching fulfillment we will not prophecy.

Below, the darkness out of which Latin America rises with difficulty, it must support a lost decade, a painful apprenticeship, and must confront severe problems such as its external debt—neutralized (from the creditors' perspective), but not resolved. Above, the power of the United States—unencumbered and strengthened after its success in the Gulf War. In between, fragile Central America—a metaphor for a world moving toward integration, which finds neither the necessary peace nor the sufficient means to attain it. And in its yearnings to achieve it, it plays all or nothing.

The Gulf War's consequences are beginning to awaken. Among them, some have inferred a loss of imagination, of prestige, from the Community's lack of cohesion and its implication. If this is confirmed, it would be a good time to learn from the consequences of another painful apprenticeship. No more.

As always when the occasion presents itself (above all, in the huge plans launched for Central America, from the United Nations or from the meetings of the Central American heads of state or the Rio Group), the EC has assumed, without reservations, the role of collaborator to put in practice (at times, using the qualification of an "extra actor," but that is to emphasize the idea of only collaborating, not because it is a more just or appropriate role).

The United States continues to be the principal actor in the Central American theatre of operations; the Community has an irreplaceable role—to make the actors get to work without letting themselves get bogged down by painful trappings. The United States enjoys proximity and power; the Community has prestige and experience. The United States supports mistrust; the Community fights against the distance.

THE IDENTITY OF THE NEW EUROPE AND THE SAN JOSE PROCESS

Laurence Whitehead

Nuffield College, Oxford

Instead of focusing directly on the EC-Central America relationship, my approach is to concentrate attention on the development of a more unified Europe as an international actor that is gradually acquiring a global role. This paper considers the motives for and limitations of this process, and the reasons why it has so much more momentum in some areas (e.g., those concerning long-term economic restructuring and convergence) than in others (most conspicuously the security dimension). This portrayal of the emerging Europe's new profile involves an exercise of comparison and contrast with other major world actors of similar weight and size (therefore in particular with the U.S.). It is only after this general Europe-focused discussion that the paper attempts to consider the case of the San José process and the implications for future European-Central American relations.

In other words, the analysis presented here follows the hypothesis that the course of European-Central America relations is best understood by first considering internal processes of the European Community. These do much to shape and drive the underlying relationship, whereas internal processes of Central America and interactions between Central America and the EC play a less fundamental role. The latter no doubt define the detailed content and rhythm of the San José process, and they certainly deserve the careful analysis they will be receiving from other participants in this conference. But the argument I wish to develop is that a purely bilateral interpretation risks overlooking or misinterpreting both the origins and the structure of the relationship.

Central American policymakers, and their scattered European allies, need to make a careful and realistic assessment of how the San José process really works if they are to promote their chosen objectives. It may do no harm to remonstrate with the EC for its insularity and the gap between its rhetoric and its performance. But it is as well to keep in mind that regional perceptions of international affairs are almost invariably highly self-regarding (indeed it can be argued that for various socio-cultural reasons Europe is somewhat more "disinterested" toward Central America than any of the great power alternatives—e.g. the U.S., the U.S.S.R., or Japan). What requires attention is not so much the overall and unsurprising self-absorption of the Europeans, but the significant though limited areas in which they genuinely have something of value to offer (non-discrimination, institutionalization, multilateralism, and a preference for political over military solutions to regional problems). The reasons why the Europeans have something to offer in these areas may have more to do with processes internal to Europe than with the felt needs of the Central Americans, but that is unimportant so long as the Central Americans understand what is on offer and act to maximize their opportunities.

The Emerging Europe

It took both Germany and Italy the better part of a century to complete their internal processes of unification and to settle on a pattern of relations with the rest of Europe and with the outside world that was not highly disruptive. Similar observations could be made about Japan, and even the United States took at least half a century to mutate from a physically quite isolated sub-continent turned in upon itself and focused on its internal frontier to a dominant superpower assuming the mantle of global hegemony. Small wonder, then, that the new more unified Europe born out of the ruins of the Second World War should have made no more than fitful and lopsided progress toward its self-realization in the first couple of generations.

What is of most importance to our discussions here is the remarkable extent to which the pace has quickened, and European integration has broadened and deepened, over the past decade. The San José process can be viewed as a significant barometer of these larger stirrings. In fact, as recently as the mid-1980s it was feared that the integration process was losing momentum, vision, and popular support. The decision to create what was somewhat propagandistically labelled a "single European market" by 1992 was adopted not out of self-confidence, but to overcome these nagging self-doubts. This decision coincided with the accession of Spain and Portugal, a geographical enlargement that also represented a substantial redefinition of the contours and priorities of the future EC. Since then the bandwagon has gathered speed once more, this time with truly breathtaking and unforeseeable repercussions. East Germany joined the Community (without adding any additional representatives to the commission or the Council of Ministers) as a result of last autumn's reunification. Austria seems next in line for enlargement to the East, with every likelihood that the coming decade will also witness expansion northwards (into Scandinavia) and perhaps southward (into the Mediterranean) as well as into Central Europe. This broadening is accompanied by an equally remarkable deepening, with plans reportedly advancing rapidly for a European Central Bank to round off the convergence of most economic institutions and practices.[1] Major political reforms are also under review, to strengthen and re-balance the commission and the council, and perhaps

[1]EC President Jacques Delors has even proposed that the Eurofed could start operations as early as 1994, although the latest German draft for a treaty of monetary union merely envisages converging the existing committee of twelve central bank governors into a "Council" which would supervise lasting progress towards convergence in price stability and improved public finances. According to this draft, the Eurofed would not be created before 1997.

to reinforce collective accountability through the European Parliament. Among the proposed revisions of the Treaty of Rome the commission envisages foreign policy coordination, including guidelines intended to link aid to developing countries with their observance of human and democratic rights.

All this is remarkable, startling, and apparently unstoppable. (At least Mrs. Thatcher proved unable to stop it.) But the process has been so rapid that most of Europe's political leaders are now struggling to catch up with it. As for public opinion, it lags far behind. A unified Europe remains more an aspiration (vision, dream) strongly desired by a relatively limited range of well-connected insiders than an achieved reality or a deeply felt popular demand. Even the enthusiastic minority have only a sketchy picture of what their eventual product may be like, and if this is true in general it applies with particular force to the definition of Europe's prospective international role. Just as the emergence of earlier great powers proceeded in fits and starts, with pauses for introspection and with intervals of great disruption to the outside world, so we should on a longer view expect Europe's recent rapid advance to be followed by renewed hesitation and debate. It would also be unrealistic to expect the Europeans, while wrestling with the profound issues raised by their internal processes of accommodation and convergence, always to act with due consideration and responsibility towards the outside world.

Two recent episodes dramatize these general strictures. Viewed from a purely internal perspective, drastic long-term reform of the Common Agricultural Policy is both a vital necessity and an extremely painful and conflict-generating test of Community willpower. However, if the Uruguay Round of GATT negotiations is not to collapse in a way that might unleash a world trade war, the Community will soon be required simultaneously both to agree on a profound domestic overhaul of its agricultural policies, and to complete the most complex and delicate trade negotiations with external partners, who stand exposed to tremendous disruption if the EC disregards foreign farm interests.

It has proved extremely difficult to coordinate the timing of the two sets of agricultural negotiations, one within Europe and the other outside. Although the EC shifted its ground in February 1991 to allow the GATT talks to restart it seems unlikely that internal European reforms will be agreed before 1992, which means that this segment of the international trade negotiations might drag on almost indefinitely.

Quite apart from the substantive details of these negotiations, the formal process is most eloquent for the purposes of this paper. Hitherto there has been one particularly influential voice shaping GATT negotiations. The U.S., as the largest single trading partner with the biggest market, was accustomed to presenting its main demands in non-negotiable form. Under the U.S. Constitution the Congress could always refuse to approve concessions offered by its negotiators if they bent too far to foreign pressure. The European Community has now introduced a second trade negotiating party of approximately equal weight, equipped with roughly the same tough mandate for negotiations. If the GATT Round emerges unscathed from these consequences of the creation of a more unified Europe, it will be a remarkable achievement for the negotiators and a stroke of good fortune for the international system. It will not be because at the global level the EC is an inherently trade-liberalizing undertaking.

Similarly the Gulf War has highlighted the other great incognita connected with the emerging EC's international role. Can Europe really act like an economic and political superpower while remaining a pygmy (or more accurately a band of squabbling pygmies) on security matters? This is in reality a complex question that I have posed in unduly simplistic terms, although these do reflect popular perceptions. It would be more accurate to say that until the collapse of the Warsaw Pact the EC conducted its security policy through the agency of NATO, under the leadership of the United States, and with attention focused on the threat from Moscow. In the future European security policy will have to be redesigned to cater to different and as yet relatively undefined sources of danger. The Gulf War has merely dramatized and rendered more urgent the nature of the rethinking that would in any case have been necessary. Is NATO still the most appropriate agency for maintaining European security, now that any future theatre of military operations is less likely to fall within its jurisdiction? (The West European Union offers one possible alternative agency if the U.S. is to disengage from Europe.) How are the very separate national military establishments, with their widely differing orientations and capabilities to be coordinated into a more unified security stance? If such coordination is slow to develop, then what will remain of the aspiration to construct an EC-wide foreign policy? How far, and in what ways, is it possible to coordinate foreign policies while abstaining from the collective capacity to project force? What kind of relationship would the EC have to establish with other major powers that do have the capacity to project force, in order to conduct foreign policy in those areas where no European military presence is contemplated? These are obviously very broad issues, but they are also of very direct application when considering the prospective future role of Europe in Latin America in general, or in Central America in particular. And, of course, they are not just regional or bilateral questions, but they touch on the central issue of the emerging Europe's prospective relationship (or division of labor) with the U.S.

Latin America and the Emerging European Community

The Gulf War may have brought this to the fore, but the underlying problem is nothing new. Indeed these issues were already apparent in at least an equally visible form at the time of the Falklands/Malvinas War. On a lesser scale they have been present throughout the eighties in Central America, as demonstrated by the continuing presence of British military forces to safeguard the territorial integrity of a now independent Belize.

Fortunately Latin America is a much more peaceful

area of the world than, say, the Middle East or Southern Africa, so that such isolated episodes of military activity do not normally dominate the European-Latin American relationship. Indeed, viewed from Europe, Latin America may well seem the most favorable setting in the so-called "Third World" for the application of those political and diplomatic formulae in which the EC has developed a comparative advantage (multilateralism, peaceful resolution of disputes within a framework of international law, economic convergence and integration, etc.) If Europe is to establish itself as a major and unified actor in global politics, it is through the promotion of such formulae that its influence is most likely to be felt.

Of course, it cannot be stressed too heavily that the search for a redefinition of Europe's global role is still at an early stage; as the Gulf War dramatized there is certainly no consensus either on the applicability of the EC formulae or on the price the Community would be willing to pay to back them in the different parts of the Third World. As far as Latin America is concerned the sub-continent is a low priority and the EC is unlikely to pay too high a price for the application of its distinctive policies in this area of the globe rather than elsewhere.

Nevertheless, provided the price is not too high, there are some good reasons why the architects of an emerging external policy for a more unified Europe could find Latin, and particularly Central, America a promising arena for action. A key motivation would be to demonstrate to a skeptical audience in Europe that it is possible to achieve worthwhile progress in the promotion of values held widely throughout the EC, through the disinterested application of common European policies. The relatively tractable condition of Latin America makes it a suitable focus for such efforts. Moreover, although the sub-continent is of the most marginal economic or strategic significance for the EC, it does have a significant hold upon the European political and cultural imagination. The episodic reasons for that hold (passions aroused by human rights violations, or civil wars, that stir memories of recent European history) may now fade, but there are also structural reasons that should prove more durable. These include shared languages and religious traditions, the widespread presence of emigrants from Europe, and the existence of strong historical ties that are kept alive through such agencies as the international party organizations (Christian Democracy, the Socialist International, etc.) and quite intense programs of education and cultural exchange. Indeed it could be argued that it is to Latin America far more than in any other part of the Third World that European models and values have been most effectively transmitted. If so, then the emerging Europe will feel a pull of solidarity and will need to demonstrate the effectiveness of its policies for Latin America, in order to establish its credentials as a global presence.

The San José Process

To achieve visible results in Latin America as a whole would require an input of EC resources far in excess of what is likely to be available. From this standpoint, then, it was almost a matter of good fortune for the EC that one small sub-region of continent presented itself to world opinion as in particularly acute need of solidarity and targeted external assistance. The aftermath of the Sandinista revolution catapulted Central America into world headlines and played up precisely those themes on which an emerging EC would be best placed to take a stand. From 1984 onwards the foreign ministers of the Community have established a remarkably high profile and have sustained a complex program of support for reconciliation and reconstruction on the Central American isthmus. In contrast to the U.S., the EC obviously had no intention of sending force, of violating international law, or of discriminating between sovereign states on purely ideological grounds. Moreover the EC's prolonged absence from the Central American scene made it far less responsible than the United States for the circumstances that had led the region into crisis. So although a few critics assumed that European initiatives must be motivated by hegemonic aspirations, these were clearly paltry by comparison with the vested interests that could be associated with U.S. policy.

The main cost to the EC of its involvement in the San José process was not the limited financial commitments involved but, the investment of scarce foreign ministerial time and resources, in particular when their efforts risked offending Washington. Yet if the new Europe was to assert itself as an autonomous global actor, some divergences with the U.S. would have to be courted and sustained. From that perspective, Central America offered a relatively favorable opportunity since U.S. opinion was deeply divided (with many Democrats closer to Brussels than to the White House in their definition of the issues); since a successful European policy could hardly be rated a mortal affront to the United States; and since a surprisingly diverse array of European governments were able to convince themselves of the merits of a distinctive common policy. The Esquipulas Peace Plan offered substantial vindication of the European diagnosis of the regional crisis, but fortunately for the EC the U.S. was not humiliated, and the outcome was satisfactory to both parties. With hindsight, an unkind but not entirely fanciful way of characterizing the San José process in the 1980s would therefore be to say that joint western interests were best served by the adoption of a "carrot and stick" policy, and that through a process of tacit cooperation the EC acquired the function of offering the carrots, leaving the U.S. free to concentrate on administering the sticks. It is unlikely that such an international division of labor could have emerged through premeditation, but it developed rather naturally from the distinctive military and geopolitical orientations of the two parties and from the very different profiles of the interests they had at stake in the sub-region.

Obviously these are extremely summary reflections on the San José process, intended to open a debate and perhaps to provide a frame for other much more precise and detailed discussions at this conference. The process by which the EC formulated its common stand, the way in which it was negotiated with the Central Americans, its place within the broader array of EC external relations (e.g. vis-à-vis Southern Africa, the Middle East, etc.) and the detailed political and economic provisions all require attention.

The key significance for Europe of the San José process was that it offered an unusually favorable context for the Community to present itself as a disinterested actor. From the military and geostrategic viewpoint the EC was disinterested in that it lacked both a capacity and a need for force projection. From the economic viewpoint it was disinterested in that the financial costs of the policy were quite modest and the economic interests at stake were minimal. (Note, for example, that whereas the U.S. spent the 1980s designing trade preferential schemes such as the Caribbean Basin Initiative, the EC bent its comparable energies to the Lomé accord from which Central America remains excluded.)

Finally, from a demographic viewpoint, the emerging Europe's relationships with Africa, Asia, and the Middle East may well be dominated by the wish to restrict uncontrolled migration. This becomes an even higher priority for European policymakers as the specter of mass emigration from the U.S.S.R. and Eastern Europe looms. But so far as Central America is concerned, if there is continuing outmigration it will be to the U.S. and not to Europe. Here too, then, the EC in uncharacteristically disinterested.

Prospects for the 1990s

One distinctive feature of the EC's cumbersome and formalized decision-making procedures is that it not only takes a long time to set any given cooperation agreement in motion, it also takes just as long to change course or deviate from past commitments. After seven years of build-up the San José process has now acquired considerable inertia. Not even the upheavals in Eastern Europe are likely to interrupt its pre-established course. Since 1984 the custom of holding regular annual summit meetings at foreign ministerial level (including last April in Dublin and this March in Managua) has become ingrained and will tend to lock the EC into its commitments. The formula has proved so successful that it has recently been extended to the "Rio Group" of 11 South American countries, plus Mexico, who will henceforth also hold annual meetings with the EC at foreign ministerial level. Just as the Central Americans used to express frustration over the EC's unresponsiveness to crisis conditions on the isthmus, other regional lobbies have begun to protest that their immediate needs are greater and yet Central America seems to have acquired preemptive rights. In fact, it is as difficult to make the EC slow down as to make it speed up. This is a marked contrast with Washington's policy-making style, which favors the rapid deployment of resources to tackle whatever may be judged the crisis of the moment, but which often lacks the stamina to achieve follow-through when a crisis goes off the boil.

With the defeat of the Sandinistas in the February 1990 election and the hesitant steps toward negotiations in Guatemala and El Salvador, many in Europe and America believe that the Central American crisis has finally gone off the boil. The inhabitants of those three troubled republics may be forgiven for taking a more cautious view, but here we are concerned with international perceptions. There would have to be a very major and spectacular setback to the Esquipulas process to convince outside observers that Central America had plunged back over the brink. By far the most likely prospect for the next few years is that, however unpleasant conditions on the isthmus may continue to be, European opinion will regard Central America as having slipped well down the hierarchy of regional trouble spots compared to the recent past. The urgency of its reconstruction needs will be thought to rank far behind those of the Middle East, Eastern Europe, Southern Africa, and quite probably also the Mahgreb. Moreover, all of the four just-mentioned regions are of far more direct economic and political concern to the emerging Europe than Central America, which already has a patron and protector in the form of the U.S. Even within Latin America, Central America's claims to priority have come under challenge, notably, when the EC admitted the Dominican Republic and Haiti to the Lomé accord in 1989 and when it extended duty free access to tropical products from Andean countries in 1990 to assist in their anti-narcotics programs. San José VII has not fully compensated Central America for these concessions to other regions.

Over the medium run we can anticipate that two conflicting forces are likely to shape EC relations with the isthmus. The force of inertia will tend to sustain and even somewhat increase the levels of European support committed so far, whereas European strategic self-interest will argue for a redirection of attention toward higher priority problems. The Central Americans will argue, with good reason, that having followed much of the advice they received from Europe they are now entitled to claim their promised rewards. My forecast, for what it is worth, is that the EC will indeed somewhat expand the resources it commits to Central America—these are, after all, still very modest as a proportion of Europe's potential. Moreover it may be possible for Brussels to achieve relatively pleasing results in Central America as a consequence of these quite modest outlays. In some quarters there will be a sense that the EC needs to be seen to honor the promises that it made, and it could be useful in the search for an attractive new international identity to have at least one showcase of "disinterested" generosity. Most of the EC's other international initiatives are unlikely to exemplify all that much altruism.

However, the *pattern* of European activism in the region is quite as revealing as its *scale*. This pattern expresses both the inherent biases of the EC as an international actor and in equal measure European perceptions of what Central America really needs to achieve reconstruction and reconciliation. So long as the pattern of EC specialization coincides with European perceptions of regional need the San José process should retain momentum.

We can therefore conclude this brief discussion paper

with a summary of the EC's external policy profile and its apparent relationship to isthmian requirements for assistance.

1) The EC will have no military role; it will not offer "police training," nor seek bases, nor plant spies. (Individual European governments may conduct their own bilateral policies on these issues, and indeed the British have bases in Belize and provide the services of Scotland Yard to an investigation team in El Salvador. Britain has also been designated Caribbean coordinator of the European Anti-Narcotics Committee by the U.N., both a reflection and a reinforcement of the fact that the British policy profile is closer to that of the U.S. than the European norm.)

2) The EC will play no more than a background role in any negotiations over Central America's external public debt. This is an area explicitly reserved by treaty to the Community's individual member states, and in practice it is the IMF and the World Bank who largely channel European initiatives on this question. The U.S., as the largest creditor, plays the leading role here.

3) The EC will be reluctant to offer one way free trade concessions to Central America in imitation of Washington's Caribbean Basin Initiative. (Last year the EC raised about $130 million from tariffs on Central American exports to the Community.) EC trade preferences related to the region's traditional agricultural exports are all slanted the other way under the recently renewed Lomé Accord, which grants privileged access to sugar, bananas, and other tropical foodstuffs produced by the recent ex-colonies of Africa, Asia, the Pacific, and the West Indies. The EC will be on the defensive here, since Community enlargement threatens to exclude competitive Central American exports from an

ever increasing proportion of the world market.[2] With regard to nontraditional exports, the EC's policies will be filtered through the Uruguay Round (where the twelve have begun to negotiate as a single party) and the Generalized System of Preferences, neither of which particularly favor Central America.

4) On the positive side the Commission has budgeted 2.9 billion ECUs for aid and cooperation with Asia and Latin America over the 1991-1995 cycle (an 82 percent rise over the previous cycle) and has stressed the need to restore Latin America's share of a growing aid budget. Within that budget Central America has received highly preferential treatment (worth about $140 million last year). The sums remain modest, of course, but the EC points to various features that make this assistance particularly worthwhile. On a per capita basis Central America already receives more EC economic aid than any other region of the world, with a further 80 percent rise planned for 1991-1995. All aid is given in the form of donations, priority goes to aiding the poorest countries, and targeting the poorest strata of the population. Food aid, aid for reconstruction, emergency relief, and aid to refugees are favored (hence the concentration on Central America). Moreover, in addition to the EC's direct expenditure on cooperation, many individual European countries also have substantial aid programs with large Central American components. Taking both sources of aid into account, the EC countries claim to be devoting 0.5 percent of their GNP to Third World cooperation, and there are plans to raise this to 1 percent in the next few years. (Compare the 0.2 percent spent by the U.S.—mostly on a handful of strategic clients, and the 0.3 percent spent by Japan, although this is now also rising rapidly.)

---

[2]In mid-February 1991 Central American banana exporters meeting in San Andrés therefore set up a "common front" to demand EC tariff reductions by 1993, and Guatemala is also pressing for a reduction in the EC's 4% tariff on coffee imports.

5) Finally, on the political side, the EC can point to at least three distinctive features of its isthmian policies, which seem to dovetail with the sub-region's particular needs. First, EC policies are formally nondiscriminatory, which is why Nicaragua was never subjected to European sanctions and indeed even Castro's Cuba remains technically eligible for assistance. This was very important during the 1980s when U.S. policy sought to benefit El Salvador and penalize Nicaragua, but when EC nondiscrimination helped keep alive the institutions of Central American cooperation. The second feature, then, is that the EC believes it has a special mission to encourage schemes of regional integration such as have been repeatedly attempted in Central America ever since its independence. Thirdly, European experience suggests that progress on the relatively technical questions of regional economic integration can promote much broader goals—reducing militarism and the threat of local wars; eroding ideological polarization; widening the basis for political toleration and pluralism; strengthening constitutional and representative government and the rule of law; and forging an extra-national sense of loyalty and identity. The EC believes that it has established an attractive model for other once strife-torn regions to imitate and that Central America is well-placed to benefit from this European experience. (This belief may help explain some of the more eccentric features of EC policy, such as the stress on the establishment of a Central American Parliament.)

If Central America does make progress along the lines just indicated, that will be a fulfillment of longstanding isthmian aspirations and a vindication of the Esquipulas formula. But it will also be seized on as a confirmation of the emerging Europe's vision of itself and the world. That is why the San José process needs to be viewed as part of a European effort to define a new identity and not just as a Central America-focused initiative.

TO THE BACKBURNER: THE EUROPEAN COMMUNITY-CENTRAL AMERICAN RELATIONSHIP

Pierre-Henri Laurent

Tufts University

Throughout the 1980s the relationship between the European Community (EC) and the Central American states has evolved and developed into an important factor in each group's international interests and goals. Since the Iberian enlargement of the Community, and in part dependent upon it, this rapprochement has gained further momentum and substance. This paper aims to explore and interpret this recent history in terms of the realistic prospects in the 1990s for more intensive, elaborate, and ambitious economic ties than might constitute a full-fledged development cooperation convention. It asserts that there are possibilities of reciprocally meaningful augmentations to the past efforts, but it focuses on the numerous and weighty limitations from the EC perspective on future large-scale involvements and commitments by the Community. The result posits that the presence of several undeniable EC priority ventures over the next decade will mitigate anything more than a very secondary role by the EC in Central America.

There is no doubt that Central America, let alone the Rio Group and Latin America as a whole, has emerged as a new part of the EC agenda in terms of relations with developing countries. In particular, the events of 1989-90 indicate a new stage in cooperation between the Community and Central America.[1] One need not here enumerate the swift steps since the late 1970s that drew the EC and Central America more closely together in a series of programs, projects, and policies. The more recent emergence of political stability and peace in the region, particularly in the last few years, has played a major role in attracting the EC to Central America. The engagement of the EC in the development processes of that region has accelerated from isolated and specific bilateral arrangements to a more comprehensive long-term overall dialogue and strategy. The connections have moved beyond charity, awareness, and even short-term emergency measures. What exists as the 1990s begin is a growing interdependence between the two regions and a shared desire to enhance various bonds and develop new mutually beneficial opportunities.[2]

Inside the EC, particularly in the wishes of Madrid and Lisbon, and certainly in Central America, there are hopes that the linkage can be deepened in terms of more preferential trade concessions and aid and investment

---

[1]"Relations CE/Amérique Centrale," Commission de la Communante Europeenne, Memo 16/90, 6 avril, 1990. Alfred Tovias, *Foreign Economic Relations of the European Community: The Impact of Spain and Portugal,* (Boulder and London: Lynne Rienner, 1990), 53-71, in giving what he considers a possibly "too optimistic view" about Iberian input into EC policies nevertheless gives much space to cautionary aspects of future EC/Central American relations. See also Rheinhard Rummel, "Concentric Integration? The Impact of Greek, Spanish and Portuguese Membership on Western Europe as a Foreign Policy Actor," paper presented at the Conference of Europeanists, Washington, D.C., November 1987.

[2]"The Europe-South Dialogue," Commission of the European Countries, 1988. See also "Joint Economic Communique Issued by the European Community and the Countries Party to the General Treaty on Central American Economic Integration and Panama Resulting from the Conference on Political Dialogue and Economic Cooperation between the European Community and Its Member States, the States of Central America and Panama, and Colombia, Mexico and Venezuela as Cooperating Countries, Held in Dublin on 9 and 10 April 1990 (San José VI)," Commission of the European Communities Press Release, 10 April 1990.

privileges such as those found in the EC/ACP Lomé Conventions. These ambitions for the European/Isthmus relationship require that we explore the EC future to assess these prospects.

The questions posed are the following: Before the next millennium what chances are there for a significant increase of EC involvement in the ten states of Central America? What obstacles hinder not a more active EC (which is possible, even probable), but an EC with a primary and critical role in the region's economic and political transformation? The contention of this paper is that EC financial constraints interact with first-line internal and external priorities, which result in a much-diminished capability of EC engagement in this hemisphere. When combined with the posture and policies of the United States, these circumstances result in the near necessity to confine (not forsake) EC obligations much more severely than the enthusiastic and dynamic eighties allowed.

There are no doubt positive motivations and rationales for pressing on with a more detailed and inclusive relationship. The influence and growing power of the Spanish and Portuguese member states are the foremost reasons, and their wants and concerns will not be totally denied. The Community's commitment to *mondialisme contemporaine*, to the Third World *in toto*, is more than rhetoric and pushes the Twelve to augment its relations throughout the developing world. But even these compelling worldwide responsibilities, in one sense, work against further and deeper ties and, in fact, do not themselves combine to produce the significant pressure to make the EC/Central America connection one of cardinal importance for the Community. Spain and Portugal may want and seek such an expansion of the Central American priority, but their position within the needy southern rim EC states will more and more produce conflicts about the distribution of increasingly scarce resources outside the Community.

One can also add other factors that appear to support greater EC/Central America links, but they too are all fraught with a dubious side or contradictory aspect. If one argues, for example, that the EC is well versed and by now even a global expert in development cooperation, especially with its practiced staff, there is the flip side of the coin to that contention, which results in the assertion that this same involvement could result in EC overstretch if too many additions were placed on DG VIII and the EC budget. Similarly, to argue that Washington has supported EC activity of late in aid, trade, and investment in the region is to avoid evidence that there are obvious qualifications to this basically supportive premise of U.S. foreign policy. What is more likely to emerge is an EC-U.S. joint-collaboration process in Central America with the U.S. in the lead. What is not likely to evolve is the EC as a counterweight to the U.S. in the region.

Even the contention that strong internal support for Central America exists beyond the Spanish and Portuguese fails the test of deeper scrutiny in that France, Germany, and the Netherlands (and to a lesser extent, the U.K.) are more and more reluctant to press that region into higher gear for the EC. The French will support the Latin thrust of Madrid and Lisbon but only to the extent that it does not injure Black Africa and her own less developed southern areas. The German involvement in Eastern Europe, as I point out, has demanded overnight far more than expected, and for a longer period, and the Dutch enthusiasm can wax and wane depending on critical internal and regional circumstances. Gaining any EC consensus on feasible directions for Central America would be difficult; a decision to aid substantially some of the least developed like Honduras or Nicaragua via a fund for export promotion would gain some member states' approval and some disapproval, as would the idea of EC participation in the capital expansion base of the Central American Bank for Economic Integration. Internal differences among the Europeans were most recently demonstrated in the Bonn and London resistance to transferring Iberoamerican debt responsibilities to the EC, fearing the repercussions that would come from the World Bank, IMF, and/or the Club of Paris.[3]

What works against Central America from the EC point of view? The financial limitations for the short term for all EC activities involve decelerated growth and accelerated inflation, in addition to the uncertain implications of the U.S. and U.K. recessions for Western Europe. The economic outlook is not just less favorable for the EC; the time has come for budget constraints which did not so severely hamper their wishes in the mid and late-eighties when Brussels jump-started its Central American involvement process.

This admittedly short-range grey picture is aggravated by existing compulsory internal and external EC programs. First, are there substantially deeper pockets for the 1992 project with all of its demands, some extending beyond 1993? The completion of the internal market has reached the stage of its hardest decisions. National adjustments to Community directives, and thus EC law, entail hardships that will continue into the mid-1990s. Secondly, the new EC tasks that concern the former Soviet satellites of Eastern Europe have only recently begun to yield a realistic assessment of the depth and scope of the burden the Twelve have assumed through this decade. Suffice it to note here and now that virtually every EC budget squabble for the foreseeable future will involve a trade-off between the much-valued and highly important job of converting the wreckage of the command economies to viable market systems and promoting democratic governance on one side and any other EC venture at home or abroad on the other.[4] The EC must be preoccupied with Eastern European reconstruction, and more likely will be drawn into the Russian process of economic rebuilding, too. Whether the Soviet Union remains a viable central authority or it ex-

---

[3]*The London Times*, May 7, 1990; also see Tovias, op. cit.

[4]"EEC/Central America: Member States Underline Analogy Between Situations in Central America and in Eastern Europe," *European Report*, 12 April 1990.

periences decentralizing disintegration, the forecast for the EC in the 1990s does call for increasing investments and other commitments once the political situation stabilizes.

One sizable EC involvement of long standing makes up a third formidable obstacle for the Central American/EC upgrade. This is the foremost Third World commitment of the EC in the Lomé Convention partnership with 68 African, Caribbean and Pacific countries. Lomé IV signaled a deeper and wider relationship for the Twelve which forms the main component of the Community's development policy. It is the symbol and much of the substance, historically, of North-South relations for the EC. It comes first, and it cannot be diminished. Most concretely and unhappily, the ruinous African economic conditions of the 1980s can safely be projected throughout the 1990s. This takes on a greater importance when one remembers that Lomé IV financial arrangements will be renegotiated in 1995, when the 10 years convention term is half through.

The United States cannot be left out of this consideration concerning the EC and Central America. The long historic interests of the Americans with their southern neighbors have resulted in an often "extensive promises and actual neglect" end result. And yet, the recent initiative of President Bush does combine with the legacy of American economic involvement to produce a continuing primary, nay, central role, for the U.S. Europe is not unaware of Washington's "Latin America Rediscovered" policies and the newfound attention to its own hemispheric problems. Whatever the outcome of the American "Enterprise for the Americas," the EC views itself as a secondary actor in that region. There are indications that EC help for Latin America is sought by Washington and that some Central American nations might "feel more comfortable with distant superpowers than with the giant next door," as John Chipman has put it.[5] These points do not, however, change the basic fact

---

[5]Quoted in Peter Rashish, "Economic Burden Sharing," *Europe*, January-February 1991.

that the EC will move slowly with prudence and with caution in that region, given American presence and policies. Northern EC member states are particularly aware that "rocking the boat" of Washington with expansive Central American moves could be counterproductive in an era of continuing trade issues among those economic giants. The Europeans do not want to offend the Americans over this secondary priority and region at a time when the transatlantic trade rivalry will most probably produce some much more serious bilateral economic divergences. Therefore, this fourth major factor mitigating large increases of economic and financial ventures of Europe in Central America is best understood in that Central America will not be a "competitive rivalry" ground for the EC, but an area where the U.S. takes the lead, as does the EC in Eastern Europe with American consent.[6]

There are three other related considerations for the Twelve when they assess their Central American policy. The Gulf War has resulted in some substantial, unplanned for EC contributions and more likely reconstruction bills that the Europeans will not want to avoid. More cogently, the post-Cold War era has stimulated efforts in the military/security dimension, pushing them to the forefront for Western Europe. Both will require new costs, especially if the war and reconstruction are lengthy and/or the security resolutions foster the creation of a true "European pillar."

Secondly, the EC must view its input of any kind and size in terms of Central American endeavors within the context of its total Latin American programs. The EC now gives about one half of its Latin American aid to the Isthmus countries, but that amount is only 5 percent of all EC aid worldwide.[7] It is difficult to imagine the Central

---

[6]See Linda Robinson, *Intervention or Neglect?: The United States and Central America Beyond the 1980s*, New York: Council on Foreign Relations, 1991; Abraham F. Lowenthal, "Latin America Rediscovered," *Foreign Affairs*, Vol. 69, No. 4, Fall 1990.

[7]*Central America Report*, XVI, No. 46, 24 November 1989.

American countries as anything other than a segment of Latin America in the eyes of the Europeans and therefore eligible for a portion of the attention the EC gives to Latin America as a whole.[8] One might even demonstrate that the Community has greater and more compelling economic interests in the nations south of the Isthmus.

Third and finally, it is evident that North-South relationships in general have triggered a complex and vigorous debate within the EC about economic aid and trade ties and the alternative forms that they might most effectively employ in the 1990s. Questions of debt and structural adjustments are only two major issues among many that are being discussed and reevaluated. The EC experiences, primarily in Black Africa, have not resulted in an amelioration of those sub-Saharan economies. Even though one can contend that each case of addressing developing economies is a separate issue, the past does provide economists and policy makers valuable lessons. It would be going too far to say that the Lomé past has soured the EC on First-Third World conventions, but it is fair to conclude that prudence and caution now dictate the day in matters of EC development programs, given the real results of three Lomé pacts.

The major point is that a more vast undertaking in Central America would require an EC decision about what development theories and methodologies could be translated into pragmatic and efficient policies for the Isthmus states. There is reason to believe that this would not be an easy task and would result in serious bickering at minimum within Berlaymont and the capitals of the Twelve. It is not therefore that there is no room for Central America in EC plans; future directions of development cooperation are basically unclear and will continue to be so until after 1993.

If Commissioner Matutes were correct in late 1990

---

[8]"Guidelines for Cooperation with the Developing Countries in Latin America and Asia," Commission of the European Communities, COM(9) 176 Final, 11 June 1990.

in characterizing recent EC action on Central America as a "qualitative leap," does this mean that the EC cooperation policy will be substantially enlarged in the future?[9] To move beyond the Rome Declaration would require increased political will and economic ability. This observer feels that in the tenuous and uncertain 1990s there may be some of the former and less of the latter. This is not a gloomy forecast about EC backing Central American efforts but a skepticism about its marked increase. Western Europe wants ties strengthened as a means of opening the region's access to European markets, stimulating expert diversification etc., but it must be remembered that European exports to the region have recently diminished and the imports into the EC are heavily in the banana and coffee sector that the EC already has access to through the Lomé partnership. This is merely to hint that there are other Central American conditions such as some political instability and macro-economic problems that will continue to cause EC circumspection, even wariness, vis-à-vis Central America.[10]

In sum, another appreciable qualitative leap is unlikely given the EC requirements of greater financial discipline and the highest priority tasks within the Twelve, in Eastern Europe, in the ACP, and in the sensitive diplomacy with Washington. The support of the Twelve for Central America has been very modest, although increased as the 1980s ended and 1990s commenced. It will most likely remain very modest, a small fraction of the EC global development cooperation budget. In contrast to some of the positions propounded in this collection, such as Whitehead and Grabendorff, there are strong indications that the EC will be pressed to contain and possibly even marginalize its Central American policy. If the concentric-circles concept is employed, Central America is not only geographically

[9]*Europe-Informations Generales*, No. 5399, 28 Decembre 1990, and *International Herald Tribune*, December 21, 1990.

[10]*Central American Report*, XVII, no. 33, 31 August 1990.

distant and thus several layers away from Western Europe, but it is also several circles away from the EC in terms of its "must-do" agenda in the 1990s.

THE CENTRAL AMERICAN POLICY OF THE EC: BALANCE AND PERSPECTIVES (A SPANISH VIEW)

Albert Galinsoga Jordà

University of Barcelona

> One must see in reality, before one's very eyes these entities which appear dead, yet nevertheless are internally active; one must observe how they search, attract, destroy, unite, consume and then, from their intimate union, take back a revitalized form, new, unexpected; then they are granted eternal life.
>
> J.W. Goethe, *Elective Affinities*

THE EUROPEAN POLICY

What has been called the "Central American policy" of the European Community (EC) has as its point of departure European support for the Contadora Group's negotiations to resolve the Isthmus's conflicts, although it counts on the antecedents derived from the progressive opening toward Latin America as a whole. The balance of the policy is reflected on three planes: political, economic, and development cooperation.

Political Level

On the political plane, the principal contribution of the EC is directed at cooling of the conflict and progressively limiting foreign intervention. The European position has been marked by the promotion and support of appropriate solutions for the Central American actors (Esquípulas process) and by the United Nations (U.N.) organs (Special

Economic Cooperation Plan for Central America [PEC] and United Nations Observer Force for Central America [ONUCA]).

European Cooperation Policy (CPE) and the Political Dialogue

Characterized from its beginning as "pragmatic and flexible," European Cooperation Policy (CPE) chose the course of establishing processes directed at promoting a common position before international events of "general interest" to the member states. This was the only position possible if they did not wish to see the policies that the member states of the EC had planned and developed dismembered. The evolution of this model of joint diplomacy has demonstrated how interaction inevitably occurs between the political and the economic, on one side, and the political and legal, on another.

The secondary interest of the EC member states in the sub-region has permitted maintaining something extremely difficult in European foreign relations: segmentation of economic cooperation around common political objectives. Even when generic coincidences arise on the political plane, as is the case of the patterns observed in Latin America, it should be taken into account that the respective national interests define the order of priority expressed by the EC member countries. Thus, with respect to the Latin American states, notable differences manifest themselves in aspects as relevant as those regarding the level of cooperation relations. In this sense, the affirmation is fully valid that the European countries practice very different policies that have certain common elements. One of the most noteworthy examples of this diversity is that British Official Aid to Development (OAD) to Belize and the Malvinas Islands is only slightly less than the sum given to all of Latin America.

Precisely because of this the CPE appears based upon a mysterious theorem: the lesser the interests of the member states in a region, the greater the degree of consensus achieved. Said another way, the base of its success is also the base of its weaknesses. Applied to the whole of Latin America, very diverse interests can be discerned regarding the importance of the region in the foreign policy of the member states, and in fact with respect to those Latin American countries that maintain greater links with one or another of the European countries.

The flexibility that is increasingly revealed by the Community structure for hooking up with the initiatives linked to the CPE permits combining mixed meetings of both structures, specifically in the case of certain common organs. Thus, there developed recent "formal" and "informal" joint meetings, which are added to the work carried out within each structure.

These characteristics are especially evident in the institutional dialogue between both regions. On April 9-10, 1990, the Sixth Conference ("San José VI") took place in Dublin. This was attended by the member of the Commission responsible for relations with Latin America, Abel Matutes, and by representatives of the Twelve, the five Central American countries, and Colombia, Mexico, and Venezuela as "cooperating countries," a fact which supposes recognition of the disappearance of the Contadora Group. Along with this significant fact must be pointed out the parallels on the political and economic plane, given that Panama ended—due to its situation after the United States intervention—its role as a "cooperating" state and was contemplated as a Central American nonmember country of the Central American Common Market (MCCA)—exactly the same as in the framework of the EC-Central America Cooperation Accord.

The usual political declaration and economic communique were effected, and an accord for European support to the Central American System of Payments was signed, with the end of revitalizing intraregional trade, the convenience of which had been established at the previous meeting. The financial donation to cover the objectives of the accord supposes a commitment with a value of 120 million ECUs over a period of two and a half years.

On the political plane stands out the satisfaction over the growing commitment of the U.N. and the Organization of American States (O.A.S.) to Central America, the support for the implementation of the new agreements adopted by the Central American presidents in the summits at Tela, San Isidro Coronado, and Montelimar, as well as recognition for the development of "free, democratic, and honest" elections in Nicaragua. Similar acceptance was demonstrated for the electoral processes in El Salvador, Honduras, and Costa Rica.

The start of the activities of the Central American Commission on the Environment and Development (CC-AD) and the signing a week before in Montelimar of the "Regional Cooperation Agreement for the Eradication of the Illicit Drug Traffic" were received as new signs of cooperation and subregional integration in the direction supported from Europe.

The Community's package of cooperation measures for Central America had already been approved by the Commission. As Commissioner Matutes indicated, the project, although it did not carry political conditions, demanded for its application at a minimum a situation of stability. Among said measures were included, in addition to the support for the Regional System of Payments, the creation of the special Honduras-Nicaragua Fund, with an endowment of 30 million ECUs to mitigate their strong trade deficits and balance of payments situation. In addition, a specific reinforcement of cooperation with Nicaragua was foreseen, directed toward the revitalization of the economy, the return of refugees, and the improvement of food supplies, possibly reaching a total of between 15 and 20 million ECUs.

Other compromises not yet finalized and in the process of research and quantification are aimed at the financial support of the Central American Bank for Economic Integration (BCIE)—which amounted to six million ECUs in 1989—as much by the EC as by its member states individually, with the progressive reduction of tariffs for certain tropical products (adopted by the EC under the framework of the Uruguay Round negotiations), and cooperation with the CCAD in concrete projects and matters in the industrial, energy, fishing, and tourism sectors.

It was also agreed, likewise, to harmonize Community measures through the commission with those adopted by the three neighboring states of the region (Mexico, Colombia, and Venezuela), which definitively appear to occupy the role that in its day the Contadora Group played.

An important theme which remains to be developed is the creation of the Central American Parliament, something promoted by the Community. European support materialized on the financial plane with an allocation included in the 1990 Community budget destined to finance actions that reinforce the democratic process in Central America, as affirmed in the fifth point of the Political Declaration of the Dublin Conference.

The European Parliament and the Commission

A recent study has demonstrated that qualitatively and quantitatively interest in Latin America and Central American matters is relatively high among the European parliamentarians. Taking as a criteria the analysis of two types of parliamentary acts that furnish a good reference in this respect—inquiries made to the institutions with the greatest decision making power and resolutions—its author determined that between 1963 and 1988 the following relevant facts can be identified:

> * A total of 629 inquiries were produced relating to Latin America (one of every 38 consultations of the European Parliament). Of these, 369 had to do with South America, 260 with Central America, and 191 with the Caribbean.
>
> * The inquiries were directed principally to the Commission (450), while the rest were directed almost entirely to the CPE

(128) and the council (127). From 1985 a rise in the number of inquiries directed to the CPE can be observed, which by 1988 received a greater number than the commission.

* Of the inquiries related to Central America, 89 referred to development cooperation policy, 89 to economic issues, 69 to political questions, and 48 to the protection of human rights.

* A total of 213 resolutions on Latin American matters were adopted, an average of 20 per year being produced from 1982 (one of every 18 in the PE). The matters included were: 78 on human rights, 64 on economic issues, 64 on political questions, and 34 on development cooperation policy.

Something significant revealed by the study is that Spanish Eurodeputies—with independent political affiliation—are extremely active with respect to South America and Central America. Their written inquiries on European policy toward both areas, in only three years, ranked third in absolute terms (45) and second (43) with respect to those by parliamentarians grouped by nationality during a total 25 year.

The assignment of specific responsibilities regarding Latin America in the Commission to the Spaniard Abel Matutes has contributed to a dynamic role in relations with Central America. These countries also have an accredited representative group in Brussels, the Group of Heads of Mission of the Central American States (GRUCA), formed June 5, 1976.

Economic Relations

On the economic level the conclusion and subsequent application of the Cooperation Agreement has not resulted in a revitalization of the limited European trade with Central America. The principal instrument for its development, the Generalized System of Preferences (GSP), has only caused delays and slight concessions on the main export products such as green coffee.

The provisions of the Cooperation Agreement call

for the establishment of a new differentiated link for EC-Central American relations, the content of which is far from the intense ties which unite the Community with those states or groups of states to which it gives preferential treatment, such as the Mediterranean countries or those of the African, Caribbean, and Pacific (ACP) Group.

The minimum framework that the agreement constitutes has important consequences, which reflect the Community's position in the course of its Central American policy. In the first place, it produces a fission between the political and economic aspects, whose interdependence characterized the first steps in relations since 1983. This break does not constitute an abandonment of the political aspect, given that the institutionalization of the dialogue called the "San José Process" guarantees its continuity, although on a different plane than the legal compromise.

The weakness and lack of specificity of the obligations imposed by the legal framework permit a greater degree of discretion in the implementation of the same and, therein, a greater directed articulation, with probably a greater degree of adaptability according to the course of events. This adaptability constitutes an influential reciprocal factor in the sense that the community would intensify its trade and financial concessions to Central America to the extent that the region's states are able to assure their stability and evolution toward political ends publicly commended by the European countries (pacification, democratization, social reforms, respect for human rights, subregional integration, etc.). Put another way, Central America will obtain greater political and economic support only if its states adopt effective measures in this direction.[1]

Trade stagnation is reflected in the figures for 1977-1987, which show, moreover, the peculiarity of these relations, given that in the trade balance—which differs from the chronic deficit the EC has in its exchanges with

---

[1]The type of relation which I am trying to define could be formulated by the symbol of the "double implication" of logical-formal language.

the whole of Latin America—there is currently a trade surplus with Guatemala and Nicaragua.

Other proof arises from the notable disequilibria according to the countries, which were also registered insofar as the utilization of the GSP (in 1985 on a coverage rate of 9 percent Costa Rica used 6 percent, the relationship for the remaining countries was, respectively: El Salvador, 3 percent and 1 percent; Guatemala, 15 percent and 6 percent; Honduras, 11 percent and 6 percent; and Nicaragua, 4 percent and 1 percent).

The improvement in coverage and utilization rates appears quite relevant for the Central American exports, inasmuch as the scheme is estimated to cover only 10 percent (official Community sources estimated that in 1986 it was only 7 percent) compared to 50 percent for the whole of Latin America and up to 80 percent for other developing countries which also do not benefit from preferential relations.

This situation was altered favorably with the inclusion of a quota for green coffee in the GSP scheme, offering a theoretical coverage of 60 percent to Central American

Table 1
EC-CENTRAL AMERICAN TRADE

	1977			1982			1985			1987*		
	imp	exp	tot	imp	exp	tot	imp	exp	tot	imp	exp	tot
Costa Rica	202	107	309	224	72	296	209	136	345	290.52	151.36	441.88
El Salvador	385	116	501	191	70	261	144	84	228	133.42	85.27	218.69
Guatemala	293	164	457	220	123	343	172	129	301	169.67	186.80	356.47
Honduras	127	54	181	132	56	188	207	94	401	205.88	88.54	294.42
Nicaragua	188	85	273	94	76	172	88	91	179	84.58	132.40	216.98
MCCA	1195	526	1721	861	397	1258	820	534	1354	884.07	644.37	1528.44
Panama	148	304	452	218	685	903	296	660	954	328.20	433.13	761.33
TOTAL	1343	830	2173	1079	1082	2161	1116	1194	2308	1212.27	1078.50	2289.77

imp = imports of the EC
exp = exports of the EC
tot = total EC-C.A. trade
*in millions of ECUs
Source: for 1977, 1982 and 1985 - IRELA; for 1987 - CES: 1990b, annex I

exports that could yet be improved if Panama were included in the total production credited to the five MCCA members.

If indeed the trade stagnation is not singly and principally attributable to the Community's trade policy, one still cannot ignore the European lack of will to impose a significant turn in the situation. This proof is highlighted by the marginalization of Central America in the application of the System of Compensation for Export Earnings (COMPEX).

With respect to two fundamental issues for the Isthmus countries, the investment flow and debt problem, the EC does not have the necessary mandate to take significant actions, since they correspond to its member states. It is clear, in this respect, how limited and paradoxical the Community's legal instruments are, since—on one side—trade and investment are increasingly related and the Latin American debt crisis constitutes the principal obstacle for the revitalization of trade with the region.

Development Cooperation

On the level of development cooperation, if indeed a notable increase in the generosity of Community funds has occurred (50 percent of those destined for the whole of Latin America), these remain well below those from the United States and indeed those contributed by the member states bilaterally.

Nevertheless, the objectives and types of Community cooperation appear quite adequate to relieve some of the Isthmus's necessities, especially those assigned to the relaunching of Central American integration and in support of the subregional projects and institutions, as well as those directed to rural development and aid to refugees and displaced persons.

The recent approval by the European Commission of the proposal for the cooperation program with the unassociated Asian and Latin American countries for the period

1991-1995 establishes global funding of 2.9 billion ECUs, a figure that constitutes an increase of 85 percent with respect to the prior program funded at 1.58 billion ECUs in 1976-1990. The Latin American share is projected at 30 percent. The increase reflects a willingness to maintain attention on the development problems of the region, but shows at the same time the marginal importance of Latin America in European development cooperation policy since the quantity given cannot be compared with the funds assigned annually, for example, to aid the Central and Eastern European countries.

The channeling of Community aid to the Central American countries for projects of a regional interest has exceeded the limited forecasts established in Article 932 of the EC budget, passing to become an element present in all the projects. Thus, while the regional actions represent just a little more than 10 percent of the total in 1983 (3.54 million ECUs out of 34.83 million ECUs) they came to signify a third (27.3 million ECUs out of 82.23 million ECUs) of which furnished in 1987.

The elements reviewed show a certain "conditioning" of aid in the general sense expressed recently by the developed countries. It can be observed, however, which the conditioning does not appear to be colored by ideological or political discrimination. It appears as much an application of political criteria to the area of development aid—in compliance with the objectives of political dialogue—as an optimization of the resources in the methodological line of financial engineering followed in other areas.[2] However, the parallels drawn with the AOD area should be geared toward the generation of endogenous development in the targeted countries.

Finally, there is a specific element in Community aid

---

[2]This has been defined by the Commission as "the determination to use in the best possible way the resources available, taking into account strict budgetary obligations," reducing them to the indispensable minimum so that they can serve as catalysts for investment by private firms and independent financial institutions.

that emerges precisely in the framework of cooperation with Central America, though it is not exhausted there. It has to do with aid to refugees and displaced persons. Created in 1984, with the inclusion of Article 936 in the Community budget, it constitutes an intermediate stage between emergency aid ("post emergency aid") and long-term cooperation. This incorporates very diversified actions directed to integration and self-sufficiency in the receiving country, return and settlement in the country of origin, or relocation to a third country. The Community aid also includes displaced persons, absorbing around 25 percent of the total in projects, the initiative for which must come from the governments of the affected countries and the Non-Governmental Organizations (NGOs).

Its funding has risen from an initial three million ECUs in 1984 to 23 million ECUs in 1989 for all developing countries (PVDNA). The total volume of aid for Central America through this financial instrument in 1984-1989 was 27.68 million ECUs (43.3 percent of the total) assigned to 34 projects, of which 11 were jointly financed with the United Nations High Commissioner for Refugees (U-NHCR) (16.83 million ECUs, 61 percent), 13 with NGOs (7.29 million ECUs, 26 percent), three with interested governments (3.13 million ECUs, 11 percent), and one with the OIM-IOM (0.42 million ECUs, 2 percent).

Insofar as the most tangible results of European policy it must be agreed which it has favored contact and reconciliation among the representatives of the five governments, involving them in the search for common positions to present to the Europeans and contributing to the opening of the Isthmus toward multilateralism on the foreign plane and pluralism on the internal plane. The impact in financial areas is still limited, but it is recognized which without pacification and democratization there is no viable development strategy. In sum, from Europe there is active contribution on the political plane to the integration of the Central American societies, broadening the participation of the ideological and social sectors, which were traditionally denied a voice and which the Sandinista revolution has allowed to become legitimized. On the economic plane. it also does so in the efforts to overcome the obstacles which interfered in the subregional integration and development project begun in the 1960s by the Central American countries themselves and which the centrifugal pressures linked to the actions of external actors threaten to make unworkable.

SPAIN-CENTRAL AMERICA RELATIONS

Spain has participated in the elaboration and application of this policy since its beginning—even though it was not yet a member of the EC—with growing intensity. The Spanish government has moved from ideologically based positions to more pragmatic ones.

The Political Level

On the political plane, the special relations with Cuba—more intense than those with any other Western state—and the support for the Sandinista government gave weight to the greater distancing of the United States position within the EC (proof of this is which cooperation with the governments of El Salvador and Guatemala was practically nonexistant until 1989, while Nicaragua became the major recipient of Spanish aid).

During the 1980s the Spanish government, for its part, followed a policy of "de-ideologization", which led to a more realistic and effective state policy. A situation that began with a rupture of diplomatic relations with Guatemala and the absence of effective contacts with the other governments of the Isthmus (El Salvador, Honduras, and Costa Rica) has developed into one of solid relations with the majority of them, although lack of communication and difficulties with the interlocutors in El Salvador, and to a minor extent Guatemala, persist.

The United States intervention in Panama, the results

of the Nicaraguan elections, and the cooling of relations with Cuba have led in the course of 1990 to a refashioning of the parameters guiding Spanish diplomacy toward the subregion. Nevertheless, the continuation of cooperation with the new government of Nicaragua, heightened relations with Costa Rica and Honduras, and the climate of understanding with two countries interested in Central America, Mexico and Venezuela, permit foreseeing which the trend started recently is a question of nuance, which appears to fit in with the recent pronouncements of the United States, whose most significant apologist is President George Bush and his "Initiative for the Americas."

Economic Relations

On the economic level, although in absolute terms it may be limited, the proportion of trade and investment in Central America is greater globally for Spain than is the case for the other respective member states. Investment, however, has always been focused on certain states in the region (Guatemala, for example), being almost nonexistent in others (El Salvador). The private flows have been reduced in recent years to historic lows. Because of this it appears clear which without a substantial change in the situation and government intervention, it will be difficult to revitalize this area.

With regard to the debt problem, the absolute value and relative weight of the Central American debt to Spain is variable, depending on the country in question. For the whole of the MCCA the risks assumed by the Spanish state reach 57.538 billion pesetas, amounting to close to 3 percent of the total Central American debt. The absolute figures by country show a marked parallelism with the rest of the Spain-Central America economic flows, distinguishing Guatemala and Nicaragua by their intensity and reaffirming the low profile—almost nonexistent—of relations with El Salvador. This risk affects only 0.1 percent of Salvadoran, 0.7 percent of Honduran, 2 percent of Costa Rican, and 2.7

percent of Nicaraguan debt—in the enormity of which Spanish efforts are diluted—and a significant 9 percent of Guatemalan debt.

Table 2
CENTRAL AMERICAN DEBT WITH SPAIN
Risks Taken by the State Through 9/30/88
(in millions of pesetas)

	AP	AU	R(B)	R(CD)	Total	CFAD	Total
Costa Rica	1519.4	1693.2	2012.1	2853.4	8078.1	829	8907.1
El Salvador	171.8	33.8	--	--	205.6	--	205.6
Guatemala	13424.6	12203.7	--	--	25628.3	--	25628.3
Honduras	1322.9	472.5	--	--	1795.4	478	2273.4
Nicaragua	2903.3	10696.0	2316.2	3667.9	19583.4	941	20524.4
Total CA	19342.0	25099.2	4328.3	6520.3	55290.8	2248	57538.8
Panama	7979.2	72.3	--	--	8051.5	557	8608.5
Total LA	3487711.3	77502.7	19420.6	84734.8	530429.4	54849	585278.4

AP = Amount Promised AU = Amount Unpaid R(B) = Refinancing (Back) R(CD) = Refinancing (Coming Due) CFAD = FAD Credits
Source: Government Response to a Parliamentary Action in 1989[3]

The distribution of banking risks and resources demonstrated, as of December 31, 1987, the diverse composition of the Central American debt to Spain, given which a dominant debt stood out from the economic relationship with Guatemala—20.7 billion pesetas—as against the reduced risks and resources committed to the remaining countries: 5.0 billion pesetas to Costa Rica, 4.8 billion to

[3]Complete table for Latin America reproduced in: "La evolución del problema de la deuda externa en Iberoamérica," *Política Exterior*, Vol. III, No. 10, Spring 1989, p. 251.

Nicaragua, 1.9 billion to Honduras, and 400 million to El Salvador.

During the last two years Spain pursued a policy, initiated previously with Bolivia, consistent in reducing the debt of Latin American countries with insurmountable difficulties in meeting their payments. Thus, on April 27 during the visit of Nicaraguan President Daniel Ortega, in a meeting between Commerce Secretary Apolonio Ruiz Ligero and Nicaraguan Economic Planning Minister Alejandro Martínez Cuenca, an agreement to forgive a third of which country's external debt (estimated at 22 billion pesetas) and reschedule the remainder over 14 years with an eight year grace period was reached. A 4.0 billion peseta Spanish Development Aid Fund (FAD) credit was also agreed upon.

Development Cooperation

The disparity between political will and the resources mobilized produces an apparent contradiction that has resulted in serious frictions within the EC because of Spanish demands which the community increase its cooperation efforts with Central America substantially.[4]

The figures on Spanish cooperation with Central America reveal this contradiction, as well as the concentration in some countries and the passing over of others for political reasons, principally regarding respect for human rights and fundamental liberties.

---

[4]In the course of the San José IV Conference held in Hamburg at the beginning of March 1988, the media became aware of the following question, posed by a high ranking commission official: How can Francisco Fernández Ordóñez complain when Spain does not even teach by example, because the aid it provides to that region (Central America) is not only four times less than that given by Italy, but in fact is 35% below that granted by Holland? (*El País*, Madrid, March 1, 1988).

Table 3
OFFICIAL SPANISH DEVELOPMENT AID
TO CENTRAL AMERICA

	1983	1984	1985	1986	1987	1988	1989
Costa Rica	57.5	109.2	166.9	29.1	256.7	n.a.	128.6
El Salvador	0	0	2.7	0	22.7	n.a.	10.4
Guatemala	0	0	0	0	22.7	n.a.	76.2
Honduras	4.4	42.8	120.3	93.8	238.5	n.a.	121.3
Nicaragua	123.9	162.9	220.9	210.9	269.0	n.a.	132.8
Total CA	185.8	314.9	510.8	333.8	809.7	n.a.	469.3
Panama	5.4	30.6	31.0	9.6	91.5	n.a.	33.7
Belize	0	0	0	0	0	n.a.	5.2
Total LA*	750.0	1308.7	1611.7	14955.7	3751.7	n.a.	2918.9

Table elaborated by author drawing from various sources
n.a. = not available
* includes generic amounts assigned without specifying a certain country

The objective interest in Central America—combined with the symbolic nature of Central America within Latin America—produced a notable unfolding of Spanish initiatives as much bilaterally as through the EC that have had an uneven incidence. The following stand out:

* The assignment of an independent EC budget entry for Latin America (previously it was joint with the Asian countries), with a subsequent increase in the share of cooperation for the region.

* The maintenance of favorable shares for the exportation of some products, such as coffee, in the exchanges with Spain and the improvement of GSP application in the whole of the community.

* The formal proposal for application to Central America of the COMPEX, rejected for fear of a "contagion effect."

* The proposal, covered in the appendix of the Conclusions of the European Council (Madrid, June 1989), to undertake favorable initiatives for the reduction of the Latin American debt.

Spanish actions outside the Community's limits have resulted in a commitment to the pacification of the subregion, participation in the International Commission for Support and Verification (CIAV) and the United Nations Observer Force for Central America (ONUCA), and a substantial—though limited—increase in bilateral cooperation.

PERSPECTIVES

From the European Community

As for the perspectives, it appears clear which the Central American policy of the EC can lead to greater effects in pacification, stability, democratization, and development in the region, given which the objectives of Central American integration appear to be assured within the system of payments supported by Europe. The continuity of the objectives established by the Contadora and Esquípulas processes should now enter a new phase (given which the problems at the root of the Central American conflicts remain unresolved).

The balance of relations permits a glance in passing at a series of aspects, which present themselves as strong points of Community action.

Support for the Subregional Integration Process

The establishment of the Central American Parliament appears a priority objective in this direction. It should be completed along with the strengthening and reform of the existing organizations, as well as with the consolidation of those recently created in areas such as environmental protection or the fight against drug trafficking.

The Community should push, likewise, starting from its own experience and which of its member states, for the creation of representative bodies and actions by the economic and social forces. Business groups, labor unions, cooperatives, etc., should receive support in the process of Central American integration building and see in the EC Economic and Social Committee (CES) a more active interlocutor. This body, whose importance in relations with Latin America in general is undeveloped, should receive greater powers in the foreign relations plan of the EC.

Opening of New Limits in Economic Cooperation Relations

The instruments for Community economic cooperation are excessively limited. The GSP cannot continue to be the principal instrument in economic relations with Central America. The maintenance of cooperation should increase with complementary actions in sectors, such as tourism or fishing, which can lead to new limits in development, in this way compensating for the absence of a public economy structure within the EC. This is one of the few areas in which the Community could adopt the cooperation models of some of its member states, especially Spain. It is the large Spanish public enterprises that present themselves as interlocutors in the relationship with Central America through their participation in infrastructure projects with a subregional scope. Also, there must be included in this section the definitive opening of European Investment Bank (BEI) financing for Central American projects and activities.

The vacuum produced between undeniable political attention and growing effective development cooperation requires the setting into motion of actions that are strictly limited to economic cooperation and which pass through two planes: actions driven by public bodies toward the creation and improvement of public infrastructures and services, on one side, and increasing contact between private actors, directed to promoting the diversification of activities and the activation of socioeconomic segments (PYME, cooperatives, etc.).

Maintenance and Increase of Development Cooperation

The existing lines of cooperation appear adequate, but their impact is still insufficient. Support for subregional integration, rural development, and aid for food, refugees, and displaced persons should be strengthened and the utilization of other kinds of assistance whose incidence is only symbolic should be increased. The area of professional formation, sanitary cooperation, scientific and technical cooperation, etc., permits a greater presence of effective private actors such as NGOs, universities, etc.

The strengthening of the CES and its greater involvement should result in an intense relationship, as well as the participation of European businesses, labor unions, and cooperatives in projects of a mutual interest with the support of financial instruments such as those derived from the "Cheysson facility." The experience of Commissioner Matutes in the field of PYMEs should lead to more intense financial support for taking to its conclusion this activity in relations with Central America.

From Spain

Spain will continue playing an active role in pushing initiatives originated in the subregion and in the whole of Latin America—the role of the Río Group should expand in this sense—to intensify the dialogue and relations with the Community and manage a "triangulation" with a United States policy, which appears to be distancing itself increasingly from the positions of "roll back" and "negative contention" that marked the 1980s.

On the Political Level

Spain, for its part, should continue to follow its line of participating in the democratization of the Isthmus. For this, an intensification in relations with the countries most removed from the Spanish government's political parameters is required: Guatemala and El Salvador. Institutional contact and transnational relations should surpass the "ideologization" phase that dominated policy toward Central America in the 1970s and 1980s.

A state policy requires continuity. This aspect should have priority before political changes and opportunities. In the case of Nicaragua it appears which this is the line followed by Spanish diplomacy. The continuation of talks and contacts with the United States on the Central American situation and concerted action with Mexico, Venezuela, and Colombia should increase, as well as the maintenance of links—from a critical position—with the Cuban government. In both cases, a "perestroika" in the subregion should be advocated, which permits promoting and supporting the United States initiatives for democratization and with respect to human rights, and the defense of social forces and movements which seek greater social justice and participation.

On the Economic Level

The dominant policy of Spain-Central America economic relations appears inescapable. Its implementation through public financing and by way of public enterprises should be complemented with the sponsorship of private actors in pilot projects. Trade will play a minor role compared to which which investment could potentially play. The connection or "dragging" of private actors into investment depends on the creativity and effectiveness of actions developed in the public sector. The principal attractiveness, together with a Central American market waiting to be developed, is favorable access to the markets of the United States and Canada. The risk of not meeting this objective would be costly given Spain's limited financial capabilities.

The sectors in which Spain has experience and adequate technology (agriculture, tourism, textile design, etc.) should take priority in the participation of private actors.

Development Cooperation

If one aspect of Spanish policy requires substantial change, it is this one. Spain should—for reasons of solidarity and international prestige—increase geometrically its financing of development in general, and in Central America in particular. The first stage of inexperience and lack of coordination has been surpassed. With an adequate institutional structure (Secretariat of State for International Cooperation and Iberoamerica [SECIPI], Spanish Agency for International Cooperation [AECI], Annual Plan for International Cooperation [PACI], etc.) and a limited but active core of NGOs, the means are in place for Spain to situate itself in the middle level of countries in the Committee for Aid for Development (CAD).

The epicenter of "soft" credits should give way to financial and technical cooperation, thereby paving the way for detecting needs of relevant governments and actors and for developing and implementing projects. Scientific, technological, educational, sanitary, and institutional development cooperation can and should be activated immediately before 1992—the date the government has set itself for maturing Spanish cooperation—although with minimal expectations for the effectiveness of its potential cooperation.

CHAPTER III

ECONOMIC AND POLITICAL SITUATION OF CENTRAL AMERICA

INTEGRATION AND DISINTEGRATION OF REGIONALISM IN CENTRAL AMERICA: FROM 1950 TO 1991

Mitchell A. Seligson

and Ricardo Córdova Macías

University of Pittsburgh

The dramatic successes of the European Economic Community in rebuilding the war-torn economies of Western Europe and in stimulating unprecedented economic development among those countries has overshadowed similar attempts at regional economic integration in other parts of the world. Unfortunately, other efforts at regional economic integration have not met with the same degree of success; indeed, most of the other regional common markets have failed and have been abandoned. However, there is at least one case, that of the Central American Common Market (CACM), in which a considerable amount of progress was made in a relatively short time span, even though the early success was not sustained in the long run. The case is one that is all but forgotten by analysts of regionalism, having been overshadowed by unfortunate events within and among its members, including an international war, a civil war, a revolution, and a protracted guerrilla war. Despite the difficulties that emerged in the Central American case, there is hope, even at this juncture, that the nations in the region might once again return to their former successful efforts at economic (and potentially political) integration. This paper examines the case of integration and disintegration in Central America from an historical perspective, tracing its early success, its later decline, and the prospects for its eventual resurrection.

Background

Central America, comprised of the five countries of Guatemala, El Salvador, Honduras, Nicaragua, and Costa Rica, emerged from colonial rule under Spain united in the Central American Federation founded in 1824.[1] The individual units in the federation shared many similarities. As a result of their common experience of some 300 years of Spanish colonial domination, Spanish was spoken throughout the region, almost all residents were at least nominally Catholic, and the legal systems throughout the region reflected the Spanish tradition. Moreover, even though there are differences in size among the nations, with Guatemala having the largest population and Costa Rica the smallest, compared to the great diversity in population and physical size with countries both north and south of Central America, these five countries appear practically indistinguishable. These similarities would seem to have boded well for the development of common interests and the emergence of a single political and economic unit. Such was not the case, however, and the federation proved to be ephemeral, collapsing entirely by 1839. From that point until the early 1950s repeated unsuccessful efforts were made to reunite these countries.

After World War II, Central American visionaries once again took up the cause of regional integration. This time, however, they limited their immediate goal to economic as opposed to political integration. The argument used by the proponents of a move toward integration was strictly pragmatic; individually, the economies were simply

---

[1]Geographically, Panama and Belize are also part of Central America. Panama, however, formed part of Colombia until the early years of the twentieth century when it was split off as part of the arrangements to build the Panama Canal. Belize, formerly known as British Honduras, remained a British colony until the beginning of the 1980s. Most Belizians speak English and consider themselves part of the Caribbean rather than Central America.

too small to sustain significant industrialization, whereas united in a common market the benefits of economic development could be achieved.

The key institution that promoted the new integration program was the United Nations Economic Commission for Latin America (ECLA), a subcommittee of which, the Central American Economic Co-operation Committee (CCE), was formed to handle Central America's program. The CCE was able to use the technical resources of the United Nations with which it planned a program of development for the region. The years between the establishment of the CCE in 1951 and 1958 were spent largely in planning, and on June 10, 1958 the "Multilateral Treaty of Central American Free Trade and Economic Integration" was signed. This treaty was the first step taken to reduce the tariffs that had served as a barrier to intra-Central American trade. The treaty was, however, highly cautious, freeing only a few items out of the many listed in the Standard Central American Tariff Nomenclature (SCATN). In this respect there is some similarity between the Central American treaty and the Montevideo treaty that established the Latin American Free Trade Association (LAFTA). As is the case with the Montevideo treaty, the free items were those that were not manufactured in the region anyway, and thus, in terms of trade creation, the effects were not substantial. The situation was to change drastically, however, on February 6, 1960, when El Salvador, Honduras, and Guatemala signed a far-reaching agreement (Treaty of Economic Association) eliminating tariffs on a much larger number of goods. Later that year the "General Treaty on Central American Economic Integration" was signed.[2] It took a tack different from that of the Multilateral Treaty, the former freeing all goods produced in Central America with the exception of those stipulated on a special list, a total of 5 percent of the items on SCATN's list. The General Treaty was initially signed by four countries, and

---

[2]December 13, 1960.

Costa Rica signed on 23 July, 1962.

Table No. 1
Trade Growth in Central America
(in thousands of U.S. Dollars)

Year	Total Imports of the five countries	Total Intra-Regional Imports	Per cent of Total Imports	Intra-regional trade per cent increase from previous year
1950	223,50	8,290	3.6	---
1951	268,77	9,735	3.3	16.9
1952	310,21	10,287	3.1	6.2
1953	252,89	11,379	3.4	10.7
1954	362,86	13,416	3.5	17.5
1955	410,35	12,791	3.1	-4.5
1956	460,80	13,481	2.9	5.5
1957	514,69	16,555	3.2	23.0
1958	500,67	20,545	4.0	23.5
1959	464,89	27,993	5.9	36.6
1960	514,14	32,674	6.4	16.8
1961	495,78	36,802	7.5	12.5
1962	552,13	50,366	10.9	37.0
1963	652,58	72,098	9.0	41.2
1964	770,44	106,399	7.2	47.6
1965	889,70	135,976	10.0	27.8

Source: Seligson (1968).

Table No.1 shows the rapid growth in both total trade and in regional trade in the region. The impact of the common market on regional trade was dramatic. As shown in Table No.1, regional trade skyrocketed. In part as a result of the rapid growth of trade within the region, industrialization and economic development were spurred.

In July 1969, harsh political reality in the form of nationalism was to overcome economic success. In that year a long-festering dispute between Honduras and El Salvador was to break out in the form of the so-called "Soccer War" (Durham, 1900). It was a short but bloody conflict. The first major aftershocks were delivered to the CACM. Trade between Honduras and El Salvador was halted, and the Inter-American Highway, the major road link among the five countries, was blocked. Trade within the region began to fall and special arrangements had to be made to keep the market from collapsing entirely. As a consequence of the Honduras-El Salvador war, the Economic and the Executive Councils—chief institutions for the integration framework—stopped functioning, and the legal system that regulated the economic integration broke down.[3]

In 1970 a meeting of Economic Ministers of Central America took place in an important effort to reactivate the CACM. They reached an agreement, in principle, but the results had limited positive impact.

During the 1970s, the normalization of Central American integration was not possible due to the border dispute between Honduras and El Salvador. However, in 1981 a peace treaty was finally signed, and initiated (at lower levels) the commercial relations between the two countries.

A decade later, as the CACM appeared to be finally overcoming the impact of the 1969 war, Nicaragua was in flames as the Sandinistas fought to overthrow the Somoza dictatorship. In July 1979 they succeeded. While the dictator was gone, the problem of economic development was far from resolved, and indeed worsened in the years to come, in part as a consequence of the Contra war supported by the United States.

By 1980 the Central American panorama was grim indeed. But the situation was to grow worse still. The international debt crisis, in which developing nations began to default on loans made during the days in which banks in the United States, Europe, and Japan were awash with "petro-dollars," began to affect the region. Costa Rica,

---

[3]By 1971 Central America had signed twenty-nine agreements of economic integration, and twenty-eight were in effect. Twenty-nine were the multilateral instruments of economic integration signed by the Central American countries, of which twenty-eight were in effect for three countries at least, and twenty for all the countries.

experiencing neither war nor revolution, was plunged into its most severe economic crisis of the century as it struggled to repay loans made by foreign banks.

The nature of the Central American crisis during the decade of the 1980s was characterized by the following features:

1) The existence of three armed conflicts (in Guatemala, El Salvador, and Nicaragua), although each one with its own characteristics, has produced a process of militarization in the entire region. The budgetary impact of this process of militarization has been enormous (Córdova, 1987). Moreover, the war has generated an enormous migratory movement of refugees and internally displaced citizens (Torres-Rivas, 1985).

2) Deterioration of the economies of the region, as defined by decline in GNP growth, GNP per capita, increasing inflation, unemployment, currency devaluation, and foreign debt. This economic picture has affected all of the countries and all social sectors, but undoubtedly the sectors with fewer resources have been more affected. For 1980, at the start of the conflict, ECLA estimated that about 63.7 percent of the population lived below the poverty subsistence level; that is to say, nearly two-thirds of the population did not have sufficient income to buy the basic "basket" of products and services (CEPAL, 1983, p.18). This is the social sector most affected by the economic crisis and the war.

3) In this context of militarization, war, and economic crisis, the volume of intraregional commerce has fallen. In 1985 intra-Central American commerce had the same value—in current dollars—as ten years before; just 15 percent of the total exports of Central America were sent to other Central American countries (Fuentes, 1987, pp. 16-17). Since 1981 there has been a decrease in the transactions realized through the Central American Chamber of Compensation. According to the Instituto para la Integr-

ación de América Latina (INTAL),[4] in 1984 the intra-regional exports fell by 6.1 percent, and the Central American imports experienced a reduction of 10.7 percent. The regional exports fell from $936.8 million in 1981 to $413.2 million in 1986.

In this critical stage of Central American history, the theme of integration has been debated as a means for solving the most serious crisis in the region's history.[5] Integration can be a means for economic recovery (Cepal, 1985), and contribute to the search for a political settlement to the armed conflicts. An understanding of the challenge and prospects for regional integration at present demands a review of the evolution of the conflict itself and the possibilities of solving it.

Political and economic crises have directly impacted the growth of regional trade. Stagnation and decline has been the pattern of recent years. From the perspective of these data, one might conclude that regional integration is a lost cause. We believe, however, that the very crisis itself has generated new possibilities for the emergence of an even stronger regional unit. In the pages that follow, we outline the motivation for this belief.

---

[4]INTAL (1986). *El proceso de integración en América Latina en 1985*, (Buenos Aires, Argentina: INTAL-BID), p. 112.

[5]Menjívar (1988) makes reference to the integrationist desire present in Central American history since the last century, arguing that there have existed cyclical movements, alternating trends of crisis/bilateralism, and prosperity/integration. Nevertheless, in the 1980s, as a consequence of the magnitude of the crisis, both trends have been expressed at the same time. The bilateral approach has sought a better understanding with, and more aid from, the US. On the other hand, other political actors have expounded upon the importance and need of integration.

The Central American Integration in the Context of War and Militarization (1979-1990)

Our working hypothesis is that the crisis of the 1980s was conducive to a search for political accommodation and the promotion of regional integration, on the basis of two principles that have increasingly gained prominence: multilateralism and pluralism.[6] By multilateralism we understand the process of accommodation and political negotiation that emerged in the region, examples of which are the Contadora and Esquipulas peace processes and the economic negotiations with the European Economic Community (EEC). In all of these cases the Central American governments negotiated as a block, rejecting isolationist or divisionist approaches that seek better treatment or position for a given country, or that admit principles of conditionality or exclusion.[7] The second principle is pluralism, understood as an acceptance of the political realities with which the countries of the region had to coexist, such as the Nicaraguan revolution. Pluralism implied recognition of the Sandinista regime by its neighbors, and the admission of Nicaragua as a negotiating partner. The acceptance that Central America is not a homogeneous region but one exhibiting different economic models and political regimes has been a significant achievement. The way in which these principles came to predominate will be examined below, in a review of the forums and proposals for the resolution of the conflict, as well as of programs and initiatives for Central America's economic recovery.

---

[6]This is not to ignore conflict and confrontation in regional negotiations. However, our interest lies in accommodation and agreement, despite existing conflicts.

[7]This approach of discrimination and conditionality in aid has only been in place in the bilateral relations of the United States with the governments of the region, excluding Nicaragua from aid. It was also present in the Caribbean Basin Initiative, the regional proposal of the early 1980s, which functioned on the basis of discrimination.

Consequently, the nature and content of future regional integration will differ from those of the immediate past. A first difference that becomes readily apparent is the political dimension of the current process, which requires a solution to the conflict based on the principle of a non-monolithic and nonhomogeneous region. In the past, integration was expressed at the economic level, on the basis of similar political regimes and without the existence of armed conflicts generating a dynamic of militarization and war.

Second, with regard to the debate on the similarities and differences within the region, it is necessary to clarify that the strictly political elements of the crisis have accentuated those differences, while the economic elements have highlighted even more the similarities. There are, of course, variations in degree, but there is a common economic problem clearly expressed in the similar behavior of macroeconomic indicators.

The political process throughout the 1980s has highlighted the need to view Central America as a region. In addition to shared structural historical and geopolitical elements, the events of the 1980s have evidenced the interdependence of the Central American countries, and underscored the need to search for a joint solution to the crisis.

The need to overcome the crisis by accepting pluralism and multilateralism has enabled Central America to begin to become a region in order to solve its problems, and to come together as an interlocutor to negotiate the terms of international cooperation. The improbability of finding individual national solutions will continue to be a key factor as Central America faces the future.

Simulating Scenarios

An important element in this discussion is the relationship between continuity and/or intensification of the armed conflicts and the problem it poses for economic recovery. The problem lies in the impossibility of economic recovery and the promotion of development without a solution to the military conflicts. This situation has been particularly complicated by the policy of the United States in the region, which has favored military instruments over political negotiations, applying its strategy of "Low Intensity Warfare".

However, important efforts have been undertaken in order to seek a political alternative of demilitarization and negotiations. In this regard, it is important to mention the results of the economic model simulated by the Policy Alternatives for the Caribbean and Central America (PACCA) for the period 1986-1992, contrasting two scenarios of Central America's potential for economic growth and the external aid required: 1) continuation of the "Low Intensity War," and 2) negotiated demilitarization of the region (Fagen, 1987). The findings of the model are illustrative of the complex situation: economic growth for the region as a whole could average 3 to 4 percent per year between 1986-1992 under conditions of peace, and less than 2 percent if the low intensity wars are maintained. The per capita economic growth under the scenario of demilitarization could recover and grow by a total of 4 percent over the entire period, but if the conflict continues, it could decline by 4 percent. These results clearly show that economic recovery is impossible under conditions of continuing war:

> without negotiations and demilitarization, there can be no reconstruction of the economies and societies of the region; without reconstruction, there can be neither economic growth nor enhanced political participation and social justice; without growth, participation, and justice, there can be no lasting peace and no political stability (Fagen, 1987, p. 6).

The Contadora Process

One of the Contadora Group's main contributions was bringing the different governments of the region to the negotiating table. The dynamics of regional negotiations, from the creation of the group to the signing of the Esquipulas II agreement, were contributing factors in the development of pluralism and multilateralism. Even though, for reasons we cannot analyze in depth here, the Contadora initiative did not result in the adoption of any of the peace proposals advanced, it paved the way for the signing of Esquipulas II. The weakness of the negotiations promoted by the Contadora Group lay in the fact that they could not advance beyond the political will of thc Central American governments.

The Contadora Group was created on the invitation of the Panamanian chancellor to the foreign ministers of Colombia, Mexico, and Venezuela to meet on January 8-9, 1983, with the objective of examining the complex panorama of the region. They in turn called on the countries of the area to reduce tensions by means of dialogue and negotiation. Deriving its name from the island in which the meeting was conducted, the Contadora Group, comprising Colombia, Mexico, Panama, and Venezuela, was established. In July 1983 the presidents of the member countries came together to discuss the general guidelines of a peace negotiations program to be proposed to the Central American governments. Two months later they made public the *Documento de Objetivos* (Document of Objectives), containing the 21 points to be pursued through regional negotiations. They included aspects of regional security, as well as issues of socioeconomic development. Finally, in January 1984 the Contadora Group announced the rules for the implementation of the commitments assumed in the Document of Objectives, which had been approved earlier by the governments of the region. The norms of immediate application referred to security, political, and socioeconomic issues.

On the basis of this platform, the Contadora Group continued to work with the Central American governments, until the presentation of a first draft of an *Acta de Contadora para la Paz y la Cooperación en Centroamérica* (peace agreement), in August 1984. The agreement was objected to by the governments of El Salvador, Guatemala, Honduras, and Costa Rica and was initially accepted only by the

Nicaraguan government. This gave way to a process of negotiations and discussion of several revised versions of the Contadora agreement, which never received the backing of the U.S. government and were rejected by almost all the Central American countries (Benítez and Córdova, 1989).

One of the most important features of the Contadora initiative was that it emerged outside of the framework of the Organization of American States (O.A.S.). The Contadora initiative and its Support Group constitute the most important Latin American diplomatic efforts toward a political settlement of the Central American conflict.

The Esquipulas II Agreements

On May 24-25, 1986, the Central American presidents held a meeting in Guatemala. The most important product of the meeting was the Esquipulas Declaration, in which they agreed to sign the Contadora agreement and announced their decision to "formalize the meetings of the presidents as a necessary and convenient mechanism for the analysis of the problems" of the region.

A second regional peace process, parallel and complementary to Contadora, was started in February 1987. Costa Rican President Oscar Arias convoked the Central American presidents and presented his peace proposals, which they agreed to discuss at a future meeting in Esquipulas, Guatemala.

On August 7, 1987, the Central American presidents signed the "Procedure for the Establishment of a Firm and Lasting Peace in Central America," better known as the "Esquipulas II" agreement. The accord establishes a commitment to work for the achievement of peace, and sets a time frame for the promotion of measures to that effect. President Arias's proposal was successful in part because the scope of the negotiations was less ambitious than that of the Contadora initiative and also because the actors in this process were the presidents themselves, that is, the highest decision-making political authority (Córdova and

Benítez, 1989).

Esquipulas II expounded "national reconciliation" in those societies experiencing profound divisions on the basis of three simultaneous measures: a dialogue between the "unarmed political opposition" and the respective governments, a declaration of amnesty, and a cease-fire to coincide with the beginning of negotiations. In addition, the agreement recognized the need to "initiate an authentic democratic process, pluralist and participative." Although an exhaustive analysis of the evolution of and the adherence or lack thereof to the Esquipulas agreement is beyond the scope of this paper, we can at least make reference to its repercussions. From our viewpoint, the political dynamic generated in the region, which promoted the development of the principles of multilateralism and pluralism, is more important than the fact that the agreement by itself has not completely resolved any of the armed conflicts of the region.

The interstate character of the Nicaraguan conflict and the fact that Nicaragua's political regime and economic system differ from those of the rest of the region made this country the "test case" for the Esquipulas II agreement. The presidential meetings in El Salvador, Honduras, and Nicaragua between 1989 and 1990 revolved around the Nicaraguan case. The Sandinista government implemented the measures contemplated in the Esquipulas II agreement and agreed to negotiate with the domestic opposition and the counterrevolutionary forces, signing the Sapoá accords in March 1988. In February 1989 the Nicaraguan government decided to hold presidential elections at an earlier date, February 1990. The agreement to hold free and fair elections became the key factor in the political negotiations. In exchange for these concessions, the Sandinistas obtained recognition and acceptance from the other governments of the region as well as a political solution to the "Contra" problem. As a consequence, at the presidential summit in August 1989, a joint plan for the demobilization and repatriation or relocation of counterrevolutionary groups based in Honduras, was approved.

The free and fair elections of Nicaragua on February 25, 1990, produced an unexpected result, the electoral defeat of the "Sandinista Front" (FSLN). A crucial decision for the future of the regional peace process and the Nicaraguan democratization was made by the Sandinistas when they recognized their defeat and decided to transfer peacefully power to Violeta Chamorro. The FSLN remains as the primary political force of opposition at the national level. Under the Chamorro administration Nicaragua has moved in a transition process toward an economic and political system closer to and homogeneous with its neighbors of Central America. Nonetheless, some basic institutions and policies have not been reversed, such as the land reform or the Sandinista orientation of the army. Another consequence of the change in the Nicaraguan government is the end of the Contra war supported by the United States and the reinitiation of U.S. assistance and cooperation, albeit at moderate levels.

The political change in Nicaragua is part of a more complex process of political changes undertaken by the region in the last two years. The United States invasion of Panama in December 1989 produced the downfall of General Noriega and the installation of Guillermo Endara. The electoral processes between 1989 and 1991 have in addition resulted in the rise of conservative forces: Alfredo Cristiani in El Salvador; Violeta Chamorro in Nicaragua; Rafael Callejas in Honduras; and Rafael Angel Calderón Fournier in Costa Rica. This new and different Central American leadership met for the first time during the Antigua, Guatemala summit in June 1990. This conservative trend has been strengthened with the unexpected electoral victory of Jorge Serrano Elias in the presidential elections in Guatemala, in 1991.

On the other hand, the process of negotiation and verification of the Esquipulas II agreement, together with the parallel negotiations on international cooperation with Central America, were key factors in the emergence of propitious conditions for the development of multilateralism and pluralism as the basis for the promotion of Central

American integration. As early as the May 1986 presidential meeting, the intention to "promote and foster joint positions to confront common economic problems" was reaffirmed, and the decision to "reinforce institutionally and financially the organizations of Central American integration" was made. Subsequently, the Nicaraguan presidential declaration of April 3, 1990, stated that "the consolidation of democracy, once the obstacles in the way of peace have been overcome, demands a resolute confrontation of the economic challenge." With this in mind, it was proposed that at the next presidential summit the following issues be discussed:

> 1) Restructuring, strengthening, and reactivating regional economic integration;
> 2) Evolution toward a productive system integrated at the regional level;
> 3) Reconsideration of the external debt problem;
> 4) A better distribution of the social costs inherent in the necessary adjustment of the region's economies (*La Prensa Gráfica*, San Salvador, April 6, 1990).

The presidential summit of Antigua, Guatemala was centered on the theme of regional economic integration, with the commitment of the presidents "to restructure, strengthen, and reactivate the integration process."

An important aspect of the process of negotiations generated by "Esquipulas II" is the institutionalization of presidential summits as a forum for debate and political agreement among the presidents of the region. The following table contains information on the different summits attended by all the Central American presidents.

Table 2
Summits of Central American Presidents

Summit	*Place*	*Date*
1st	Esquipulas, Guatemala	24-25 May 1986
2nd	Guatemala, Guatemala	6-7 August 1987
3rd	San José, Costa Rica	16 January 1988
4th	San Salvador, El Salvador	13-14 February 1989
5th	Tela, Honduras	5-7 August 1989
6th	San Isidro de Coronado, CR	10-12 December 1989
7th	Montelimar, Nicaragua	2-3 April 1990
8th	Antigua, Guatemala	15-17 June 1990
9th	Puntarenas, Costa Rica	15-17 December 1990

During the last presidential summit at Puntarenas, the Central American presidents agreed to have a rotating presidential summit each semester with the host country assuming the secretariat of this forum, acting as its spokesman, and coordinating relations with other countries and international organizations.

The Central American Parliament

The creation of a Central American Parliament was approved at the presidential summit of May 1986, within the framework of the efforts in the search for political understanding, peace, and Central American integration. The task of drafting a proposal began in August 1986, and in October 1987 the "Project of a Treaty for the Creation of the Central American Parliament and other Political Mechanisms" was officially presented (Córdova and Benítez, 1989). This project has been ratified by the Legislatures of Guatemala, El Salvador, Honduras, and Nicaragua, while Costa Rica's paradoxically delayed doing so. Finally, the treaty came into effect on March 1, 1990, although Costa Rica has not yet ratified it. Nevertheless, at this time not all the countries have elected their representatives to the Central American Parliament. Honduras was the first one to elect its representatives, and El Salvador decided to elect them in March 1991 elections.

The importance of the creation of a Central American Parliament must be seen in the context of the need to have a political mechanism to promote, support, and strengthen regional integration, as well to develop a forum for high-level political debate as a means of regional communication and accommodation. It has been proposed that "this mechanism be the only instrument established in the framework of the peace plan," (Abraham, 1989, p. 44) which would make it the only permanent institutional legacy of the Esquipulas II process.

The parliament was designed to be only a deliberative body, since the various national governments would not be bound by its agreements. Nevertheless, the very nature of the parliament might serve as a point of departure for a gradual enhancement of its powers.

On the other hand, a positive aspect is that for the first time in the history of Central America political parties will have an important role to play in the framework of regional integration. Representation in the parliament would not be based on nationality, whereby each country would send a block of deputies, but on ideological tendencies. This would open avenues for the participation of political parties that they never had before. This innovative proposal may contribute to the consolidation of regional political parties and political pluralism, and to the development of ideological debate. Nevertheless, there is an inherent contradiction in this arrangement, for even though the deputies must be elected in fair and free elections,[8] in agreement with the laws of each country—which may contribute to advancing the process of democratization in the region—the parliament's powers are extremely limited (Aldecoa, 1989, p. 39).

---

[8]This applies exclusively to the 20 deputies from each country. The rest of the members of parliament are not elected: former presidents and vice-presidents.

The International Cooperation

The third contributing factor to the revitalization of the project of regional integration on the basis of multilateralism and pluralism is international cooperation, because it has forced the Central American governments to act as a block despite existing political polarization and intolerance.

In 1985 the Agreement of Cooperation between the EEC and the Central American countries, including Panama, was signed. This was the culmination of a process of negotiations that began at the Conference of Ministers of the EEC and its member countries, the Central American states, and the countries of the Contadora Group, in San José, Costa Rica, between September 28-29, 1984. Prior to this summit (San José I) the Central American governments held several meetings in order to adopt a common position. This process culminated in Luxembourg on November 11-12, 1985, with the "Second Conference on Political Dialogue and Economic Cooperation" between the countries of the European Economic Community, Spain and Portugal, the Central American countries, and the Contadora Group. The Conference approved the agreement of cooperation between the EEC and Central America, and reaffirmed the objective of "contributing to the reactivation, restructuration, and strengthening of the process of economic integration of the Central American countries." The accord establishes the most favored nation clause both for imports and exports. The agreement gives preferential treatment to Central America only "in the framework of the programs (that the EEC) reserves for nonassociated developing countries" (Fuentes, 1987). However, even though the agreement is general and vague in the areas of economic and commercial cooperation, the process and the results of the negotiations strengthened regional integration. The most important factor was that the Central American countries had to adopt a common position on developmental issues.

As part of the agreement, the "Joint Commission" was established. The commission has held three meetings: Brussels on June 17-18, 1987; Managua on June 24-25, 1988; and Brussels on June 28-29, 1989. In these meetings the evolution of commercial exchange has been reviewed, the Central American countries have identified problems and obstacles that emerged since the Luxembourg agreement, and recommendations to improve relations between the partners have been made.[9]

In 1987 the General Assembly of the United Nations passed two resolutions toward the preparation of a "Special Plan of Economic Cooperation for Central America" (SPEC) in order to promote the pacification and development of the region and to serve as a channel for funding from the international community. The plan was approved by the U.N. General Assembly on May 12, 1988.

Reacting to these initiatives from the international community, the Central American governments have worked together to set priorities for international cooperation with the region. In January 1988, a conference of vice-presidents with the ministers of foreign affairs, planning, and those responsible for economic integration approved the "Plan of Immediate Action" (PIA). The plan is understood as

> part of a strategy of regional development at the short, medium, and long term, having as basic objectives to identify and give priority to international aid in those areas and sectors of most interest for the Central American region, framing the efforts in a direction defined by regional criteria of economic rationality and efficiency (SIECA, *Carta Informativa*, Guatemala, No. 316, February 1988).

---

[9]See CEPAL (1989). "Informe sobre la cooperación de la Comunidad Económica Europea a los países del istmo centroamericano."

The purpose of the PIA was to set, with a unitarian approach, priorities for international cooperation, according to areas of the greatest regional interest. The plan was incorporated into the Special Plan of Economic Cooperation and served as a general framework for the proposals presented to the European Economic Community.

Both the Plan of Immediate Action and the Special Plan of Economic Cooperation for Central America

> give priority to the so called Program of Emergency which includes five points: food aid, an emergency fund for the economic reactivation of Central America, energy security, foreign debt, and aid to refugees and displaced people (INTAL 1989 *El Proceso de Integración en América Latina en 1988*, Buenos Aires, Argentina: INTAL-BID, p. 79).

It is not possible to give at this point a thorough assessment of the U.N.'s Special Plan of Cooperation for Central America, but it is worth noting that one of its weaknesses is the uncertainty about the financial requirements, and even the fact that, given the serious needs of the region, the resources contemplated in the plan are clearly insufficient.[10]

On November 29, 1987, the "Compromise of Acapulco for Peace, Development, and Democracy" was signed during the first summit of eight Latin American presidents in Acapulco, Mexico. The eight countries that participated were the members of Contadora and its Support Group: Argentina, Brazil, Colombia, Mexico, Panama, Peru, Uruguay, and Venezuela. With regards to Central America,[11] the Latin American presidents agreed to implement an emergency program that contains

---

[10]Roughly $4 billion.

[11]The most important precedent was the "Plan of Energy Cooperation from Mexico and Venezuela for the countries of Central America and the Caribbean" (San José Pact), signed in August, 1980 and renewed annually since then. This pact has been considered as example of South/South cooperation without political conditionants.

measures to promote Central America's inter-regional commerce, and to facilitate trade access of member countries of the common market to the countries of the Group of Eight.

The Prospects for Central American Integration

We have outlined in this paper the major benchmarks in the evolution of regionalism in Central America. We have shown that despite many similarities in history, size, culture and economic development, prior to World War II the efforts all met with failure. The Central American Common Market, formed in the 1960s, proved to be the most successful of all of the efforts to date, but it too succumbed to nationalist pressures and is currently moribund.

Despite the failures of the past, we believe that regional integration offers a significant opportunity to overcome problems of economic underdevelopment. Moreover, we see evidence that reactivation of the CACM is a distinct possibility. We are particularly encouraged by the democratic elections that have taken place in all of the five countries. For the first time, all of the countries are ruled by civilian governments. We are also encouraged by the winding down of the Contra war and some evidence that the armed conflict of El Salvador may also be drawing to a close. In the decade of the 1990s and beyond, we may see a reactivation of the CACM and a move toward greater regional unity.

Bibliography

Abraham, Gloria (1989). "El Parlamento Centroamericano: Su incidencia en el desarrollo futuro de la región." *Polémica*, San José, Costa Rica, segunda epoca, No. 8 May-August. pp. 41-46.

Aldecoa Lazarraga, Francisco (1989). "El Parlamento Centroamericano: A la luz de la experiencia europea." *Polémica*, San José, Costa Rica, segunda epoca, No. 8 May-August. pp. 35-40.

Benítez Manaut, Raúl y Ricardo Córdova Macías (1989). *México en Centroamérica. Expediente de documentos fundamentales (1979-1986)*. México: Universidad Nacional Autónoma de México.

Booth, John and Mitchell Seligson (1989). *Elections and Democracy in Central America*. Chapel Hill: The University of North Carolina Press.

CEPAL (1985). *Centroamérica: Bases de una política de reactivación y Desarrollo*. Mimeo, México D.F.

CEPAL (1983). *La crisis en Centroamérica: Orígenes, alcances y consecuencias*. Mimeo, México D.F. September.

Córdova Macías, Ricardo y Raúl Benítez Manaut (1989). *La paz en Centroamérica: Expediente de documentos fundamentales, 1979-1989*. México: Universidad Nacional Autónoma de México.

Córdova, Ricardo (1987). "Los efectos económicos de la militarización en la región centroamericana (1979-1986)." *Occasional Papers Series* 20 (March). Miami, Florida: Latin American and Caribbean Center, Florida International University.

Durham, William (1979). *Scarcity and Survival in Central America: The Ecological Origins of the Soccer War*. Stanford: Stanford University Press.

Fagen, Richard (1987). *Forging Peace: The Challenge of Central America*. New York: Basil Blackwell, for PACCA.

Fuentes, Juan Alberto (1987). "La integración económica centroamericana. Nuevas perspectivas a partir de la turbulencia." *Polémica*, San José, Costa Rica, segunda epoca, No. 1 January-April. pp. 15-34.

Menjívar, Rafael (1988). "Centroamérica: Hacia una integración para la paz." *Polémica*, San José, Costa Rica, segunda época, No. 4 January-April. pp. 14-27.

Seligson, Mitchell (1968). "Central American Economic Integration: Problems, Theory, and Prospects."

Seligson, Mitchell (1973). "Transactions and Community Formation: Fifteen Years of Growth and Stagnation in Central America." Journal of Common Market Studies, Vol. XI, No. 3 March. pp. 173-190.

Torres-Rivas, Edelberto (1985). "Report on the Condition of Central American Refugees and Migrants." *Occasional Paper Series*, Hemispheric Migration Project. Washington DC: Georgetown

Table No. 3
Central America Intra-Regional Commerce, 1970-1985
(US Millions of Dollars)

	Central America		Guatemala		El Salvador		Honduras		Nicaragua		Costa Rica	
Year	Exp	Imp	Exp	Imp	Exp	Imp	Exp	Imp	Exp	Imp	Exp	Imp
1970	286.3	299.3	102.3	65.0	73.8	60.6	18.0	54.9	46.1	50.1	46.1	68.7
1971	272.7	276.4	92.0	66.4	81.0	63.6	5.4	16.3	47.4	53.6	47.0	76.5
1972	304.7	306.7	98.7	68.8	92.5	75.3	5.8	22.3	56.2	60.8	51.4	79.5
1973	383.3	388.2	130.0	89.6	112.5	92.6	10.1	32.4	60.3	89.9	70.5	83.7
1974	532.5	526.0	163.2	122.1	149.8	117.3	23.7	42.0	91.5	130.7	104.3	114.0
1975	536.4	519.1	168.2	103.1	141.8	136.9	26.6	51.7	92.6	112.7	107.2	114.7
1976	649.3	611.3	189.0	106.4	176.1	170.4	35.7	58.4	117.8	140.3	130.7	135.6
1977	789.9	719.8	222.5	105.4	215.5	210.3	43.5	71.2	134.0	164.5	174.4	168.0
1978	862.5	886.3	255.0	207.6	233.6	239.9	48.9	96.8	146.3	138.9	178.7	203.0
1979	879.6	879.8	354.0	199.9	192.6	256.9	56.5	98.5	108.1	111.2	168.4	213.1
1980	1177.8	1177.9	530.3	222.3	201.9	344.7	86.8	104.4	82.0	267.8	276.8	238.7
1981	936.8	972.4	355.5	186.4	206.5	304.8	65.9	118.4	70.9	210.5	238.0	152.3
1982	765.5	796.9	320.1	219.9	174.2	260.8	51.9	86.8	52.1	116.9	167.2	112.4
1983	766.7	811.0	308.7	229.4	164.9	233.1	61.4	104.7	33.5	123.6	198.2	120.2
1984	719.7	724.5	285.2	186.6	156.2	251.4	47.6	98.8	37.7	72.9	193	114.9
1985p	490.3	538.2	207.8	90.0	95.7	216.8	17.5	74.8	24.2	56.7	145.1	99.8

Sources: SIECA, CEPAL and INTAL.
(p) Preliminar.
Note: The export figures are given in prices FOB, and the imports in CIF.

THE POST-CRISIS POLITICAL AGENDA:

CENTRAL AMERICA FACES THE 1990 DECADE

Gabriel Aguilera Peralta

FLACSO - Guatemala

Central America's presence in the international arena was characterized by a crisis situation throughout a decade. Beginning in 1979 with the triumph of the Sandinista Revolution, a societal organizational paradigm, different from the market economy and liberal democratic one that had homogenized the region, was presented for the first time at a state level. This diversified model was initiated in a plus-sum game of non-compromise between the concurrent models, a situation which was translated to the internal politics of the states as a violent search to disrupt the existing order, as happened in El Salvador and Guatemala.

The basis of this conflict was, of course, the extreme inequality in the population's access to society's goods and services, as well as the authoritarian and, in many cases repressive character of various political regimes in the area, which made the democratic political principles that they nominally defended worthless. Nevertheless, since the international context was also one of confrontation, the Central American situation was drawn by the United States into the East-West dispute, leading to the superpower's intervention in the conflict.

As the conflict developed both internally and externally with the involvement of extra-regional actors, the problem became a complex one of grave proportions, transforming itself into a situation comprised of internal wars, militarization, and interstate confrontations, provoking serious economic losses and the near paralyzation of the integration process, as well as high human costs, not only in dead, wounded or injured victims, but also in the displacement of large numbers of internal and external refugees. All the Central American countries were eventually involved, including those like Costa Rica, which because of their stable political and economic regimes were not originally implicated in the crisis, but were also affected by its development.[1]

During the climax of the crisis, the Central American actors seemed unable to find their own way out of the escalation of armaments, war, and superpower intervention. At this critical juncture, during the first half of the 1980s, external actors with different perspectives had an important influence. The Mexican and Venezuelan initiatives, and later those of the states that made up Contadora and the Support Group, had the attention of the European Community, which had a bearing on the regional situation, with each one trying to promote a negotiated solution to the different levels of the conflict and trying to relocate the development and democracy issues in the Central American agenda. The largest effort on the part of Latin America was the Contadora Act, and even though it was not accepted by the conflicting states, this initiative is recognized as central in restraining the acceleration of the crisis, especially in relation to the possible military confrontation between the U.S. government and the Sandinista regime, and was the basis for later peace efforts.

The European political participation in support of Contadora also originated one of the early efforts of international cooperation in the region, the "San José" meetings,

---

[1]Literature on the crisis is abundant. The titles include: Edelberto Torres-Rivas *Centroamérica, la democracia posible* (Central America, Possible Democracy) (San José: EDUCA, 1987); George Irving and Xavier Gorostiaga, eds., *Towards an Alternative for Central America and the Caribbean* (London: George Allen and Urwin, 1985); Morris Blachman, et al., *Confronting Revolution: Security Through Diplomacy in Central America* (New York: Pantheon Books, 1986); Richard Feinberg, ed., *Central America: International Dimensions of the Crisis* (New York: Holmes and Meier, 1982); Cristina Eguizábal, ed., *América Latina y la crisis centroamericana: En busca de una solución regional* (Latin America and the Central American Crisis: In Search of a Regional Solution) (Buenos Aires: GEL, 1988).

from which sprung a two-pronged policy of participation: policies favoring peace and democratization and developmental cooperation.

As it is known, the crisis was solved by the concerted efforts of these actors, beginning with the Esquipulas process. The action of third parties served as a catalyst, giving movement to the leading states. In synthesis, Esquipulas, at its early stage, was a movement to plus-variable positions by the countries, at least at the state level. The procedure not only constituted a scheme for negotiation but also developed a societal model accepted by all the actors, who put it in motion through a complex process of two year's duration, which was advanced by reciprocal concessions. This paradigm contains a proposal for a democratic society, understood as such not only in the political dimension, but also in a socioeconomic one.

Although the procedure's execution had its ups and downs, due principally to the insistence of external agents in manipulating it towards a logic of confrontation, it achieved its main objective: to reestablish the actors' consensus regarding a societal model oriented towards peace, democracy, and development.[2]

The Post Crisis Situation

Just as the Sandinista triumph in 1979 signaled the beginning of the crisis, the electoral defeat of this political

---

[2]The initiative of Esquipulas is analyzed in depth mainly in: Enrique Gomariz, ed., *Balance de una esperanza: Esquipulas II un año después* (Balance of a Hope: Esquipulas II After One Year) (Costa Rica: FLACSO/CSUGA/UNIPAZ, 1988); Andres Opazo and Rodrigo Fernández: *Esquipulas II: Una tarea pendiente* (Esquipulas II: A Pending Matter) (Costa Rica: EDUCA, 1990); Guido Fernández, *El desafío de la paz en Centroamerica (The Challenge of Peace in Central America)* (San José: Editorial Costa Rica, 1989); Gabriel Aguilera, ed., *Balance de Esquipulas: Un debate* (A Balance of Esquipulas : A Debate) (Guatemala: FLACSO/F. Ebert, 1989).

force in the elections of 1989 marked its conclusion. This presentation is without doubt unilateral, since Nicaragua was only one of the leading actors of the crisis, not the only one, a dimension which, at least during the foundational stage of the procedure, was present when the crisis was defined as a situation that affected all of the actors, who were equally responsible for its resolution. Nevertheless, the importance of the Nicaraguan elections of November 1989 lies in the fact that they signaled the conclusion of the armed conflict in that country, aided at the same time by the successful negotiations between the government and the irregular forces, and the subsequent free decision of the population by electoral means of the government they desired.

It cannot be concluded that the numerous problems that were present at the beginning of the crisis and which contributed to its origin are already solved. Some of the issues are of a structural character such as the aforementioned highly unequal organization and income concentration of the economy,[3] a situation which worsened during the crisis years; other problems are still part of the crisis even though they tend to be forgotten, such as the internal wars in El Salvador and Guatemala, or the violent resolution of differences between the hegemonic power and the regional actors,[4] as well as the persistent violation of human rights in several countries of the Isthmus. Also in the political realm, where there has been more advancement in the electoral processes, the decisive military influence on the

---

[3]The population of the six Central American countries (including Panama) in the mid 1980s was 22.592 million, of whom 14.199 million lived in poverty. *Central America in Pictures*, (San José: FLACSO/IICA, 1990).

[4]For example, in El Salvador, the November 1989 FMLN offensive caused 2,000 deaths, 30,000 houses destroyed or damaged, and $120 million in economic losses; the US invasion of Panama left 655 dead, 14,000 houses damaged or destroyed, and $2 billion in economic losses. Figures from "Social Disasters," *International Central America*, Vol. 3, FLACSO, April-May 1990.

state and society has not been solved and continues to be a reflection of the internal wars.

In other words, if Esquipulas promotes the prototype of a peaceful, democratic, and developed society, this objective is still a goal to be reached even if the international and regional framework is favorable given the conciliatory tendencies and the peaceful arrangements that seemed to prevail in the international arena between the end of the Cold War and the start of the Gulf War.

The Central American states face the challenge of constructing a different agenda than that of the crisis, which even in its seriousness was relatively simple: to stop the armed conflict escalation, to construct a common model, and agree on a negotiating mechanism that could be applied both among the different states and internally to their societies in order to achieve a political solution to the situations in dispute.

Actually, in a phase that we can define as post-crisis to signify its transitional character rather than its stability, the difficulty lies in the precise definition of the themes of the new agenda and later in the process of facing them.

According to our criterion, these elements could be the following:

Which Integration?

Integration has been for the Central American countries both a paradigm and an illusion. Springing from historical elements, especially the Central American Federation experience after independence from Spain (1821-1830), the idea of the constitution of a state reflecting the ideals of a divided nation has been ever present in the political projects of the majority of the Isthmus states for many generations. In the nineteenth century and at the beginning of the twentieth century it was thought that political integration determined by the governmental and political spheres was the answer. Since the 1950s and under CEPAL's influence, it was believed that the economy had to be unified in order to create the basis for political integration. The success of the Central American Common Market is well known, which increased intra-regional trade and raised growth rates indicating that the road to development had started. Nevertheless, regional income distribution disparities and the international economic crisis seriously slowed the process that terminated with the crisis.[5]

But paradigms are longlasting, and now in the post-crisis restructuring the integration project has been reassumed by the Central American actors and their foreign supporters. The strategy seems to be that both political and economic systems must be approached simultaneously and that the pace must be accelerated.

Once again, the international climate is favorable for the effort. In all of Latin America integration processes have been used as a basis for the search for an answer to the region's imbalance in view of the shift in power worldwide.

The political integration dimension is now focused on the Central American Parliament (PARLACEN) project, initially proposed by former Guatemalan President Vinicio Cerezo and later incorporated into the Esquipulas Procedure.[6]

At the time of the original proposal, the PARLACEN logic was to institute a permanent space for dialog-

---

[5]On the Common Market, see Juan Alberto Fuentes K., *Desafíos de la integracion centroamericana* (Challenges of Central American Integration) (San José: FLACSO/ICAP, 1989); Victor Bulmer-Thomas, *La economía politica en Centroamérica desde 1920* (Political Economy in Central America since 1920) (Costa Rica: BCIE, 1989); Metchilld Minkner, "Central American Integration: Evolution, Experiences and Perspectives," *German Yearbook of International Law*, Vol. 32, 1989.

[6]On the PARLACEN see Lorenzo Fernández, Coordinator, *El Parlamento Centroamericano y la experiencia europea* (The Central American Parliament and the European Experience) (Madrid: Fundación Ebert, ICI, 1989); Rocío Barahona, "La Comunidad y el Parlamento Centroamericano" (The Community and the Central American Parliament), *Cuadernos de Ciencias Sociales* 20, Costa Rica, 1989).

ue and exchange between the Central American governments, creating the opportunity for understanding in a confrontational context. As this situation has already been overcome, its mission now would be to act as an embryo of interregional government, with the European Parliament serving as its logical model.

PARLACEN has been facing problems, such as Costa Rica's delay in ratifying the treaty that created the organization, springing from the distance between the integrationist discourse and the persistence of the perceptions of national interest, which probably do not fit in with today's world. In effect, PARLACEN, while it could initiate action would have no other governmental function than appointment of officials to the integration agencies, being for the most part a forum for debate and the exchange of opinions, despite of which there is a resistance on the part of the actors to take the first step in the direction of political unity.

On the contrary, the other dimension of integration, the economic one, has been adopted by the governments in the sense of the times, trying to reactivate it by starting from understandings based on opening their economies to the world market, promotion of preferable agricultural exports, and keeping the maquila industry. This policy discards the old CEPAL import substitution and industrial protection through state intervention model, which at one point was considered necessary for defending regional interests and expanding international margins of action. The new perception, which identifies itself with Initiative for the Americas proposal is congruent with the unanimous adoptions of neoliberal policies.[7] The search for free trade agreements with Latin America, and especially with Mexic-

---

[7]The unanimity of the governments on this approach is shown in *Declaración de Puntarenas*, Documento de la cumbre de presidentes de Centroamérica y Panama, Ministerio de Relaciones Exteriores (The Puntarenas Declaration, Central America and Panama Presidential Summit Document, Ministry of Foreign Relations), Guatemala, 1991.

o,[8] are included within this strategy.

In this dimension, a new regionalism management must be included. The Central America of the past is not sufficient, at a time in which international power tends to be concentrated in large groups of states that have tightened the margins of operation for smaller actors. In this sense, the incorporation of Panama, already begun, to the new schemes of integration, must be accompanied by that of Belize, a country which has the dual characteristic of being Central American and Caribbean and could promote connections between the Isthmus and Caribbean region.

In this way, the first issue of the new agenda will define an integration process that is pragmatic and congruent with the times, which definitively incorporates the political dimension and that will advance toward its goals at a good rate in order to obtain more autonomy for the Isthmus countries in the world arena.

Unfinished Tasks

The possibilities of a new form of integrated action springs from the premise that political and economic homogeneity have been reached. This is correct at the political level, but not necessarily at the societal level. The persistence of a dual phenomenon of internal wars and human rights violations shows the incapacity of the states to provide for basic popular demands and a rejection by segments of the population of the legitimacy of the states. These situations are part of the problem Esquipulas identified as "profound divisions within society," and for which it offered national dialogues as a solution.

In view of the long duration of the armed conflicts

---

[8]Within this framework, the Central American countries have initiated formation of a free trade area with Mexico. See: *Declaración de Tuxtla Gutiérrez* (Tuxtla Gutiérrez Declaration), Presidential Summit of Central America and Mexico Document, Ministry of Foreign Relations, Guatemala, 1991.

and the impossibility of contending parties to agree on military matters, the only possible solution are negotiations leading to political agreements. The feasibility of this process was demonstrated by the ending of the Nicaraguan War, but the intention to replicate it in El Salvador and Guatemala has been unsuccessful. In the latter cases there have been two types of problems: first, the narrow interpretation of the Esquipulas terms, in the sense that insurgent forces must surrender their arms and turn into a "non-armed internal opposition," prior to starting negotiations and second, when this interpretation has given way to a more expanded one, that of initiating a dialogue with recognition of the belligerency, the difficulty has been defining the parameters, not only of the reconciliation process, but also of the concept of social reorganization.[9]

As social reorganization directly affects the power of the armed forces, these processes—as has occurred in the experiences of other Latin American countries—run the risk of becoming swamped in the contradictory situation that growing democratization can end the war, to the extent that insurgent forces, partially influenced by world changes, have abandoned their revolutionary paradigms of violent change in society to claim reforms compatible with the Esquipulas spirit. A sector of the power groups refuse this type of transformation, since their interests are being affected.

This dispute explains the nonmovement of the

---

[9]On Central American negotiations see Gabriel Aguilera, "Esquipulas y el conflicto interno en Centroamérica" (Esquipulas and the Internal Conflict in Central America), in *Anuario de Estudios Centroamericanos* (Central American Studies Annual), University of Costa Rica, 14 (1-2), 1988; Martha Elena Salguero, "Perspectivas de la paz en Centroamérica a la luz de Esquipulas" (Peace Perspectives in Central America in the Light of Esquipulas), *Debate Notebooks*, 7, (Guatemala: FLACSO, 1990); Ricardo Córdova Macías, "El Salvador: Análisis sobre las negociaciones de paz bajo la mediación de las Naciones Unidas y perspectivas politicas," (Analysis of Peace Negotiations under United Nations Mediation and Political Perspectives), presentation made at the FLACSO International Relation's Workgroup II Reunion held in Cancun, Mexico, 1991.

negotiating processes, which were also given in the Nicaraguan case. Notwithstanding, in this case the impasse was broken by the rest of the Esquipulas actors and extra-regional factors, which acted over the contending parties pressing them into the negotiations. But the same situation has only been created weakly in the other cases. This has something to do with the terminating of the Cold War and ending the possibility of the domino effect, which the hegemonic power had used to explain the development of the insurgencies, and with the way that the Esquipulas process had in 1989 of turning around the Nicaraguan crisis.

As the persistence of war situations are directly linked with the violation of human rights and the difficulty of establishing the primacy of civil over military power, it is clear that the resolution of these problems is a prerequisite to obtaining a united society that will permit the consolidation of the democratic transition and from there the facing of development tasks.

Democratic Security

The concept of security adopted by the governments during the crisis was conventional in terms of its definition vis-à-vis external and internal threats to the survival of the government's political and economic structure, springing from armed opposition groups.

The new agenda calls for the introduction of a new concept of security that could be inspired in the administration of democratic security, at present being discussed in South America.[10]

In other words, it must be perceived in the light of risk factors in Central American societies, a list which could include three elements.

---

[10]For this concept see *Seguridad democrática regional*, (Regional Democratic Security) (Santiago, Chile: South American Peace Commission, 1988); Peter Calvert, ed., *The Central American Security System: North-South or East-West?* (London: Cambridge University Press, 1988).

The first real threat is high poverty levels, slow economic growth, and scientific and technological recession. To prolong this situation would reduce not only the quality of life of the population but the governments' capacity for action as well. Increased social violence, adopting more perverse forms, and extended criminality involving important sectors of the marginalized youth population can also be included here.

A second issue is the importance of drug trafficking and production in the region. With different levels of intensity, all countries in the area are involved in cocaine trafficking from producers, countries to the United States. As in other similar instances, capital gains obtained from drugs are such that they are able to exert a strong influence at the local, regional, and national levels, affecting political and civil societies alike. The outcome is likely to be the distortion of the political system,[11] resulting in additional obstacles for achieving genuine democracy.

The problem reaches serious proportions when countries also become producers. While marijuana is presently cultivated in various countries, it does not reach the level of importance of the poppy crop in Guatemala, a country that could well be the largest opium producer in Latin America and seventh among the world's producers.[12] Furthermore, profit margins for the new product are exceedingly superior to those obtained from marketing conventional agricultural products, generating substantially

---

[11]For an analysis of how drug power affects a Central American country's political system see: "Legislative Assembly, Informe de la Comisión sobre el Narcotráfico" (Report by the Commission on Narcotraffic) (San José, Costa Rica: UNED, 1988).

[12]US General Accounting Office. *Drug Control: U.S. International Narcotics Control Activities*, GAO/NSIAD-88-114 (Washington, D.C.: Government Printing Office, March 1988); "Puente del Narcotráfico" (Narcotraffic Bridge), *Prensa Libre*, Guatemala, July 24, 1989; "Drogas en Guatemala, descripción del problema fundamental" (Drugs in Guatemala, Description of the Fundamental Problem), *USIS Information Bulletin*, Guatemala, June 1989.

increased living conditions for poor peasants involved in the production of opium and simultaneously creating a social base which locally supports the activities of organized groups linked to international drug cartels. To the extent that this criminal power exerts influence on countries afflicted by poverty and social and political violence, the result may well tend to be "Colombianization" of society.

A third security issue is environmental deterioration. Since Central America's security agenda had been oriented toward overcoming more immediate problems it has been slow in joining the global concern about the environment. Armed conflict along with demographic pressure, poverty, and careless industrial regulations resulting in accelerated deforestation are probably the most acute obstacles to regional environment conservation. Projection maps estimate that under present conditions existing rain forests will be extinct in only 15 years.

This article on security depicts a possibly frightening short-term scenario: societies with high indexes of absolute poverty, serious problems of social and, eventually, political violence, areas of the countries controlled by drug traffickers—all within the framework of devastated natural resources.

Central America in Today's World

As pointed out in the Esquipulas document, although the actors in Central America are willing to deal with regional problems, cooperation in external elements is required. As mentioned previously, this input was central in displacing armed confrontation in favor of peace negotiations during the period of crisis.

Ending the confrontation, however, had the unexpected effect of lessening the world's attention and weakening foreign support for the area; specifically, the Central

American issue lost importance on the U.S.'s agenda,[13] and it was also replaced as other states focused on new situations, such as the political disintegration of Eastern Europe, internal problems in the U.S.S.R., expansion of Islamic fundamentalism, and, finally, the Persian Gulf War. As a result, the Isthmus risks being excluded from international debates and is now in a position where, as demonstrated, none of the three Esquipulas objectives—peace, democracy, and development—has yet been achieved.

Likewise, attention today is geared toward solving current core problems (drugs, ecology) and those of a structural nature (economic underdevelopment), all of them so overwhelming that attempting to find adequate solutions will require intensive support from external agents such as that obtained for political issues during the crisis.

There are four basic external resources in the area: the United Nations system, and the systems of other international organizations, to the extent that assistance programs such as PEC continue; Latin American countries, through the processes of free market association and the conservation and expansion of the San José Agreement; the European Community countries, bilaterally or through the cooperation agreements reached at the San José Dialogue; and nongovernmental initiatives, such as the proposal of the International Commission for the Recuperation and Development of Central America.

Maintaining and increasing these sources of support does not depend solely on the countries of the region. Nevertheless, their capacity of acting as a bloc will be instrumental in obtaining support at an appropriate level of external cooperation to the extent that they are able to resume their position in the framework of the new political agenda and solve many of their own issues.

---

[13]For a discussion see Abraham Lowenthal, "Not Berlin but Still German," *Hemisfile*, May 1991; Edelberto Torres-Rivas, Carlos Sojo, and Abelardo Morales, "Centroamérica y el tamaño de su soledad" (Central America and the Size of Its Solitude), *International Central America*, Vol. 3, April-May 1990.

This cooperation should include support for the sovereignty of the Isthmus countries, since the world arena tends towards multipolarization, but the Central American region is perceived as unipolar. Searching for a wider scope of action that would include participation of the countries of the region in solving their problems, in a form similar to the pursuit of peace by Esquipulas, should prevent the unilateral intervention of third actors—as in Panama.

The Central American countries, in general, have adopted the *Procedimiento de Esquipulas* (Esquipulas Procedure) as a frame of reference to define a new agenda. Thus, institutionalization of presidential summits, their specialization in treating economic and technical issues, reduction of political issues, the creation of new areas of discussion, such as the environment, aside from recently begun efforts to reach an agreement on a new concept of security all point in that direction.[14] Nevertheless, the central idea of the procedure must be reiterated to achieve not only political democracy but also equity in social matters.

If these norms are duly observed, the Isthmus countries, although still underdeveloped, could eventually reach the end of the century with a consolidated regional project and relatively more equal societies.

---

[14]Discussion by the Security Commision for the Esquipulas Procedures and the Puntarenas Summit Agreement is in this direction and will constitute a new regional security model. See *Declaración de la Comisión de Seguridad* (Declaration of the Security Commission), San José, July 31, 1990. Ministry of Foreign Relations Document, Guatemala, 1990 and the Puntarenas Declaration, op. cit.

THE ECONOMIC AND POLITICAL SITUATION OF CENTRAL AMERICA IN THE PRESENT INTERNATIONAL SITUATION

Guillermo Molina Chocano

CEPROD - Honduras

This study will attempt to make some reflections on Central America's economic and political situation in light of the changes that have taken place on the international scene, while examining the repercussions of trends in international cooperation toward the region. In addition, it is necessary to analyze the social and political changes which have been made within the region during recent years and, from an overall regional perspective, the modifications that are being undertaken.

Within the first aspect, there has been talk of a "post-Cold War" era, which presupposes the emergence of a new international order surpasses bipolarity and confrontation between the two great superpowers. It also presupposes taking into account the rapid social and political changes in Eastern Europe, such as German reunification and the political democratization of various socialist countries in Eastern Europe.

At the economic level, there is talk of forming large trade and financial blocs, such as the European Economic Community and the unified Europe of 1992, Japan and the Newly Industrialized Countries (NICs) of the Pacific, and more recently, the effort to create the "North American Common Market" (MCN), headed by the United States and its minor associates, Canada and Mexico. This last case involves a free trade accord that would create one of the largest trade areas in the world. The president of the United States has carried out intense discussions with Canada and Mexico, to which go two thirds of the United

States' foreign trade; North American investment in Mexico represents two thirds of direct foreign investment. In turn Mexico has signed various bilateral accords concerning subsidies and compensatory taxes, etc. And in 1990 negotiations intensified to eliminate most of bilateral trade tariff barriers, except for petroleum.

But the United States seeks an even larger framework. On June 27, 1990, President Bush announced the so-called "Initiative for the Americas" which in general terms includes matters such as free trade, foreign debt, and investment. At first sight, many analysts have assessed the proposal as a new version of the Monroe Doctrine, insofar as it would strengthen the unequal interchange between countries very different in their economic capacities and technological development. Be that as it may, Bush contends that the United States needs a Latin American market to face global challenges, given the productive, financial, trade, and technological power of Japan and a unified Europe that increasingly controls more economic areas. Latin America's preoccupation with finally being absorbed by the United States is evident, although its negotiating capability remains yet to be seen given that it represents a market of almost 200 million people, possesses an enormous reserve of primary materials, and has an extremely important strategic geopolitical position for North America.

Another important element within this new continental scenario emphasizes a factor that would form part of the same global strategy mentioned previously. It concerns the new rapprochement of Mexico with Central America, also called "the Petroleum Diplomacy," insofar as Mexico represents 30 percent of the supplies to the region and along with Venezuela (70 percent) forms the Petroleum Treaty of San José. At the recent meeting of the five Central American presidents with the Mexican chief executive in Tuxtla Gutiérrez, Chiapas, Mexico, he [President Salinas de Gortari] reaffirmed his leadership and took advantage of the reunion to present a "Framework Accord" proposal for free trade with Central America, which would be gradually implemented in the next few years. The occasion was also propitious for important petroleum debt re-negotiations of the Central American countries, including operations (SWAP) or exchanges of foreign debt for national assets. Such a possibility was discussed by President Salinas de Gortari during his visit to San Pedro Sula, Honduras, in the case of a cement plant.

It is not accidental that these visits and meetings coincide with the chronology and the agendas of the North American Common Market (NACM), since Mexican foreign policy has gravitated toward signing a free trade treaty with the United States. If this Central American treaty with Mexico enters into effect, the region would have a border with the United States, with the subsequent consequence of Mexico apparently becoming an intermediary: that is to say, that regional free trade by way of the Caribbean Basin Initiative runs the risk of being substituted by free trade with Mexico.

As can be seen, the strategy of the United States works in various fronts: the North American Common Market, the so-called Initiative for the Americas, and the "Framework Accord" for a Mexican-Central American free trade treaty. The required question is to what measure this favors or restricts the possibilities of expanding Central America's trade and its access to broader and less conditioned international cooperation. In this sense, it is essential for Central America to formulate a sovereign and democratic economic and legal program that contemplates alternative development strategies and which strengthens its margin for autonomy and negotiating capabilities within the context of intra- and extra-continental blocs.

From the point of view of international cooperation with Central America one can discern diverse focuses and tendencies. As is known, the United States has a privileged position permitting it to assume and preserve its hegemonic role in the subregion, subordinating the orientation of its aid to its geopolitical and national security interests (even in the "post-Cold War" era). This is evident in the conflicts in Nicaragua, El Salvador, and Honduras (not to mention

Panama), insofar as it is a stepping stone for regional intervention and control. This is to say that aid has followed the oscillations of the geopolitical situations that have been occurring since the Cuban revolution, the Sandinista revolution, the political-military conflict in El Salvador, the presence of irregular anti-Sandinista forces in Honduras, the political-military confrontation in Panama, etc. Most of these cases concern cooperation conventions and accords concerning donations and loans in the areas of economic cooperation, military and security help, bilateral and country-by-country pacts, with various types of conditions.

In contrast, the European focus combines bilateral aid and multilateral conventions emphasizing subregional integration dimensions and ultimately, through the Esquipulas II peace accords, the political dimension has been incorporated as in the case of the Central American Parliament. The conferences of ministers from the European Economic Community, Central America, the Contadora group, the Group of Ten (Rio Group), the Group of Three, etc., have constituted important consultative, negotiating, and cooperation forums, within the uninterrupted sequences of San José I to San José VII in 1991 to discuss levels of financial cooperation with Central America.

These differences have turned into discrepancies rooted in the so-called "Declarations of Antigua," Guatemala, in June 1990 when the North American Secretary of State, James Baker, proposed an organization similar to the Group of 24 (G-24), including Canada, Japan, and the European countries to guarantee and channel all international aid to Central America. Secretary Baker affirmed "that the United States has ideas and outlines about how to support Central America financially and through coordination," (FLASCO-No. 4, July-August 1990), giving the idea that the United States would retain executive control of the G-24's actions. Obviously this statement was unacceptable for the European countries, which saw in the proposal a mechanism to centralize all aid to Central America, which would give the United States power to impose certain limitations. In turn, it was unable to decouple the proposal of the North American plan to create a free trade zone in Latin America, which constitutes in reality the underlying reason of the Initiative for the Americas. In this sense, the economic projects and the hegemonic proposals of the United States are incompatible with the European Economic Community's focus on offering help to Latin America and Central America, especially to stimulate genuine subregional integration processes to attain the potential of its autonomy and international negotiating capability.

In addition to the external conditions, which could limit or reduce the effectiveness of European cooperation, it is fitting to stress some of the principal changes have taken place within the Central American region, which detail the most acute elements of the economic and social crisis affecting the majority of the Central American population. As the Economic Commission for Latin America (CEPAL) has indicated, the Central American panorama is characterized by social turbulence, recession, and economic disintegration as the constant features of its evolution. This signifies that the levels of poverty have accentuated, affecting on average more than 60 percent of the population, which already had wretchedly low social well-being indices in rural areas and in the principal cities.

To this picture was added in the 1980s the so called "Lost Decade," which in reality for Central America meant a retreat of about 25 years in the average life span. The economic crisis and the foreign debt explosions intermixed with the socioeconomic effects of the war and political-military conflict that depressed the region for several years, resulting in thousands of refugees, undocumented immigrants, and economically displaced persons who move throughout the region and in large measure toward Mexico and the United States. This is a phenomenon of enormous proportions affecting the sending countries as much as the receiving countries in what is called the "brain drain" and the problems of services and employment it creates in places of departure and arrival.

The governmental responses to these crises follow practically the same pattern as in the rest of Latin America:

imposition of a neoliberal model of recessive adjustment intended to overcome the large macroeconomic, fiscal and balance of payments disequilibriums needed for foreign debt payments and fulfillment of the measures required by the international financial organization to merit the label of "solvent" or "eligible" for refinancing or new loans. Of course, the model does not contemplate the social costs of adjustment, even though there is timid talk of social compensatory measures, which with difficulty permit recuperation to precarious levels of life.

In this way the social debt increases, as is indicated by the fourth plenary assembly of the Episcopal Secretariat of Central America and Panama (ESCA), held in Panama from January 21 to 25, 1991:

> The scandalous increase in poverty as the direct consequence of inflation, the foreign debt, and the imposition of neoliberal economic models by governments among other causes. The application of this model has increased the number of unemployed and has raised prices of basic consumer goods, has facilitated as well, abusive practices such as food hoarding and speculation. The situation has worsened with the immoderate fuel price increases. The peace efforts in the various nations continue meeting obstacles such as manipulation of information by the groups in the conflict, the obvious failures of the administration of justice, resistance by privileged groups, civilian as well as military, to the changes which assure just, fraternal, and solidarity coexistence. It is alarming the environmental deterioration for lack of legislation and healthy habits of the population.

Further on the Central American Episcopal Conference emphasizes the inadequacies of the economic measures to the social situation of the majority of the population:

> Therefore, we cannot accept as valid and compatible with Christ's teachings materialistic, political, and economic doctrines as the object of all human activity, without concern that to achieve them measures are employed against human dignity and by trampling on people's rights.

At this level the Catholic church appears as one of the most important opposition forces at the regional level, since its structure allows it to adopt a common diagnostic-denouncing position of what it considers a truly grave and socially explosive situation.

The concurrence among countries as to the gravity of the crisis also manifests itself at the political-electoral level in what has been called the emergence of a "new right in Central America." This alludes to the simultaneous ascent of elected governments between 1989-90 that shared an image and political discourse in the denominated conservative modernization strategy that supports a radical anti-statist position and believes determinedly in the miracles of the free market and the magic of promoting exports as the only way out of the crisis. It is curious that in all the countries there are triumphant opposition candidates who win with a relatively ample electoral majority, promising reforms or not-well-defined changes to modify their respective crisis situations. Also, all, upon taking power, begin systematically applying structural adjustment programs, not mentioned or practically denied during the electoral campaigns, contending that it involves inevitable healthy economic measures. It involves a practically imitative discourse that hegemonizes the style of government at the regional level.

In this sense, the discourse assumes the traits more characteristic of neoliberal proposals: the great culprit of the crisis is the state, therefore its immediate reduction is essential as a necessary condition to reactivate the economy. Therefore, the market becomes the axis of the restructuring, insofar as it becomes the sole valid and legitimate instrument that could lead to reprivatization in all of society, the economy, the state, and even politics. It involves then the totality of the market, before which any other figure or thing becomes secondary.

According to some analysts critical of this new tendency, the leaders or managers of the new right "are more ideologues than rigorous analysts; they are more publicists than investigators. Their moving simplicity allows an easy popularization of the messages through the mediums of mass communication" (see R. Marin/S. Lopez, ALAI). Radio and television have been converted in effect into privileged channels of the images which tend to deify and mystify the adopted measures as the only salvation and which require "the unselfish sacrifice of all the population." This allows the cushioning of constant increases in the cost of living, uncontainable inflation, devaluation, increased taxes, increases in public service fares, etc. Without a doubt it involves a corporate model, which efficiently synchronizes the economic level with political propaganda, which talks of consensus and reconciliation but without any real or effective participation.

These internal tendencies in the countries are translated to the plane of regional action. It was said that Esquipulas II represented the Central Americanization of Contadora. Beginning with the eighth presidential summit of Antigua, Guatemala, in June 1990, one could say it became the "North Americanization of Esquipulas," as it drastically turned from the political toward the economic, which inaugurates a new technical language and at the same time conceals the unfulfillment of the pending political accords assumed at previous meetings. Apparently it blurred the regional political autonomy attained by the previous presidential summits which, despite foreign pressures, undertook crucial decisions which at the time prompted the regional pacification process and created bases for establishing a permanent political forum of consultation and cooperation.

If one analyzes the process retrospectively, one can see that at the fifth and sixth presidential summits in August 1989 in Tela and December of the same year in San Isidro Coronado, respectively, crucial decisions were produced which unfettered the peace processes upon approving demobilization, disarmament, repatriation, and relocation of the Nicaraguan counterrevolutionary forces ("Contras"), with an eye toward the participation of ONUCA (U.N. Observation Force for Central America) and the CIAV (International Support and Verification Commission) in the jobs of implementation and observation. At the same time the parties to the conflict in the Salvadoran civil war were encouraged to begin a dialogue and negotiate.

By contrast, the Antigua declarations shift toward the field of the "reconstruction of the economic integration program," at the same time as Secretary Baker's proposal for Central America and the launching of the Bush Initiative for the Americas. It is fitting here to ask what integration entails: of regional integration or the new insertion of every country into the Inter-American economic system and the world market? The Central American Economic Action Plan (CAEAP), which gathers diverse initiatives for reactivating commercial exchanges and promoting foreign trade, appears as a product of the summit. It establishes measures that stimulate industrial reconversion and coordination of agricultural policy, explicitly assuming the necessity of stimulating coordination processes in return for the economic adjustment programs in every country and the respective social compensation programs that minimize the impact of the former in the short-term on:

> the most unprotected groups and incorporates the sectors of fewer recourses to the development process, through access to capital, technology, training resources, to those groups that especially are connected to the informal sector, the microenterprises and associated forms of production. The preparation of rural development plans is an integral part of this instruction.

In another point it talks of "...establishing a Central American consultative and coordinating forum for foreign debt matters to find appropriate solutions to bilateral and multilateral debts."

The new tonic of the presidential summits became more obvious at the ninth reunion of presidents celebrated in Puntarenas, Costa Rica, in December 1990, which was notorious for the absence of a deliberate pluralistic and equitable attitude in the treatment of diverse actors and conflictative terms which characterize the problematic region. The approach of these discussions and declarations centered more in a reaffirmation of the privatist model and economic adjustment which is encouraged for all the region, than in a search for alternatives and answers to strengthen the region's negotiating capacity above all before the United States, Japan, the European Economic Community, and other subregional economic blocs. In the political field it showed partiality when it made a unilateral declaration of unconditional support for President Cristiani's policy and a complete condemnation of the Farabundo Martí National Liberation Front (FMLN), rather than establishing channels that would encourage more effective negotiations between the opposing parties, as it demanded of the Sandinistas and the Contras leading to the famous SAPOA Accords. This attitude was expressed by Auxiliary Bishop of San Salvador, Monsignor Gregorio Rosa Chávez as the consequence of "the reality that Central America is at this moment is in hands of governments with the same ideological persuasion and where it is easy for one single vision to dominates."

Undoubtedly the regional presidential forum has become depersonalized and has lost its image as an autonomous organization, genuinely Central American, with an appreciable margin for maneuver which would allow it to easily sort conflicting internal situations and extraregional pressures with realism, a sense of equilibrium, and pragmatism in the definition of concrete mechanisms to resolve matters of crucial regional interest. Now it shines as a uniform and hegemonic example, with little creativity and capacity for initiative, more interested in attaching itself to proposals of other powers or regional blocs. The agencies and accords fall in a vagueness and absence of definitions concerning themes as diverse and varied as they are contradictory, which appear to talk of all and nothing at the same time; it does not appear to fix upon strategies and priorities. Finally, it appears that it concerns a deliberate confusion which ends by accepting in a dissembling manner President Bush's Initiative for the Americas without balancing the advantages or disadvantages for Central America.

This climate of ambiguity appears conducive to a passive and uncritical acceptance of the economic and strategic initiatives of the United States at a time when the North Americans need Latin America in the face of the global challenges they confront in the new world order and at time when the ability is needed to negotiate an improvement in the terms of a grossly unequal relationship in the situation in which the foreign assistance resources that North America offers the region are rapidly diminishing in accordance with the cuts required by its own enormous fiscal deficit and accelerated loss of industrial, commercial, and financial competitiveness to Europe and, in particular, Germany and Japan.

In the same way, it appears not to take advantage of the potential for European aid because of their same lack of political will, by the limitations imposed by North American hegemony, and by the nature and orientation of the political forces that operate on the Central American scene. On the other hand, the new economic reality of a unified Europe of 1992-1993 surely will impose other conditions which perhaps will define new parameters for cooperation with Latin America and, in particular, with Central America.

Finally, the proposals of Inter-American Dialogue and the International Commission for Central American Reconstruction and Development (SANDFORD Commission) establish important lines to define viable and realistic policies for cooperation with Central America based on regional and global diagnosis that adequately plumb the depth of reality.

POLITICAL TRANSITION AND ECONOMIC RECOVERY IN CENTRAL AMERICA

René Herrera Zúniga

El Colegio de México

After ten years of intense political and military crisis in Nicaragua and El Salvador, Central America is now witnessing the positive effect those years had on regional politics. Engaged in the follow-up and analysis of the bellicose events, we set aside the fact that Central America has had important changes in its way of making policy, in its way of outlining and deciding economic policies, and of presenting and fulfilling social demands. Today it offers three new trends that with the past. Notwithstanding that these trends are reactions to the dangers of civilian-military confrontations, what is important is that in spite of—or as a consequence of—the crisis in the last decade, there are new horizons for the region.

The first general trend is in the political arena. The present governments are the products of broader and more open political contests. This new and greater political competition is producing governments in the five countries that are very similar. That is, Central American governments are now more homogeneous than in the past. From Costa Rica to Guatemala their rulers are very much alike, not only in their electoral origins, but also in their style of government; that is, their political discourse is based on an entrepreneurial culture. In other words, they are homogeneous in an ideological sense.

This homogeneous leadership trend corresponds to an intentional transitional period that demands to be fulfilled by men with a low political and social profile as well as low key partisan compromises in a society politically polarized and economically and socially crippled.

The second general trend in the region is market ideology; this new ideological chapel, as it has been called by Jorge Domínguez, is shared, fed, and encouraged as a fundamental economic strategy of government policies.[1] From traditionally social-democratic Costa Rica to traditionally conservative Guatemala, the political discourse is economics loaded with proposals favorable to economic internationalization and regional integration.

The homogeneity of leadership is reinforced and fed back with market ideology and trade integration. In the foregoing idea it is implicit that the private sector must assume a stronger and leading role in society, and that the state should exert less influence to achieve social-economic efficacy. Democracy is seen as a political regime and not as a type of society. The government must be looked upon in a competitive fashion, but its efficacy in the face of social and economic situations must be seen according to the attitude adopted by the groups and individuals forming the economy and society.

A third general tendency to be noted is that the five governments, sharing the same style and ideology, are ready to seek a discrete but efficient space for Central America in the new international economic order. They well know the limitations of their political mandates and consequently have to resort to the plain language of cooperation and international aid. Nevertheless, they can advance in a new political articulation designed to remove the ideological aspects of internal processes and to set the basis in the near future for a political competition that is less polarized. In other words, they press for the need for regional economic recuperation to support internal political reform[2]—they are obliged to follow the political transitions with caution and

---

[1]Jorge Domínguez, "Teoría y cambios internacionales; implicaciones para América Latina," en *Foro Internacional*, El Colegio de México, Vol. XXIX, April-June 1989, p. 650.

[2]William Ascher, *Interactions Among Regional Integration Initiatives: North American Integration and Its Impact on Other Blocs* (CIDR, Duke University, January, 1991), p. 3.

moderation. The search for a place in the new international economy is full of integrationist moves, free trade, and regional cooperation. This economic space can only be found if they can count on previous agreements for political stability. As long as these political agreements are not stabilized it will not be possible to have regional integration.

Could these three tendencies observed change the pace of the domestic drama that the Central American people have lived in the recent past? Can these governments be transitional governments toward democracy and social and economic welfare? I think so despite the observed difficulties that seem to doom these transitional projects to failure. To a large extent success depends on the governments moving to set the bases for national accords.

To attempt an honest response to this question it pays to study the situation that originated the tendencies we observe. First of all, Central America is rounding the curve of a most tortuous path it experienced during the last decade of upheaval while it emerges from being a zone of international ideological tension. Central America is one of the last lashes of the Cold War. The region became the focus of international attention forcing the United States to strengthen its direct influence on governmental management. The idea is shared in Central America that the United States lessened its attention in the 1970s to the region's political processes, trusting in the irreversibility of the economic successes achieved during the 1960s and first part of the 1970s. It then appeared that the impact of Cuba on the region was neutralized or diluted. The United States and the governments of that time trusted too much in the economy and did not think it convenient or wise to extend their influence to modernize the political structures.

When the economic difficulties appeared in the middle of the 1970s there also appeared difficulties in the political handling of society. The most dangerous curve was in Nicaragua in 1979; to avoid it the other countries had to learn a new way of making politics. The lesson of Nicaragua was quickly learned in other countries. While Sandinista consolidation was prevented, in the rest of Central

America there was political reform. In the face of the revolutionary threat, there developed a process of significant changes in the political process. Political parties excluded in the past, rejected political leaders, and prohibited political alliances were allowed to make a comeback with the acceptance of current governments in a more open political arena. Napoleón Duarte in El Salvador and Vinicio Cerezo in Guatemala were the first in this initial transition; an initial opening designed to give room to the militant Left of the guerrillas. Both governments advanced slowly in the face of resistance, but they advanced reforms that allowed a second round of competition among civilians. They made room for new coalitions even if they contradicted traditional parties. Alternate governments are a consequence of these efforts to make institutional reforms that will later allow for a more competitive society. Cristiani, Serrano, Chamorro, Callejas, and even Calderón are the products of new coalitions that are not disputing the past but rather are seeking a place in the present vacuum.

Thirdly, the ideological crisis, political polarization, and the civil war hurt the national economies. All accumulated modernity from economic growth in the post-war era vanished in the last decade. Nicaragua stopped being a national economy, and El Salvador only survives with foreign aid.

This brings me to the fourth item. The economy in Central America is destroyed, and it is morally just to want its recuperation and reconstruction. But we are still in a transitional mode, a period of political fragility. We cannot and should not confuse or force the tasks of the transition. Particularly a special political transition.

What do I want to say? That we should be patient in matters of cooperation and wait for the changes in the political system to settle in so that with political viability we can gain economic viability. Many people say that we should gain both at the same time. And that with help and cooperation the economy can recover and support a faster and more secure transition. However, that is not possible. And we are thinking especially of Nicaragua. There a massive thrust of resources would only help to postpone the process of de-Sandinization: they still control the institutional political apparatus (unions, professional associations) and the Army. As long as the laws that politicize the labor-management relationship, investment and foreign trade, land ownership, and the role of bureaucracy are not changed it will be impossible to reconstruct the country economically. These are hard times for a weak transitional government that has as its basic task dismantling the totalitarian and authoritarian structures inherited from Sandinism. It is a priority that does not rest in the economy but on politics per se. This makes the transition difficult, but it is the job of the present government. It is not possible to reactivate an enterprise under market criteria without first removing the political obstacles imposed by a totalitarian vision of social relations. We should start by removing and dismantling unwanted structures, because we cannot have a stable economic recovery over unremoved political debris.

The transition has the difficult task of rationalizing the tragedy lived in the past and making the institutional reforms that will afterward allow for a more competitive society. The central problem consists in how to organize and consolidate a process of dismantling undemocratic structures while starting economic recovery. My thesis is that these tasks cannot be performed simultaneously. And so the facts of the first year of Violeta Chamorro's transitional government have shown.

Other political transition processes are permitted when the country's economy is healthy and growing. The dispute for power is a limited dispute. Central America's political transition is more fragile. Governments acquire a feeling of being temporary almost in the sense of a government in custody. This is the essence of Chamorro's government in Nicaragua. She won the government, the illusions to govern, while the Sandinistas want to maintain power. But both sides are obliged to get along in a dynamic essentially political manner over which the economy does not have any influence.

The Central American crisis of the 1980s is a political crisis derived from the modernization generated by economic growth of previous decades. The governments were not able to assimilate the pressures from the population, which each time was more diversified in their interests in political participation, nor were they able to confront the pressures from the international economy. The social pluralization produced by the economic success of previous decades overtook the political capabilities of the governments to open necessary channels of political competence and participation that would lessen social pressures. The high degree of fragmentation of the groups, which were looking for participation and the lack of traditions for political organization between different and opposing interests left change in the hands of armed organizations.

A coincidence of conflicts provoked the violent rupture in the Nicaraguan system, a profound destabilization of the Salvadoran regime, and a threat of rupture in Guatemala. Honduras and Costa Rica, also involved in the crisis, received a massive flow of refugees, experienced suspension of normal economic relations, and risked becoming directly involved in the conflicts.

Ten years of conflict have passed, but the solutions adopted to overcome them have not been able to pave the way for stability and economy recovery. The situation in Central America comes just as the world is experiencing great changes with the end of the Cold War and a reordering of the international economy based on regional integration schemes. From a simplistic point of view it would seem to be an ideal external atmosphere for Central America to achieve political stability and economic recovery in a relatively short period.[3]

My argument is that there is a great distance between favorable external conditions and the internal pos-

---

[3]See materials from the "Conferencia de Cooperación entre socios desiguales," Centro de Estudios Internacionales, El Colegio de México, México D.F., 26-29 November, 1990, and especially in presentations and commentaries by Victor L. Urquidi and Douglas Chalmers.

sibilities for making use of them. Political transitions in other countries have been successful because, on the one hand, they began much later than the preceding wars or internal conflicts, and on the other hand, because economic conditions were neither so extremely bad nor foreign to the country's historical experience.

In the Southern Cone, Brazil, Argentina, Uruguay, Chile, and Paraguay are able to mix political transition and economic recovery with a single political and economic development strategy. The integration they have adopted to find solutions for different sectors is a viable way for maintaining the connection between transition and economic development. In my judgement, this is not the case in Central America. The political transition in Nicaragua is just beginning, it is maintained with difficulty in El Salvador, and experiences its first civilian presidential continuity in Guatemala. In every country, the transition has peculiarities that are not yet favorable for regional homogeneity for rapid reconstruction of regional integration mechanisms. The step from one political moment to another is a long and difficult one in which the economy has less influence than we think or wish. Central America still lives in political times.

Perspectives for Economic Recovery through Central American Regional Integration

For the moment, prospects for economic recovery through regional integration are not good. The suggestion of creatively applying a new policy of reactivation and development for Central America[4] is valid and suitable, but for the moment is inopportune.

For Central America to be able to have policies that

---

[4]Gert Rosenthal, "Fundamentos de una nueva política de reactivación y desarrollo para Centroamérica," in *Revista de la integración y el desarrollo de Centroamérica,* No. 34, 1986, BCIE, Tegucigalpa, Honduras, pp. 61-74.

take advantage of external conditions, it must first turn the transitional changes occurring during a time of intense polarization and conflict toward institutionalizing the political system. Victor Urquidi has pointed out that the two jobs must be done at the same time, that of political transition toward institutional stability and economic recovery.[5] In an ideal situation this would be fair and correct, but the imperatives of economic growth are still blocked by political realities. At least two key countries in Central America, Nicaragua and El Salvador, still find it impossible to start programs for national recovery. The economic crisis in Nicaragua is no more dramatic than its political crisis. The productive system is dismembered and the capacity for movement in economic policies is almost zero. Politically the Sandinistas still hold power. In exchange, they have given Violeta Chamorro the illusion of governing. While in politics it is a government under the custody of the Sandinistas, in economic policy the population does not notice any change. Personal income is the same as under Sandinism—that is, at the level of 30 years ago.[6] The Nicaraguan economy is no longer a national economy and its rate of inflation is unheard of on a global scale. Uncertainty discourages production and favorable signs in the economic situation cannot be seen.[7]

In El Salvador the armed conflict continues to create uncertainty in the economy and to influence the definition and execution of the political economy. In per capita terms, the GDP fell in 1988 to a level 26 percent lower than in 1978 and even lower than that of a quarter of a century

---

[5]Victor Urquidi, from his presentation and comments during the *Conferencia de Cooperación*, op.cit.

[6]CEPAL, *Centroamérica: Situación actual y perspectivas de la economía y la integración*, Mexico, September 7, 1989, p. 27.

[7]Ibid., p. 29.

before.[8] During the last decade the Salvadoran economy has been subjected to severe strangulation in a climate of political tension and armed confrontation.

The idea of reviving the common market is generally accepted by businessmen, government, and agricultural producers, not only in terms of immediate necessity. However, they do not know how to organize it in a long-term scheme acceptable to all.[9] The idea of restructuring the common market in industrial and commercial circles follows the idea of re-establishing free trade. It is only that the countries that suffered most from the 1980s crisis will confront the other ones affected. Already Nicaragua and El Salvador have sufficient reasons for seeking preferential treatment for a certain period and Honduras has made it clear that it is not willing to return to unrestricted free trade, asking for preferential treatment or some mechanism that will compensate for the disadvantages of the common market.[10] Costa Rica has also warned that because of the advantages it gained through structural readjustments during the past decade, it will have a better and more competitive position in relation to the rest of the countries in the area and expects that they will implement restrictions to defend their balance of payments.[11] For Guatemala the restructuring of the regional economy within an integrated framework must be carried out under rather simple schemes in which business agreements prevail over bureaucratic government hindrances.[12]

We are faced with a general disposition to reactivate

---

[8]Ibid., p. 14.

[9]CEPAL, *Centroamerica: Algunos problemas de la integracion economica. Opiniones de empresarios*, Mexico, July 4, 1990.

[10]Ibid., pp. 11-12.

[11]Ibid., p. 11.

[12]Ibid., pp. 9 y 11.

the common market, but this does not hide the presence of old national greed today existent in the inequality among these countries. To this we must add certain ideological values that imprint a certain rejection to the participation of the state in the making of regional economic policies. An idea in this direction is that "the ones responsible for the end of the common market have been the governments or their central banks."[13] The main restriction to trade is the rate of exchange, which means that central banks have reinforced their participation in regional economic operations. It is from this that the idea above mentioned emerges that governments hinder both trade and business agreements. In reality, the enormous monetary disorder is influencing the possibility of trading beyond the present limits. The Federation of Chambers of Commerce of Central America at their Esquipulas, Guatemala, meeting stated that only 55 percent of installed capacity is in use.[14]

Since 1987 when the Tela (Honduras) Agreement was signed among Guatemala, El Salvador, and Honduras, the national currencies have been set according to direct agreements between buyers and sellers. This has worked well between Guatemala and El Salvador, with little participation by the central banks. According to businessmen from these two countries, the central banks should be observers recording transaction statistics.[15]

The efforts to face the blockade of regional commerce imposed by monetary disorder include various agreements. Costa Rica, Guatemala, and El Salvador operate a mini-chamber of monetary compensation. In Nicaragua this situation is resolved with payments in dollars or by direct

---

[13]Ibid., p. 10.

[14]FECAICA, Exposición a la reunión de Presidentes de Centroamérica (Presentation at the meeting of the Central American Presidents). Esquipulas, Guatemala, May 24, 1986.

[15]Memorandum of the Industry Council of Guatemala, to the Directors of the FECAICA, September 7, 1989.

exchange. Honduras, despite the 1987 Tela Agreement, maintains the uncertainty of its exchange rates, therefore its trade is complicated and making its incorporation into regional integration difficult.

In general, all policies designed to stabilize trade relationships have failed. The effects that show in the region, the changes in international economy in addition to the political tensions of these countries, have not given way to successful economic policies. According to CEPAL, "the balance of payments imbalance became worse in spite of import reductions...controls increased the climate of uncertainty, discouraging private initiatives and fostering greater capital flight. In general, monetary policy has shown its limitations in these open, but small, economies."[16]

Conclusions

Central America still lives in a time of political reconstruction under transitional standards that demand caution and moderation from governments in their application of economic stabilizing policies. The urgency of economic reactivation, both national and regional, should remind us not to take on a new task before finishing the old one. Political transition is difficult, and we should not demand of governments at this time a socioeconomic efficacy while they still have the task of consolidating new institutional arrangements for political competition and participation. International cooperation for economic reactivation should first be considered according to the how governments have stabilized the political situation. Beginning a regional solution before completing the national tasks could lead to recuperation at the national level, which is incompatible with that at the regional level.

Unfortunately, it has been observed that several

---

[16]CEPAL, *Centroamérica: Crisis y políticas de ajuste, 1979-1986*, Mexico, July 15, 1988, pp. 14-15.

countries have strengthened their inequalities which negatively influences the possibilities for regional recovery. At least three of the five countries have warned, as we have shown, that they will demand preferential treatment in case of a return to regional integration. It is possible that international economic cooperation will exert pressure for internal reforms to the extent that a parallel process of political and economic recovery can be initiated, but giving first priority to consolidating political stability. I refer here to those institutional agreements that de-activate the ideological confrontation in the worker-owner relationship, in land ownership, guarantees for investment with respect for the rights of individuals, and for those agreements that ease political competition within constitutional frameworks. Nicaragua has just started this transition with a government under Sandinista custody, and El Salvador is starting negotiations under difficult conditions. However, they are heading toward a formula which, if it works, will allow in the medium-term the reconstruction of their economies. For the time being international cooperation should support this transition and should not prematurely foster the realization of economic tasks beyond the capabilities of the present governments.

The Central American governments of 1991 are more homogeneous than past ones. This offers the advantage of regional coordination of recovery plans with international aid. In this sense the urgency of economic recovery and the offers of international cooperation help to advance internal reforms in the political system. International cooperation should collaborate with transition processes in the sense of offering incentives for democratic consolidation. Although the five Central American governments are now more alike and are more inclined to make their economic policies compatible, it is clear that they should first consolidate internal institutional changes.

A rather fortunate vision of the Central American future includes at least a succession of events in the present transition:

a) Homogeneity of leadership;
b) Homogeneity of policies designed to institutionalize political participation within the framework of open and competitive processes;
c) Homogeneity of economic policies to ease the coordination of plans for regional recovery;
d) Return to a common market with rules allowing balanced development and preventing the reappearance of national egoism.

The role that international cooperation plays is fundamental and should take advantage of the present homogeneity of leadership to encourage in those governments the idea that the offer of support will help consolidate internal reforms.

STABILIZATION AND ADJUSTMENT PROGRAMS IN CENTRAL AMERICA–WHY ARE THEY PROVING SO DIFFICULT?

Victor Bulmer-Thomas

Queen Mary and Westfield College
London University

More than a decade has passed since the first stabilization programs were adopted in Central America to cope with the series of external and internal shocks which struck the region at the end of the 1970s.[1] Since stabilization is widely recognized as an essential precondition for adjustment programs leading to sustainable long-run growth, the importance of successful stabilization cannot be overemphasized. No Central American country can afford to repeat the decrease in living standards experienced in the 1980s, so growth of real per capita income in the 1990s is the highest priority. Yet the basis for sustainable long-run growth in the current decade will be fragile if stabilization has not been completed successfully.

Despite numerous attempts at stabilization, not one of the five Central American countries has succeeded in laying a really solid foundation for stable and sustainable growth. Even in Costa Rica, the republic which has made the most progress on policy reform, the annual growth rate of real Gross Domestic Product (GDP) fluctuates widely with a year of fast growth (approximately 5 percent) being followed by one of slow growth (less than 3 percent) as the economy runs up against numerous constraints that past stabilization programs have failed to remove.

---

[1]On stabilization and adjustment programs in the first half of the 1980s, see V. Bulmer-Thomas, *The Political Economy of Central America Since 1920* (Cambridge: Cambridge University Press, 1987), Chapter 11.

One of the consequences of the failure of stabilization has been a dismal growth record. Not a single country—not even Costa Rica—had recovered the 1980 level of real per capita GDP by 1990. Although the 1980s was the "lost decade" for all of Latin America, the drop in living standards was more severe in Central America with the four northern republics all recording a fall in real GDP per capita through the 1980s, which was greater than the Latin American average, while Nicaragua recorded the most dramatic decline (5 percent a year from 1981 to 1989) of any Latin American republic.[2]

Throughout the region, internal disequilibrium—manifested in budget deficits and high rates of inflation—remains a problem. The same is true, however, of external disequilibrium reflected in trade and current account deficits in the balance of payments. Furthermore, the situation is in some respects worse than a decade ago, since all republics now suffer from double digit annual inflation rates and the chances of funding balance of payments deficits with official capital flows are receding as the Bush Administration in the United States—the principal source of lending to the region—adjusts its official lending policy to the geopolitical realities of the post-Cold War era.[3] Thus, an unchanged current account deficit may imply an even greater external disequilibrium than before as a result of the expected decline in official capital flows from the major donor.

---

[2]See Inter-American Development Bank, *Economic and Social Progress in Latin America 1990 Report* (Washington D.C., 1990), Table B-2, p. 265.

[3]On the forecast decline in US official capital flows to Central America, see USAID, *Economic Assistance Strategy for Central America 1991 to 2000* (Washington D.C., January 1991).

Stabilization and Adjustment: The Record so Far

In small countries with poorly developed capital markets—as is the case in Central America—the fiscal position is often a crucial determinant of internal disequilibrium. Even a relatively modest budget deficit (expressed as a proportion of GDP) can lead to inflationary pressures as a result of the monetary implications of deficit financing. Thus, an important test of stabilization programs in Central America has to do with fiscal policy.

Since many republics in Central America went into the 1980s with a ratio of government revenue to GDP, which was low by international standards, an increase in this ratio might have seemed an appropriate way to implement a tighter fiscal policy leading to internal equilibrium. Yet, as Table 1 shows, the ratio was either stationary or falling in the last years of the 1980s. Indeed, El Salvador and Guatemala ended the decade with a ratio below 10 percent, which is among the lowest in the world—yet alone in Latin America. In Nicaragua, despite draconian tax increases in the first years of the Sandinista regime, the ratio fell sharply after 1984 as the high and accelerating rate of inflation eroded the real value of tax receipts and the burden of taxation was offset in part through delayed payments.[4]

Even more disturbing than the ratio of government revenue to GDP has been the composition of revenue itself. In a region long noted for its dependence on indirect (including trade) taxes and for its small number of direct taxpayers, an increase in the proportion of government revenue from income and/or property taxes might have seemed an appropriate route to fiscal orthodoxy. Yet the opposite generally has happened. In three republics (El Salvador, Honduras, and Guatemala) the proportion was lower in 1989 than in 1980, and in Costa Rica the propor-

---

[4]Known as the Oliveira-Tanzi effect, the impact of accelerating inflation on real tax receipts was also responsible for the collapse of the ratio of government revenue to GDP in Argentina and Peru in the late 1980s.

tion has been falling since 1983. Only Guatemala has managed to increase this ratio, but it is still one of the lowest in the region, since the republic started from such a low base (14 percent in 1980).

The failure to raise the ratio of government revenue to GDP has forced those responsible for the design of stabilization programs to put greater emphasis on cutting expenditure as the means to reduce budget deficits. Certainly substantial progress has been achieved in all republics in reducing the ratio of expenditure to GDP, but in far too many cases the reduction has come through cuts in public investment (including health and education). Since there is a growing recognition (even in neoliberal circles) of the complementarity of public and private investment, the opportunity cost of cutting expenditure through reducing public capital formation is high. Indeed, in some republics (e.g., El Salvador) public investment has fallen to the point where negative "crowding in" is far more of a danger than "crowding out".[5]

The cuts in government expenditure in Nicaragua were not sufficient, at least until 1989, to prevent the emergence of a massive budget deficit, the prime cause of accelerating inflation. In 1988 the Sandinista regime had the dubious distinction of presiding over the highest annual rate of inflation (33,603 percent) ever recorded in Latin America. Elsewhere, budget deficits as a proportion of GDP were lower at the end of the decade than at the beginning, but the inflationary implications were still considerable and the size of the fiscal deficit was a major factor behind the increase in the cost of living index in all republics (see Table 2). Indeed, Guatemala and Honduras began the new decade with rates of inflation higher than ever recorded

---

[5]"Crowding-out" refers to the risk that public investment will exhaust available sources of finance for private investment. "Crowding-in" refers to the complementarity between public and private investment. Negative "crowding-in" therefore refers to the (complementary) fall in private investment that will follow a decline in public investment.

since the 1940s.

The poor fiscal record did not reflect the lack of attempts at fiscal reform as much as the failure of such attempts. In Guatemala, for example, the efforts of the Cerezo administration (1986-1990) at tax reform were largely undermined by the opposition of a well-organized private sector. In Costa Rica numerous attempts were made in the 1980s to improve the efficiency of tax collection, but the fiscal privileges offered to exporters of nontraditional products tended to overwhelm the modest tax gains achieved under President Monge (1982-1965) and President Arias (1986-1990).

In Nicaragua any prospects of tax reform were undermined by the acceleration of inflation which—as already argued—eroded the real value of tax receipts and gave taxpayers a strong incentive to delay payments. Not a single country made any progress on negotiations with the U.S. government that might have led to taxation agreements affecting flight capital to Miami and other U.S. cities.

The problem of internal disequilibrium has been aggravated by the political constraints on tax reform and the lack of consensus on the appropriate measures to take to reduce budget deficits. By contrast, there has been widespread acceptance that external disequilibrium should be tackled by measures to promote exports rather than suppress imports. Painful choices have arisen, however, as soon as the policy debate has moved from the general question of export promotion to the specifics of how to achieve it.

Among the International Financial Institutions (IFIs), such as the World Bank and the International Monetary Fund, there is a conviction that the most appropriate way to promote exports is through a depreciation of the real effective exchange rate (REER), trade liberalization, and the encouragement of direct foreign investment (DFI). These three ingredients, part of the so-called Washington consensus,[6] have met with a mixed reception in Central America.

The commitment to depreciation of the REER has proved to be a painful pill to swallow for several reasons. First, in small open economies (such as in Central America) the depreciation of the nominal exchange rate has an important bearing on the rate of inflation; thus, a small depreciation of the REER usually requires a large nominal devaluation with serious inflationary implications. Secondly, the five republics of Central America had a long history before the 1980s of relative exchange rate stability with currencies pegged to the U.S. dollar; this nominal anchor had proved extremely useful in stimulating productive investment, avoiding capital flight, and reducing currency transaction costs.

Not surprisingly, exchange rate policy in Central America has been fraught with problems in the last decade. Honduras only abandoned its fixed nominal rate (unchanged since 1918) in 1990; Guatemala has oscillated between devaluing the exchange rate to promote exports and intervening to control inflation; Nicaragua's devaluations, both under the Sandinistas and President Chamorro, have tended to be too little too late; the Cristiani administration in El Salvador was at first wary of freeing the exchange rate because of the possible impact on inflation—only to find that capital inflows from remittances, reverse capital flight, and IFIs were producing an equilibrium exchange rate that was almost certainly overvalued in relation to the requirements of export promotion.[7] Only

---

[6]The phrase "Washington consensus" has become famous following the publication of an influential book on policy reform in Latin America by John Williamson. See J. Williamson, ed. *Latin American Adjustment: How Much has Happened?* (Washington, D.C.: Institute for International Economics, 1990).

[7]The strength of the Salvadoran currency has even led to suggestions that the country is suffering from "Dutch disease" –a phenomenon more commonly associated with energy exporters.

in Costa Rica has a consistent exchange rate policy been pursued, providing exporters with a stable REER after an initial real depreciation in the first half of the 1980s.

Trade liberalization has been equally problematic. The Common External Tariff (CET), a requirement of the Central American Common Market (CACM), had been revised in the mid-1980s, but both the average tariff rate and tariff dispersion were considered too high by the IFIs. Under its Structural Adjustment Loans (SAL), the World Bank was able to persuade Costa Rica to break ranks and reduce tariffs unilaterally; similar steps were taken in El Salvador and Honduras, but tariff policy in the region is no longer harmonized. Furthermore, measures to liberalize extraregional imports have often been matched by additional restrictions on intraregional trade so that the recovery of the CACM has been delayed longer than necessary.

Policies towards DFI have been generally liberal. In Nicaragua, the Sandinistas vacillated for years over the adoption of a Foreign Investment Law, but the lack of interest on the part of private investors made the debate rather sterile. However, Central America has traditionally adopted liberal policies towards DFI and the problem since the end of the 1970s has been a reluctance on the part of foreign investors to invest in a region perceived as politically unstable while other regions have become increasingly attractive.

Again, it is no surprise to find that the record on external disequilibrium has been rather patchy. Costa Rica has enjoyed considerable success in the promotion of nontraditional exports, but the high (and rising) propensity to import has left a gap in the current account which is almost as large as at the beginning of the 1980s. The strong exchange rate in El Salvador is making it hard for many industrialists and farmers to adjust to the shock of trade liberalization. The experiment with neoliberal policies in Honduras under President Callejas threatens to be short-lived as the losers from trade liberalization and REER depreciation prove to be far more vocal than the winners.

Just as in many other parts of Latin America, serious efforts have been made to introduce policy reform, to implement stabilization packages, and to adopt adjustment programs in Central America. It would be harsh indeed not to recognize the supreme sacrifices demanded of the Nicaraguan people in the name of stabilization both under the Sandinistas in 19881989 and under President Chamorro in 1990/1991. Similarly the Cristiani government in El Salvador deserves credit for the courageous way in which it has tackled both stabilization and adjustment since coming to power in mid-1989. Yet, at the beginning of the 1990s it is difficult to say with confidence that a single country has truly laid the solid foundation needed for fast growth in the next decade.

Why Progress Has Been Insufficient?

Numerous explanations can be found for the lack of progress in implementing successful stabilization and adjustment programs in Central America. The fragile social and political situation in all republics except Costa Rica has encouraged policymakers to postpone awkward decisions as long as possible. In the case of internal disequilibrium, measures to tackle budget deficits and accelerating inflation can be postponed almost indefinitely for a government is only forced to act (as the Sandinistas found to their cost) as hyperinflation approaches. External disequilibrium, on the other hand, must be addressed unless the country concerned has access to sufficient capital inflows to finance the deficit or is prepared to ration the limited supply of foreign exchange through draconian import controls. Both alternatives were widely adopted in Central America in the 1980s with El Salvador and Honduras in particular using official capital inflows to postpone harsh decisions and Nicaragua being the most dependent on foreign exchange rationing.

A second problem has been the lack of consensus on

the appropriate measures to take. The bitter debates over exchange rate policy in Honduras and tax reform in Guatemala have already been mentioned. Nicaragua under the Sandinistas could not reach consensus on foreign investment. The issue of land reform in El Salvador has proved deeply divisive and the lack of consensus has had numerous implications for adjustment and stabilization. Even in Costa Rica, where consensus on export promotion has at least been achieved, there remain numerous divisions over tax reform and financial liberalization. Furthermore, constitutional rigidities in Costa Rica have often prevented the executive from implementing a consistent policy even when a broad consensus has existed.

A third, and widespread, problem has been the reluctance to tackle all aspects of stabilization and adjustment simultaneously. Although such "general equilibrium" solutions are generally recognized to be preferable, they have been abandoned in favor of "partial equilibrium" solutions in which progress has been made on a limited number of fronts. Yet partial equilibrium solutions in one area can aggravate problems in other areas. For example, the use of fiscal incentives to promote nontraditional exports undermines the fiscal position; rapid trade liberalization (through tariff reductions) can also weaken government revenue; the commitment to a stable REER damages price stability, and so on.

The public external debt also proved to be an obstacle in the path of successful stabilization for much of the past decade. At best a time-consuming distraction for hard-pressed government officials, the public sector's purchases of scarce foreign exchange to service foreign debt have distorted government expenditures while widening balance-of-payments current account deficits. Although the burden of the public external debt has not been as severe in Central America as in some other Latin American republics, it has to be remembered that the region has been extremely ill-equipped to cope with even a modest debt problem—yet alone a major debt crisis.

Finally, there has been conflict between adjustment

and stabilization programs themselves. With the renewal of growth becoming the overriding priority throughout the region and with adjustment needed to underpin stable and high growth rates, there has been an understandable desire to launch adjustment programs before the process of stabilization has been completed. These programs, with their emphasis on a change in relative prices to encourage resources to shift into new activities and the adoption of appropriate incentives, can aggravate stabilization problems—as Costa Rica has found to her cost on numerous occasions in the last decade.

What Can Be Done?

The above analysis of the failures and disappointments of stabilization and adjustment programs suggests that a key problem is the inconsistency that arises from trying to do too much too quickly. The crisis in Central America has so many dimensions that it is easy to lose sight of the main priorities. Furthermore, the crisis has affected the confidence of the policy-making elite in all republics, leaving them vulnerable to pressure from outside interests. These pressures have led to a widening of the reform agenda in directions that might be desirable under more normal circumstances, but which—in the Central American context—create unrealistic expectations.

The first priority is to subordinate stabilization and adjustment programs to a long-run growth model for the region. Such a model[8] would have at least four dimensions: 1) the promotion of nontraditional exports to the rest of the world, 2) the recovery and strengthening of the CACM, 3) the exploitation of new opportunities for traditional exports

---

[8]I have developed these ideas in more detail elsewhere. See V. Bulmer-Thomas, "A Long-Run Model of Development for Central America," paper to Latin American Studies Association, Washington, D.C., April 1991.

arising from the formation of market economies in Eastern Europe and the move to a Single Domestic Market in the European Community, and 4) the broadening of the internal (national) market through a reduction in poverty and an improvement in income distribution.

The design of stabilization and adjustment programs consistent with such a long-run model would have two crucial ingredients: fiscal policy and exchange rate policy. These are the two elements that any Central American republic ignores at its peril. Other items on the reform agenda (e.g., privatization, deregulation, and financial, liberalization) can be added once success has been achieved in the two priority areas.

Prudent fiscal policy suggests modest budget deficits. With further expenditure cuts (except on debt service payments and defence) so hard to achieve, the emphasis must be put on raising revenue. Here the problem is not the introduction of an array of new taxes so much as the enforcement of existing taxes. Where tax reductions or exemptions are introduced as part of the incentives in adjustment programs, they need to be matched by additional revenue from other sources.

The need for fiscal discipline arises for a number of reasons. With nominal exchange rate devaluation expected for some years to come (see below), a tight fiscal policy is necessary to moderate the increase in domestic prices. At the same time, the need to broaden social expenditure through careful targeting of groups most in need will be self-defeating if the additional expenditure is financed through inflationary borrowing techniques. Tight fiscal policy cannot eliminate inflation in Central America, but loose fiscal policy—as Nicaragua has found to her cost—will certainly exacerbate inflationary pressures.

The need to give priority to exchange rate policy arises from the crucial role which competitive exchange rates play in the promotion of exports. Thus, an initial devaluation of the REER needs to be followed by an exchange rate policy which at least maintains a stable real exchange rate. Unless exporters are confident that the

REER will be stable or falling, they are most unlikely to undertake the investments required to shift resources towards the export sector. Other measures to promote exports will be ineffective unless exchange rate policy is consistent.

Even a stable REER implies—in the Central American context—a rise in domestic prices as a result of nominal devaluations. Thus, price stability is not an option in the medium-term. New measures must be taken (including targeted social expenditure) to protect the poorest groups in society from the impact of price increases, so that a stable REER implies the use of some government subsidies. These will quickly lead to fiscal undiscipline unless matched by tax increases. Thus, exchange rate and fiscal policy need to complement each other and must be operated in harmony.

Narrowing of the reform agenda in the first instance to fiscal and exchange rate policy may not sound very ambitious, but we have already seen the consequences of overambitious reform programs. Once these two crucial areas of policy reform are established and credible, the reform agenda can be widened. Trade liberalization should aim both to lower tariff protection and to reestablish the CET, while immediate steps need to be taken to eliminate all non-tariff barriers on trade within the CACM. Financial liberalization should set positive real interest rates as a minimum goal and property rights for small farmers need to be strengthened as early as possible.

The Role of Foreign Aid Donors

The Central American crisis drew new foreign donors into the region for the first time, while established sources of official capital (e.g., USAID) were called upon to increase their lending programs. Each donor has brought to Central America its own set of priorities and preferences for reform. As peace and political stability return to the region the donors are unlikely to depart, but they are more likely to increase the conditionality of their lending programs to ensure compliance. Thus, there is a pressing need for foreign aid donors to harmonize their policies not only with each other, but also with the priority areas in Central America.

Such harmonization will demand a certain amount of restraint on the part of donors. Central America should not be seen as a "tabula rasa" on which new ideas can be written and where new experiments can be carried out. Conditionality should be limited to priority areas *both* in terms of growth prospects (e.g., non-traditional exports) *and* in terms of policy reform (e.g., fiscal policy).

Donors also have a crucial role to play in developing the enabling environment, which will allow private sector investment to flourish. This includes strengthening existing public sector and regional institutions, helping with technical training and providing specific guidance on many policy reform issues (e.g., tax administration). Far too often donors, sometimes unintentionally, have compared Central American institutions unfavorably with their foreign equivalents and undermined them even further in the process.

Finally, in a conference devoted to the role of the European Community (EC), it is appropriate to note the comparative advantage the EC enjoys in the promotion of regional integration in Central America. Written off as at best an irrelevance by many other donors, the CACM is in fact an important plank in the long-run growth model for the region. The EC, with its special institutional interest in integration, is well-placed to help Central America establish a new integration scheme, which will promote both efficiency and equity without undermining international competitiveness.

Table 1

CENTRAL GOVERNMENT REVENUE
AS A PERCENTAGE OF GDP

YR	Costa Rica	El Salvador	Guatemala	Honduras	Nicaragua
1980	12.8	11.4	9.5	14.9	21.3
1981	13.6	12.6	8.6	13.4	24.1
1982	14.4	12.3	8.4	13.4	25.3
1983	16.6	12.4	7.8	13.3	30.9
1984	16.6	13.2	7.3	15.1	34.9
1985	16.2	13.4	7.7	15.6	32.1
1986	15.4	14.4	8.9	15.6	32.0
1987	15.7	11.9	9.4	16.3	27.7
1988	15.2	10.4	10.1	16.1	20.5
1989	15.0	8.2	9.2	15.6	18.9

Source: Inter-American Development Bank, Economic and Social Progress in Latin America 1990 Report, Washington D.C., 1990, Table C-1, p. 275.

Table 2

ANNUAL RATES OF INFLATION (percent). December to December.

YR	Costa Rica	El Salvador	Guatemala	Honduras	Nicaragua
1982	81.7	13.8	-2.0	8.8	22.2
1983	10.7	15.5	15.4	7.2	35.5
1984	17.3	9.8	5.2	3.7	47.3
1985	11.1	30.8	31.5	4.2	334.3
1986	15.4	30.3	25.7	3.2	747.4
1987	16.4	19.6	10.1	2.7	1347.4
1988	25.3	18.2	11.0	6.7	33602.6
1989	10.0	23.5	20.2	11.4	1690.0
1990	22.4	19.9	50.1	25.3	8500.0

Source: United Nations, Economic Commission for Latin America and the Caribbean, Preliminary Overview of the Economy of Latin America and the Caribbean 1990, Santiago, December 1990, Table 5.

CHAPTER IV

INTERESTS OF OTHER ACTORS IN CENTRAL AMERICA

THE EUROPEAN POLITICAL PARTIES AND THE RECONSTRUCTION OF CENTRAL AMERICA

Cristina Eguizábal

University of Costa Rica

The European presence in Latin America declined gradually from the middle of the nineteenth century, disappearing almost completely after the Great Depression.[1] The end of European influence was even more rapid and major in the Central American region, which after the consolidation of the United States as a state and its expansion toward the Pacific, became an undisputed area of influence of the United States. It was there that the international role of Washington was initially established and the Europeans allowed the new world power to first exercise its hegemony.

During the 1960s, the evolution of the international system toward more flexible structures than in the immediate post-war period offered new opportunities for the reaffirmation of European influence, even more so because the problems, economic (external deficits) and political (open and violent questioning of the legitimacy of United States leadership) generated by the Vietnam War eroded profoundly the confidence of American society in itself.

Intra-hemispheric political relations also deteriorated in those years as a result of Latin American expectations frustrated by the failure of the Alliance for Progress as an

---

[1]Eusebio Mujal-León, "Europa Occidental y los procesos de democratización en América Latina," *Síntesis*, No. 4, January-April 1988, pp. 256-263.

instrument for economic and political development, and American disinterest in the region's problems during the era of "benign neglect." Paradoxically, the Carter Administration's human rights policy contributed to the weakening of American influence because of the extent to which it antagonized Washington's more traditional allies in the region.

The relaxation of tensions had unleashed polycentric tendencies in NATO where decolonization placed the problem of development and the injustice of the existing international economic order on the agenda of the day. Although Latin Americans no longer participated very actively in the political forums of the Third World, the region's influence was indisputably felt through Latin American economic thought, which defined the terms of the North-South debate. The multipolarity emerging in the international system forced the structural contradictions between the North and South in the Western Hemisphere to rise to the surface.

The Europeans, for their part, once the economic reconstruction stage in their countries was surpassed, confronted a growing necessity for raw materials, a need which was accentuated by the loss of their colonial possessions. This situation accelerated the conscious decision in Western European capitals to develop a new profile in Latin America relevant to the emerging structure of power in the international system.

From an economic and demographic standpoint, Latin America could convert itself into an interesting market. From the political point of view, the region's cultural links to the Western world and the relevance of European political theory to understanding Latin American political structures made our countries valid interlocutors for post-imperial Europe.

In the case of the Central American countries it was this last dimension, the political dimension, which reached unforeseen heights in the 1980s during the "Central American Crisis," although economic and security considerations promoted European interest in the region cannot be underestimated. From the economic point of view it is certain that Central America no longer is of major importance for European exporters; however, with Germany and the Scandinavian countries among the principal markets for Central American coffee, there exists an interest at least on the part of importers (in general large food consortiums) of maintaining the stability of their suppliers.

As far as security interests, the important external dimension of the European economies makes them particularly vulnerable to disturbances in international communications. From this arises interest in maintaining secure free access to the Panama Canal, through which they access markets on the west coast of the United States and the Caribbean lines of navigation guaranteeing their economic link to eastern North America. Moreover, if we consider the Caribbean Basin as a geopolitical unit, European security interests in the region are even more clear since three countries (Great Britain, France, and Holland) still maintain colonial possessions there.[2]

When the "crisis" exploded, the presence of European governments in Central America as important external actors surprised more than one observer and in effect the weight of the Europeans cannot be understood unless from a certain historical distance. In the 20 years prior, the majority of the interactions between European and Central American societies had not occurred through official channels. Before 1979, the governments had maintained a discreet presence in the region's capitals, concentrating their activities mainly in the area of cultural cooperation. It was the political parties, which constituted the principal linkage groups and channels for communication between Europe and Central America, mainly from the beginning of the 1960s.

---

[2]For a more detailed analysis of European security interests, see José Miguel Insulza, "Europa, Centroamérica y la Alianza Atlántica," *Síntesis*, No. 4, January-April 1988, pp. 264-279.

Given the path of the political parties as actors in the Europe-Central America relationship, I believe they should continue and will continue playing a primary role. It is my purpose in this paper to retrace the evolution of these party links in the context of the political development of the region and analyze their impact on the regional crisis and the definition of the situation developed by the European governments, on the basis of which they designed their Central American policies. Finally, I would like to make some comments on the role of political cooperation on the democratization of Central America.

The Rise of Christian Democracy in Central America

Antecedents

The ideological presence of one of the two great European political forces in Central America made itself felt from the dawn of the 1960s. The preponderance of Catholicism in Latin America had made it propitious for dissemination of the political ideas developed by European Catholics since the struggles against the values of the liberal and bourgeois revolution, including the participation of young Catholics in the anti-fascist resistance movements. After the war, the great figures of European Christian Democracy, Konrad Adenauer, Robert Schuman, and Alcides de Gasperi, tried to recover the legacy of resistance and make of the confessional democracy a movement of a trans-European character.[3]

In Latin America, Catholic youths followed closely the development of events on the Old Continent. Influenced by intransigent Spanish Catholicism and by the French references of the 1930s (the "integral humanism" of Jacques

---

[3]For a more detailed analysis of the development of European Christian Democracy, see Etienne Fouilloux, "Les quatre étapes du parcours européen," *Le Monde Diplomatique*, February 1981.

Maritain and the "communitarian personalism" of Emmanuel Mounier), youths of a conservative stripe went on to found the first Christian parties.

In 1938 in Chile, from a schism in the Conservative Party, the Conservative Phalange was formed, later the National Phalange, which would convert itself into the Christian Democratic Party in 1957. In Venezuela, COPEI was founded on January 13, 1946, as an opposition electoral committee against the Democratic Action candidate supported by the revolutionary government of Rómulo Betancourt, one of the principal leaders of Social Democracy in Latin America. In 1964 and 1968 the Christian Democratic parties of Chile and Venezuela (COPEI), respectively, became the government parties.

In the same way that they had been growing in their respective countries, they extended their influence to other countries in the region. The Chileans participated in the formation of a first group of Uruguayans, Argentines, and Brazilians; the Venezuelans assumed responsibility for training officials in charge of organizing Christian Democratic parties in Central America and the Caribbean.[4]

Even when Christian Democratic politicians maintained their distance from the Catholic hierarchy, the great political currents present in the church after the Vatican Council II reforms had profound repercussions on the evolution of the ideological orientation of the parties in general and the Central American ones in particular. In bold strokes we find four great tendencies in the heart of the Latin American Church: 1) the conservative tendency that has discreetly supported authoritarian regimes; 2) the Social-Christian that concedes a conditional legitimacy to

---

[4]Rafael Caldera, "Un mouvement politique chargé d'avenir," *Le Monde Diplomatique*, February 1981. According to the same author, with the goal of maintaining cohesion in the Christian Democrat movement, in 1956 the Christian Democrat Association of America (ODCA) was formed in which the Chilean and Venezuelan parties participated in an outstanding manner. In 1965 the European Christian Democrat Union and the World Christian Democrat Union were founded.

the military regimes, in very qualified cases, and in general favors the establishment of democratically representative regimes; 3) the "socially compromised" tendency that gets its support from popular movements and base communities; and 4) the "politically compromised" tendency which pronounces itself clearly in favor of socialism.[5] The leadership of the Central American Christian Democratic parties has traditionally belonged to the second tendency.

Christian Democracy in Guatemala and El Salvador

The oldest party, the Guatemalan Christian Democratic Party, was born in 1955 amidst a counterrevolution as an attempt to promote a political alternative (non-military) to the defeated atheistic socialism. The founders were conservative politicians who believed that they could take political advantage of the influence of the priests and the network of Catholic Action Movements in the struggle against Communism. The ideological orientation of the party in the beginning was reflected clearly in the political alliances that it formed with the Democratic Nationalist Movement, today the National Liberation Movement.

In 1963 the first turn toward the Left occurred. The most conservative faction left the party after the majority refused to participate in a supposed redistribution of seats in the Congress, a measure proposed by Colonel Peralta Azurdia.[6] This marked a rupture with the hierarchy. From then on, in the post-council church, parallel with the growth of the progressive sectors (politically and socially compromised) of the clergy, the participation of Christian Democracy in the student struggles (Social Christian Student Front) and the labor movement (National Workers' Con-

---

[5]Raul H. Green, "Evangile libérateur pour ceux que l'on fait taire," *Le Monde Diplomatique*, February 1981.

[6]José Luis Chea, *Guatemala, la cruz fragmentada* (San José, Costa Rica: DEI, 1988), p. 93.

federation) promoted formation of blocs more convinced of the need to reform society. Thanks to its reform proposals, the Guatemalan Christian Democratic Party managed to widen its bases of support despite the vicissitudes of an active political life.

The 1970s marked the party's consolidation in a Center-Left position. For the 1974 elections, it decided in an alliance with the Social Democratic groups (United Front of the Revolution and the socialist Authentic Revolutionary Party)[7] to nominate General Efraín Ríos Montt as the presidential candidate and Dr. Alberto Fuentes Mohr as the vice-presidential candidate. Although the opposition apparently won by a landslide, the army did not recognize it.

To the extent that repression worsened in Guatemala, Christian Democratic militancy became more difficult. By the end of 1980 more than 30 leaders, local and national, had been assassinated and the top party leaders were operating clandestinely. The situation did not change fundamentally in the following years until under pressure from the Reagan administration the process of returning civilians to politics was begun with the election of the Constitutional Assembly in 1984.

The Salvadoran Christian Democratic Party was formally constituted in November 1961. Two central ideas appeared in its pragmatic platform: democracy and social justice.[8] Its conception of representative democracy was not much different from the classic conception: free elections,

---

[7]See Mario Solórzano, "El papel de la democracia cristiana en la actual coyuntura centroaméricana," *Nueva Sociedad*, 48, May-June 1980. Hilda Caldera and Benjamín Santos, "La democracia cristiana en centroamérica," (Guatemala: INCEP, n.d.), p. 50, express it thus: "In this, the rapprochement with the Social Democrats was decisive and the influence of Christian postulates was renovating, which by then were in force in other Latin American Christian Democratic parties, in particular in Chile..."

[8]Stephen Webre, *José Napoleón Duarte and the Christian Democratic Party in Salvadoran Politics 1960-1972* (Baton Rouge: Louisiana State University Press, 1979).

respect for human rights, freedom of association and thought, etc. With respect to the notion of social justice, they conceived it as the right to a just remuneration for work performed and a better distribution of property and income, which in their analysis was not possible without undertaking structural reforms in Salvadoran society and the economy.

Despite the reformist proposals, which the economic elites viewed with distrust Christian democracy in El Salvador continued to be basically a middle class ideology, coherent with the social roots of the professionals who had taken the initiative of forming the party. Their criticisms of the existing social order came from a Christian ethical position which did not question the class structure. For the Salvadoran Christian Democrats education was the ideal means for guaranteeing the process of social change to the extent that it made possible the generalization of the traditional Christian values they favored.[9]

As in Guatemala, the concrete political situation and the ever greater limitations on party work led the PDC center of gravity to shift to the left. In 1972, in the UNO's electoral platform, for the first time the PDC accepted the conclusions of dependency theory and defended the need for agrarian reform. However, it was the Christian Democratic youth that became radicalized more rapidly. Inspired by the liberation theology pronouncements, the young militants questioned not only the viability of elections as a means of obtaining power, but the structure of society itself. Many of them abandoned the ranks of the CD to incorporate themselves into the armed struggle proclaimed by Marxist youth.

---

[9]Ibid., pp. 49-69.

Christian Democracy in Nicaragua, Costa Rica, and Honduras

The Social Christian Party of Nicaragua was founded on September 25, 1957, as an option, according to the words of its founders, that opposed capitalism as much as communism on the one hand, and on the other was against the historical Nicaraguan bipartisan system. However, in the struggle against the dictatorship it did not hesitate to ally itself with the more traditional parties—in 1958 and 1966 in the National Opposition Union with the Conservative Party and Independent Liberal Party, and in 1970 with the PLI and the National Renovation Action in the National Opposition Coalition.

By the end of the 1960s the change in the Catholic hierarchy's alliances placed it in a privileged position. The new archbishop of Managua, Monsignor Obando y Bravo, gave its leadership his full moral support for the first time. However, with the radicalization of the anti-Somoza struggle, the PSCN started losing its "centralized" position in Nicaraguan politics because of the extent to which it opposed the armed struggle.[10] As John Booth well puts it, "despite having entered the '70s as one of the reform leaders, the PSCN was eclipsed and subjected to divisions since it remained reformist in revolutionary times."[11]

In Costa Rica, the presence since the 1940s of the social doctrine of the Church had a strong effect on national politics. The influence of Monsignor Sanabria, archbishop of San José, on the government of President Calderón Guardia was undeniable and the presence of members of the Costa Rican clergy in the ranks of the National Liberation Party allowed social Christianism to permeate Costa Rican political thought. In spite of this,

---

[10]In 1979 it formed part of the Wide Opposition Front and later the Patriotic Front.

[11]John Booth, *The End and the Beginning. The Nicaraguan Revolution* (Boulder, Colorado: Westview Press, 1982), p. 108.

Christian democracy remained an intellectual movement and did not present any candidates until the 1970 elections when it won a few municipal and legislative representatives.

As an independent party it did not prosper; however, it made its influence felt on the platforms of the opposition coalitions to National Liberation. The formation of an opposition party, the Social Christian Union Party, allowed them at last to exercise hegemony from an ideological standpoint over the sectors opposed to the liberationist social democracy.

In Honduras, the Christian Democratic Movement emerged in 1970 with a platform similar to those of its contemporary Guatemalan and Salvadoran counterparts. It maintains a critical position against the national union proclaimed by the army and accepted by the traditional parties since the armed conflict with El Salvador. In 1975, the Christian Democratic Party was officially organized, but did not manage to convert itself into a real alternative within the political panorama, which continued to be dominated by the traditional parties (Liberal and National).

Central American Social Democracy

Just as with Christian Democracy, Social Democracy has a long history in Latin America with some parties dating from the beginning of the century. However, differing from the first, its development in Central America, with the exception of Costa Rica, lagged, coinciding with the strengthening in Europe of Social Democracy and the consolidation of the German Social Democratic Party as the dominant party in the Socialist International.

From the first declarations of the Socialist International, founded in Frankfurt in 1951, its stated purpose was clear of becoming a "third way" among the socioeconomic systems dominant in the post-war world, offering a mixture of political liberalism and economic reform and a distinct opposition to "real socialism." This position had a double effect among the parties of a social democratic tendency. On the one hand it alienated a good part of the world's socialists who perceived the SI as an instrument in Washington's struggle against communism, while on the other hand attracting the attention of various political forces in the Third World who sought to increase their autonomy with respect to the superpower conflict.

During its first six years, the Latin American secretariat of the SI, created in 1955, was in contact with the Panamanian Socialist Party and Costa Rica's PLN.[12] From 1959 the PLN had a school for political training that in 1968 came to be known as the Latin American Center for Democratic Studies, at the same time that it increased its links to the Friedrich Ebert Foundation.

However, the importance of the Socialist International for Central America dates to the 1976 Congress of Geneva at which the European Social Democrats decided to involve themselves more actively in the Third World.

In this redefinition of the geographic focus of the SI Willy Brandt stood out (who conditioned his acceptance of the presidency to solidarity with the Third World), Olaf Palme, and Bruno Kreisky. The socialists declared themselves in favor of seeking a New International Economic Order and condemned the ethnocentrism, which until then had ruled in their hearts, alluding to the necessity of incorporating a wider definition within the concept of democratic socialism.[13]

Central American representatives from the Sandinista National Liberation Front, El Salvador's National Revolutionary Movement, and the National Liberation Party of Costa Rica were present in Geneva. (Daniel Oduber was one of the three heads of state present at the conference.)

---

[12]Felicity Williams, *La Internacional Socialista y América Latina* (México: Universidad Autónoma Metropolitana Azcapotzalco, 1984), p. 90.

[13]G. Pope Atkins, *Latin America in the International Political System*, 2nd ed. rev., (Boulder, Colorado: Westview Press, 1989), pp. 158-9.

They managed to obtain various resolutions condemning the human rights violations in El Salvador and Guatemala, and supporting the anti-Somoza struggle.

But it was the 1978 Vancouver Congress which marked the highest point of Latin American participation in the SI before the Central American crisis. Resolutions were adopted at the congress demanding an end to arms sales to the Somoza forces, especially by the United States, and supporting the parties allied within Nicaragua in the struggle against Somoza. From that point, the European Social Democratic parties offered immediate assistance to the government succeeding Somoza in its task of reconstruction. Héctor Oquelí, of El Salvador's National Revolutionary Movement, was elected a member of the SI secretariat in charge of Latin American questions and Daniel Oduber remained as one of the organization's vice-presidents.

Beginning with the triumph of the Sandinista revolution, the Latin American interest of the SI was concentrated on Central America. Nicaragua appeared in the eyes of important sectors of international public opinion as a symbol of the struggle against despotism and oppression. From the first, for the majority of the socialist parties, it promised the possibility of better living conditions in Central America.

On the other hand, the path of the FSLN, its links to Cuba, the explosion of the crisis in El Salvador, and the generalized violence led Washington to see in Central American events a strong threat to the security interests of the United States within the scope of the East-West conflict. With the arrival of President Reagan at the White House in 1981 this definition of the situation became the foundation of policy toward the Isthmus.

Europe and the Central American Crisis

At first, if indeed the European actors appeared to perceive the threats to their interests in the area as coming more from the behavior of the United States than from that of the U.S.S.R., it was obvious on one side that the differences with Washington resulted from the interpretation of the crisis and the selection of policies for confronting it, and on another that the differences with the U.S.S.R. were in the last instance irreducible. The centrality of the Central American problem in the foreign policy of the Reagan administration, the secondary importance ascribed to the region in the security considerations of the Old Continent, and the reticence of the European governments in opposing their principal ally explain the evolution of policy in the main European capitals as events developed in the region.

At the beginning of the 1980s there was hope on both sides of the Atlantic that the European socialists could create a bridge between the need of the Latin American countries to increase the limits of their autonomy and the principal concerns the European members of NATO might share in that field. That period (1981-1982) was characterized by a European policy that was active and contradicted Washington's position. The principal actors were the SI and the governments of France and Germany (FDR), each led by parties belonging to the Socialist International. The French government opted to channel its actions within the area of political cooperation, taking positions such as the Franco-Mexican declaration on the representation of the Salvadoran guerrillas or President Mitterand's speech at Cancún on the legitimacy of the use of violence in the search for liberty when all other means have failed. The German government, under the leadership of Helmut Schmidt, opted instead for a lower profile focusing on economic cooperation and reconstruction aid for Nicaragua. The Scandinavian governments also participated in a substantial manner in the reconstruction efforts.

Beginning in 1982 political changes in Europe, in particular the change of government in the FDR and the electoral difficulties of the socialist party in France, growing disillusion with the policies of the Sandinista regime, and the regionalization of the conflict supported by the Reagan Administration, led to an eclipse of European policy in the region. The formation of the Contadora Group, in part a product of the European withdrawal and the need to offer an alternative policy to the increasing militarization of the Central American conflict, accentuated Europe's tendency to retreat. The majority of governments contented themselves with supporting this Latin American initiative without reservations.

In October 1984, Europe adopted a more protagonistic role on the Central American scene with the San José summit, at which the EEC, now the principal actor, proposed an economic aid plan for the Central American countries without any type of discrimination. By this time, Christian democratic governments had been elected in El Salvador and Guatemala, making it difficult for their European counterparts to question the democratization of the political systems in which their presence constituted one of the principal elements of legitimacy.

The Political Parties and the Transnationalization of Central American Policy[14]

Very soon it appeared clear to Central American politicians that the strategy of "diversification of dependence," advocated by nationalist sectors as a means of counterweighing the tremendous influence of the United States in the region should have political dimensions. Given the difficulties encountered in the search for internal support due to the repression of any type of dissent against the established order, the political actors sought to develop

---

[14]Wolf Grabendorff, "The Internationalization of the Central American Crisis," in W. Grabendorff, H.W. Krumwiede, and J. Todt, *Political Change in Central America. Internal and External Dimensions* (Boulder, Colorado: Westview Press, 1984), pp. 155-171.

those external supports, multiplying contacts with non-governmental groups. In response to the demands of the Central Americans and given the deficiencies in the traditional pattern of bilateral relations, transnational activities developed considerably.

The German political parties and their foundations would play a primary role in this process, in particular the Friedrich Ebert Foundation of the Social Democratic Party (SPD) and the Konrad Adenauer Foundation of the Christian Democratic Party (CDU).[15]

The Christian Democrats as well as the Social Democrats accept that social change is imperative for achieving regional stability. Even so, although they call for socioeconomic structural reforms and consider these as vitally important for the construction of democracy, neither one has ceased criticizing Cuba and Nicaragua for aligning themselves with the U.S.S.R.

The former, less prone to consider the class struggle as an explanatory element of the situation and more radically anti-Communist, tended, like the Reagan Administration, to emphasize the East-West dimension of the conflict to the extent that this was popularized. The internal alliances of the Central American Christian Democrats, particularly their participation in the management of the counterinsurgency programs with the national armies, reflect very well their priorities.

The latter, thanks to their tradition of Marxist analysis, from a strategic standpoint understood the alliance of the Social Democratic parties with the revolutionary left and their support for the armed struggle as the legitimate means for conquering power. They have been more interested in facilitating the incorporation of the revolutionary groups into the political systems through negotiations, in their view to avoid greater radicalization.

---

[15]Other foundations have been present in the region to a lesser extent: the Hans Seidel Foundation of the Social Christian Party (CSU) and the Friedrich Nauman Foundation of the Liberal Democrats.

The SPD provided an organizational infrastructure for the leftist movements through the Socialist International. The youth movement has sponsored solidarity campaigns for Nicaragua, raising funds and recruiting "internationalists."

For its part, the CDU/CSU has participated in financing important political support projects, in particular a broad cooperation program by COPEI with the Salvadoran PDC. The participation of COPEI in the Venezuelan counterinsurgency experience, where a civilian regime was consolidated in an environment of armed violence, should provide valuable models for action.

Future Perspectives for Cooperation

There are multiple reasons why the political struggle in Central America, with the exception of Costa Rica, became radicalized to such an extent.[16] At this point I want to emphasize the fact that the political systems did not develop at the same rate as the economy and society during the boom period of the common market. The political structures stagnated by the elites' rejection of true diversification and circulation were incapable of integrating the rapid changes being produced in the economy and society. To the extent that the economies were diversifying and the societies becoming more complex, the political processes continued to be characterized by repression and clientelism. The political debate did not manage to overcome the ideological dimensions and feelings of the different actors, and in particular the parties were unable to establish political strategies beyond those that would eventually take them to power.

After ten years of crisis and the periodic celebration of elections held under strict international supervision, the

---

[16]For a magnificent summary of the causes of the Central American crisis, see Edelberto Torres-Rivas, "Ocho claves para comprender la crisis en Centroamérica," in E. Torres-Rivas, *Crisis del poder en Centroamérica* (San José: EDUCA, 1981), pp. 70-112.

real base of power remains in the hands of the alliance between the agro-exporting oligarchies and the region's military. The latter, today stronger than ever thanks to the enormous quantities of weapons to which they have had access, appear little disposed to give up their share of power.

The party system has not managed to root itself in the real power structure although prominent party members from the right do participate in it. The capacity of the governing parties to serve as a channel of communication between the electorate and the authorities, and therefore to develop their capacity to contribute to legitimizing the government's actions, was seen to be seriously in question.[17] This political handicap, combined with administrative inefficiency, would suffice to explain the limitations of the Christian Democratic mission as much in Guatemala as in El Salvador were it not that the situation of generalized violence has in fact frustrated the incorporation of the masses into the political system, under the leadership of governing or opposition parties, legal or revolutionary.

The failure of the counterinsurgency reform strategy has demonstrated why the Central American elites are still stubbornly refusing to accept the idea of representative democracy based on popular sovereignty. A great part of the political public continues to stay, or has returned, to the fold of the private sector, which, through its trade associations (chambers of commerce, industrial associations, banking sector, etc.) fashions a line of action. Many of the policies that concern them directly (in particular those regarding agriculture) are worked out basically in response to their particular interests; a great number of decisions, if

---

[17]The functions of the political party system to which we allude are those enunciated by Robert Scott, "Political Parties and Policy-Making in LA," in J. La Palombara and M. Weiner, *Political Parties and Political Development* (Princeton University Press, 1966), p. 335.

they reach the council of ministers or the legislative committees, arrive simply to be ratified.[18]

Despite elaborate constitutional precepts and cautious norms that govern the separation of power, the judicial powers continue to be under the domination of the executives, over which the ministers of defense, imposed by the upper echelons of the military, exercise an unquestioned veto power. With the obvious exception of Costa Rica, the rule of law is at best embryonic.

The process of democratization is long and complex. Even in the best possible scenario, in which, after a relatively short term, an agreement is reached between the insurgents and the established governments in Guatemala and El Salvador, we will not have overcome the crisis, either from the production point of view, since the necessities for reconstruction are enormous, or from the crisis of distribution. This is because the structural reforms are incomplete in the best of cases and nonexistent in the worst, while the crisis of participation, along with the growing needs of our populations, is increasing.

The necessity of improving the living conditions of the majority and their possibility of utilizing political action, which the international community increasingly guarantees them, makes organizational modernization imperative for those parties willing to represent the interests of those sectors in the political party arena. To the extent to which their efficiency in this area increases, they will increase their power resources in other areas.

In the 1960s, the Western European political parties contributed to the formation of modern parties in Central America; in the 1970s they helped them strengthen and become real alternatives to power, but could not defend them from the blows of the established powers; in the 1980s

---

[18]Paradoxically, the demands of those international organizations which today condition Central American economic policies if they are made taking into account a more general definition of interests with respect to society as a whole and not solely with respect to a specific private sector.

they contributed to the opening of political space and to making human and political rights an inescapable demand of the international system.

In addition to guarding the respect of human rights and individual liberties, the priority themes in cooperation between the European and Central American political parties in the 1990s should move beyond training in the task of taking power, to concentrating on activities that promote design and management of public policies that influence the organizational development and programs of the parties in a way allowing them to remain real alternatives when electoral results are unfavorable to them.

The electoral defeats of the Salvadoran and Guatemalan Christian Democratic parties and their subsequent weakening on the political scene demonstrate that it is not enough to have an electoral mobilization, but that permanent party work should be guaranteed. It is necessary to regulate party-government relations and parliamentary factions to guarantee a certain structural autonomy permitting each of the structures to continue fulfilling the responsibilities that correspond to them. Preoccupied with the everyday problems of running a government, the Christian Democratic leaders neglected party work and found themselves at the end of their term with an organization, which had been costly to build and maintain, on the way to disappearing. Finally, it is necessary to build a conscience over the necessity of regulating the financing of the parties with the ends of guaranteeing their independence and contributing toward preventing corruption.

The Social Democratic parties have had a different experience, but to the extent to which they maintained their democratization processes they will be closer to the responsibilities of government, a fact Guatemala's PSD is already experiencing.

The field of political cooperation is very broad. Let us hope that it continues developing between Europe and Central America.

THE ROLE OF SPAIN IN THE PACIFICATION PROCESS OF CENTRAL AMERICA

JoAnn Fagot Aviel

San Francisco State University

Traditional perspectives on the Central American crisis have stressed either the East-West or North-South aspects of the conflict. While there are aspects of each in the crisis and while each contributed to European and Spanish interest in the area, a spiderweb model of conflict can be useful to explain the internationalization of the crisis and Spanish involvement in it. According to this model, the source of the conflict, the center of the web, is the confrontation between groups over establishing a legitimate nation-state and distributing goods and benefits. Analysis must thus focus on groups, not just nation-states and internationalization occurs from the linkages that domestic groups establish with other groups, governments, and international organizations. These linkages provide an additional source of power for contending groups (Fernández, 3-8).

Societal Support for Role

Under the Franco regime the principal societal contact was through the large number of Spanish religious working in Central America. With the transition to democracy new nongovernmental organizations were formed to support the Third World, and within the Third World, Central America received the greatest attention and aid. Funds were also spent in Spain to increase Spanish awareness of Third World needs and problems (Arahuetes, 9-11, 19). Polls taken of Spanish attitudes showed increasing support for an active Spanish role in Central America. In

1984 51 percent felt that the government should do something to resolve the crisis in Central America, while in 1986 66 percent responded affirmatively to a similar question (C.I.S., 1984, 1986). Although there were relatively few business links with Central America, Spanish labor unions had links with labor unions in Central America, monitored human rights violations, and even participated in a boycott to support Guatemalan workers in a labor dispute with *Coca-Cola* (Pérez, 125). Spanish political parties had links through their Internationals with political parties in Central America.

1979-1982

Although solidarity groups had pressured the centrist government of Adolfo Suárez, which had sold planes to Somoza in 1977, to break relations with his government, Suárez refused to do so but did increase aid to Nicaragua after the Sandinista victory in 1979. Relations were broken with the Guatemalan government after its assault on the Spanish embassy, which had been occupied by a group of peasants and students in January 1980 (Bayo, 18-20). While in opposition, the Socialist party criticized the government for not doing more to aid Nicaragua. As vice-president of the Socialist International and head of its Committee for the Defense of the Nicaraguan Revolution, Felipe González had a strong personal interest in Nicaragua, had visited the region frequently, and had helped formulate socialist policy on the region (Mujal-León, 32-33).

1982-1986

Upon assuming office, González first sought a more active role in Central American diplomacy. However, with the rejection by the United States as well as some Latin American nations of a Spanish proposal in 1982 to host a conference on Central America in which both the U.S. and

Cuba would participate, Spain assumed a less public role while still expressing its desire to collaborate in negotiations to end the conflict. Spain backed the Contadora nations' attempt to resolve the Central American crisis and worked to gain the support of other European nations for the Contadora initiatives. Costa Rican President Monge, on his visit to Madrid in 1984 pleaded, "We need the help of Spain to bring peace to Central America" (*Diario 16*, June, 12 1984). Although only a prospective member of the European Community, Spain met with EC members and Portugal, together with the Central American and Contadora nations in San José, Costa Rica in 1984 to discuss increasing relations between the two areas and solutions to the crisis in Central America. Despite U.S. pressure to exclude Nicaragua, the EC had granted Nicaragua more financial assistance than any other Central American country and included Nicaragua in the EC/Central American Cooperation Accord signed in 1985 (Puig, p. 288).

Together with other European nations, Spain encouraged Nicaragua to hold elections in 1984 and sent technical personnel to advise the government on election procedures, but recalled them when Spain became discouraged at the pace of negotiations between the Sandinistas and the opposition. Spanish socialist leaders met with other opposition and Contra representatives in Costa Rica and participated in unsuccessful negotiations between opposition leader Arturo Cruz and the FSLN commander Bayardo Arce. González declined an invitation to attend Daniel Ortega's inauguration and suspended credits to Nicaragua for several months in 1985 owing to Nicaragua's failure to pay earlier debts. However, González was careful to keep communication lines open and continued to facilitate talks between opposition leaders and the Sandinistas (Mujal-León, 40-42).

Increasingly critical of the Sandinistas, Spain was also critical of U.S. policy towards Nicaragua in speeches in the United Nations as well as in diplomatic notes of protest such as one sent in April 1984 after the mining of Nicaraguan ports. González met with President Reagan in Washington in 1983, and when they later met in 1985 in Madrid, González expressed his concern both for the grave deterioration in relations between Nicaragua and the United States and the U.S. support of the Contras (Pinol 1988, 12). When the U.S. announced an embargo on Nicaragua in May 1985, Spain, the European Community, and the Socialist International rejected the embargo and called for continued assistance to Nicaragua (Vanderlaan, 256).

As part of its commitment to take a more active international role, after ceasing to be an aid recipient in 1977, Spain decided to begin an aid program to developing countries. Aid increased from $161 million in 1980 to $327 million in 1987 and $470.7 million in 1989 (ICE, November 13-19 1989, 4225). Central America was declared a priority area for aid, and a plan to coordinate aid to Central America was drafted in 1984. From 1983 to 1986 Nicaragua was the largest recipient of technical cooperation funds in Latin America (AECI, 43). During this period El Salvador ranked last among countries receiving aid and Guatemala was the only Latin American country not to receive any funds at all. In 1984 Spain resumed relations with Guatemala after the new government accepted responsibility for the assault on the Spanish embassy in 1980, and thus, resuming relations with all Central American governments. Although aid to other Latin American countries increased from 1986 to 1990, Nicaragua continued to be a major recipient of Spanish aid funds (PACI, 1989-ranked fourth; PACI, 1990-ranked fifth).

1986-1990

Frequent meetings with Central American officials and opposition leaders kept Spain well informed on developments there. While working to get the support of the Democratic party in the United States for his peace plan, Costa Rican President Arias also traveled to Europe to seek support. Although González said at the time that he would only study the plan, he later met with Arias and Fidel

Castro in Caracas where they convinced Daniel Ortega to move forward the date of elections. Arias stated, "Felipe, with his good knowledge of Latin America aided very much" (*El País*, May 6, 1990). Spanish participation in a commission of verification as provided for in the 1987 Esquipulas agreement based on the Arias plan was sought by both Costa Rica and Nicaragua, and was agreed upon by Spain after consultation with all relevant parties (Piñol 1988, 35). Spanish General Quesada was named to head the U.N. Observer Group in Central America and Spanish Colonel Maldonado de Arjona was named to head the mission in Nicaragua (*Ya*, Abril 18, 1990). General Quesada's work during negotiations between the Sandinistas and the Contras to put an end to the war was commended by all parties.

After its entry into the European Community in 1986, Spain preferred to act through the EC in regard to Central America, thus giving its actions greater weight and avoiding U.S. hostility directed at it. Spaniards were appointed to key EC posts dealing with Latin America. They worked with Spanish government officials to institutionalize continued meetings with Central Americans and to elaborate on an EC aid plan for the area. Foreign Minister Ordóñez stated that the aid which the European community has given to Central America was due "in great measure thanks to the petitions of Spain" (*Ya*, May 7, 1990). EC aid increased from $72.7 million (63 million ECUs) in 1987 to $102.5 million (93 million ECUs) in 1989 and was conditioned on progress being made towards peace (CEC, 3). During its presidency of the Council of Ministers from May 1988 to April 1989 Spain sponsored a program to promote interregional commerce, which would be supervised closely by the European Commission (*Expansión*, January 15, 1990).

In his capacity as EC representative, Foreign Minister Ordóñez made clear to Secretary of State Baker in a meeting on May 13, 1989, that the European Community sought the rapid dismantling of the Contras, expressed support for elections in Nicaragua, and offered to mediate to resolve differences between the United States and Nicaragua (Piñol 1989, 54). Although nothing came of the offer to mediate, European concern for the resolution of the conflict was evident to the United States. Although an attempt by Spain to mediate the Panamanian dispute was rejected by Noriega, Spain, prompted by public opinion in Spain as well as in Latin America, was the only EC member to vote in favor of the U.N. resolution deploring U.S. intervention and calling for the withdrawal of U.S. troops from Panama (*Diario 16*, December 31, 1989).

Elections and After

Spain, together with the rest of the European Community, had pushed for elections to be held in Nicaragua. Senator Laborda, spokesperson for the socialists in the Senate, stated:

> Our participation with Nicaragua...is extraordinarily high. Thanks to it we are capable of demanding that the Nicaraguan directors evolve politically towards actions which, in our judgement, are positive for consolidating a progressive democratic regime...We cannot support a revolution which finishes deriving toward a totalitarian regime (Peréz, 26).

However, González denied that he had pressured Ortega to democratize but instead "had many times interchanged points of view with Ortega on the things in which he believes and I believe" (*El Mundo*, March 11, 1990). At the inauguration of President Callejas in Honduras, Foreign Minister Ordóñez met with both U.S. Vice-President Quayle and Nicaraguan Minister of the Interior Bórge to discuss the importance of having elections with results that would be honored by all (*El País*, January 27, 1990). Ordóñez later stated:

> We have worked in favor of these elections with all our forces in order to aid in defending the dignity of Nicaragua and avoid any type of foreign intervention, which would have been catastrophic. We [Spain] have aided the entire region and have succeeded in obtaining the European Community's economic support for the

> Central American region, and, thus, for Nicaragua (*ABC*, March 5, 1990).

However, opposition leaders stated:

> It has been the blockade and the economic crisis which has forced the dictator Ortega to celebrate elections ...The aid of the PSOE government of millions of pesetas has served to retard elections and has prolonged the dictatorship (*ABC*, March 7, 1990).

While the precise contribution of each cannot be assessed, it appears that both the "carrot and the stick" played a role in bringing about early elections.

Spanish and other European contacts with both the government and opposition helped to create a climate in which peaceful elections could be held. Before leaving on a trip to Europe in April 1989, Ortega told reporters, "This is a good time for Europe to play a more active and aggressive role in Central America, to stimulate this peace plan and stimulate the United States to support it" (*San Francisco Chronicle*, April 4, 1989). UNO opposition candidate Chamorro wrote European leaders to put any aid in a trust so that it would not be used for "propagandistic purposes" and later traveled to Europe herself to seek agreement to maintain the same level of aid if she should win (*La Prensa*, April 22, 1989; *Diario 16*, February 22, 1990). Spain and other European countries pledged $55 million in new aid to Nicaragua and later promised $1.8 billion in aid to Central America conditioned on progress being made toward peace and democratic reforms (*Barricada*, May 13, 1989; *San Francisco Examiner*, August 13, 1989).

Public opinion in Spain appeared to support the Sandinistas and expected them to win. UNO vice-presidential candidate Godoy was quoted as saying, "If the Sandinistas had elections in Spain, certainly they would win, but not here" (*El Mundo*, February 14, 1990). In Spain articles were written and petitions signed calling for the United States to respect the results of the elections (*El País*, February 20 and 21, 1990). Three Spanish technicians programmed the 67 computers given by Germany and Spain to make the final count of votes in the elections (*Tiempo*, March 7, 1990). Over 200 Spaniards traveled to Nicaragua to observe the elections, including official observers from the European Parliament, the International Liberal Party, the Socialist Party, the Congress, the Ministries of Health, Defense, and the Interior as well as mayors from various cities and others who came on their own (*Diario 16*, February 23, 1990). Both aid from official sources and from solidarity committees was delivered (*ABC*, February 23, 1990).

Spain joined with others to try to assure a peaceful transition of power after the surprise victory of Chamorro. The Spanish foreign minister stated that

> We have made efforts to achieve a smooth and peaceful transition and we are going to aid all, including giving economic support. It is a country which has suffered much, and if an occasion to bring peace is presented, we have the duty to aid them (*ABC*, March 5, 1990).

When President-elect Chamorro was questioned about the future relations with Spain in light of the support given to the Sandinistas, she replied that she had received

> messages from my friend Felipe González congratulating me for the triumph. We hope to have a very close relation with the Spanish government; we need the support of all countries, but we will not consent to interferences in internal affairs (*El Mundo*, March 7, 1990).

During a press conference in Venezuela, González assured that Spain would continue to cooperate with Nicaragua and stated that "Spain has been the Western country which has most aided Nicaragua" (*El Mundo*, March 12, 1990).

González took advantage of his trip to Venezuela, Chile, and Brazil soon after the elections to work towards a peaceful transition of power. A flight to Chile with Presidents Peréz of Venezuela, Ortega of Nicaragua, Arias of Costa Rica, and Callejas of Honduras on González's chartered plane was used to obtain agreement on the necessity of dismantling the *Contras* in accordance with the U.N. plan before Chamorro's inauguration in return for Sandinista collaboration in a peaceful transition. González informed U.S. Vice-president Quayle of the discussions and helped to facilitate his meeting with Ortega (*Ya*, March 13, 1990; *El Mundo*, March 13, 1990). While these efforts facilitated communication between parties to the conflict, the demobilization and disarming of the *Contras* did not begin until April 1990, and did not terminate until the end of June (*La Vanguardia*, June 29, 1990).

González supported those who wanted to transform the Sandinistas into a European style party. On his return from Chile, Ortega announced that the Sandinistas would attempt to change their status from observer to member in the Socialist International with the help of González (*ABC*, March 20, 1990). The Spanish Socialist party's secretary of international relations declared that her party would support its entry now that it is "a progressive force" but that it should hold a congress to redefine its program (*El Independiente*, March 20, 1990). However, the greatly divided Sandinistas have not yet joined the Socialist International, and their first congress is not scheduled until July 1, 1991.

González did not attend Chamorro's inauguration, but instead sent his foreign minister who flew to Nicaragua with the presidents of two principal opposition parties during which they attempted to reach a consensus on Spanish policy towards Central America and particularly Nicaragua (*ABC*, April 25, 1990). In a meeting with Chamorro, Ordóñez declared that Spain wanted to reunite the mixed commission charged with bilateral cooperation to prepare a new plan to aid in the reconstruction of Nicaragua by providing about $60 million of which $40 million would be FAD credits (*ABC*, April 25, 1990; *La Vanguardia*, April 25, 1990). Chamorro told a small group of Spanish journalists hours before her inauguration that the Spanish transition is a good example of what she wished to do in Nicaragua (*Diario 16*, April 25, 1990). Meetings with Vice-President Godoy, who had been the most critical of Spanish aid to the Sandinistas, and other UNO leaders together with the promise to maintain and even augment aid contributed to improving the image of Spain held by the new government (*El Mundo*, April 21, 1990). Nicaraguan Foreign Minister Dreyfus when interviewed on a private trip to Spain in June 1990 stated that,

> As far as our relations with Spain, I believe they are guaranteed and without doubt will be good because the government of Felipe Gonzalez has contributed to the democratization of Nicaragua. This assures a continuity in the relations between our two countries (*El Independiente*, June 11, 1990).

The Spanish embassy in Managua has served as an intermediary between the Sandinistas and the government of Chamorro during the civil unrest after her inauguration. In May 1990, a seminar on the political transition in Spain gave representatives of each the opportunity to debate each other as well as to listen to the experiences of Spaniards ranging from an retired army officer to a Communist party official and including academics, journalists, and the subsecretary of the interior ministry. The Spanish ambassador stated that

> Although historical experiences are never equal, however, at the actual moment in Nicaragua with such a transcendental change of government, it is very possible that the Spanish experience of social and labor understanding could serve as an element of reflection for this nation (*EFE*, May 14, 1990).

Nicaragua's need for aid as well as the Sandinistas own strength contributed to the government's search for accommodation with the opposition. Previous aid givers including the Soviet Union as well as the EC expressed willingness to continue aid if the new government did not dismantle the reforms of the previous. In May UNO director Alfredo Cesar, the minister of tourism, and a group of businessmen met with González to request Spanish cooperation and his support in forming contacts with Spanish businessmen who could invest in Nicaragua (*El Mundo*, May 17, 1990). In June, Nicaraguan Foreign Minister Dreyfus accompanied by the Central Bank president and the

Sandinista ex-vice-president stopped in Spain on their way to Rome to participate in the II Conference on Aid to Nicaragua to ask Spain to be the spokesperson for the support group to be formed. The Spanish foreign minister repeated that Spain would maintain the same level of aid as in past years, which in 1989 amounted to 90 million dollars including the condemnation of a third of Nicaragua's 200 million dollar debt with Spain (*El País*, April 25, 1990). The United States had granted $263 million in emergency aid and the Soviet Union $288 million (*Envío*, June 1990). In Rome, the Nicaraguan government obtained a pledge of $135 million in emergency aid and a support group composed of Spain, the United States, Japan, Norway, and Sweden was formed (*La Vanguardia*, June 14, 1990). Problems with the stabilization plan and confrontations between the government and labor unions have increased the need for aid. At the Paris conference in December 1990, donors refused to approve $300 million sought by Nicaragua until after a delegation had traveled to Nicaragua to study the government's plan of adjustment and economic reform measures based on economic and social *concertación* agreements between the government and the opposition signed in October 1990 (*Barricada*, February 2, 1990).

After meeting with Chamorro in New York, González met with President Bush and proposed that Venezuela and Mexico reconsider their agreements on supplying petroleum to Nicaragua and that the United States and Spain would collaborate in financial aid (*Diario 16*, October 1, 1990). Agreements for Spanish aid to the police and military demonstrate the trust in Spain held by both the government and the Sandinistas. In June 1990, Spain agreed to collaborate in the restructuring and expansion of the Nicaraguan police force (*El País*, June 22, 1990; *Ya*, June 23, 1990). A Spanish army captain and an officer of the Civil Guard are advising on the creation of a rural mounted police charged with preventing cattle thefts. Spain had helped in the drastic reduction of the Sandinista army by donating $5 million to the professional retraining of 5000 Nicaraguan officers and by providing scholarships for ex-military officers. In November 1990, during the visit of Spanish Minister of Defense Serra to Nicaragua and Honduras, agreements were reached on strengthening military cooperation with each country and providing assistance in professionalizing each army. A Spanish military attaché will be sent to Managua charged with relations with all Central American countries (*El País*, November 26 and 27, 1990; *La Vanguardia*, November 26, 1990).

While Spanish attention has focused on Nicaragua, Spain has also had a role in the pacification process attempted in the conflicts in El Salvador and Guatemala. As in the case of Nicaragua, Spain has maintained contact with both the government and the opposition in these countries and has tried to encourage dialogue between them. In Guatemala, Spain's role in promoting dialogue was recognized by ultra-right extremists who threatened the Spanish ambassador with death in April 1990. Although the Guatemalan government promised to guarantee his safety, Spain sent three police agents to protect him (*ABC*, May 9, 1990; *El Mundo*, May 10, 1990). Both Guatemalan government officials and opposition leaders have visited Spain. In June 1990, Spain hosted talks between the government and guerilla leaders in which the guerrillas agreed to suspend attacks for six months and the government agreed to convoke a constitutional assembly in 1991 in which the guerrillas would participate (*El Mundo*, June 2, 1990). Ordóñez met with the Salvadoran FMLN representative in charge of international questions in Mexico in January 1990 before meeting with Salvadoran President Cristiani in Honduras. Likewise, in April 1990 before meeting with the Salvadoran foreign minister in Dublin for the Central American-EC summit, Ordóñez met with a delegation of the FMLN in Madrid after they had signed an agreement in Geneva for negotiating with the Salvadoran government (*El Independiente*, April 6, 1990).

These contacts are likely to continue until a settlement is reached. While denying publicly its own role as mediator, Spain has supported U.N. mediation. If the Salvadoran government accepts the peace plan presented in

U.N. sponsored talks in Mexico in February 1991, Spain will have played some role in bringing this about and is likely to contribute to the peacekeeping troops needed to implement the plan (*San Francisco Chronicle*, February 15, 1991).

Human rights abuses have aroused Spanish public opinion, especially the assassination of the six Spanish Jesuits in the Central American University in November 1989. Spain sent a police team to collaborate in the investigation together with teams from England and the United States (*El País*, May 9, 1990). On the first anniversary of their death, Spain sent a high level delegation to the memorial ceremonies in San Salvador. In the face of calls to break relations with El Salvador, the government decided to issue an ultimatum in November 1990 that the case be satisfactorily resolved in six months and to call for increased pressure on the government by the European Community and the United States. The Spanish ambassador's good relations with the Salvadoran government was criticized by journalists and relatives and friends of those assassinated who called for his removal (*La Vanguardia*, November 19, 1990; *El Sol*, November 20, 1990; *ABC*, November 17, 1990). However, the Spanish government's concern for maintaining relations with the Salvadoran government could be seen in its proposal to increase its aid to El Salvador from 10,350,000 pesetas in 1989 (ranking it last among 20 Latin American nations receiving aid from Spain) to 51,033,650 pesetas in 1990 (thus, raising it to fifteenth) (PACI, 1989 and PACI, 1990).

Conclusion

The Fifth Centennial celebration in 1992 commemorates old ties and attempts to create new ones through increased aid to Latin America and the institutionalization of summit meetings between Spain and Latin American leaders. As long as the many ties between groups in Spain and Central America exist, Spain will continue to play a role in the pacification process even as the EC integrates further and ties are increased with Eastern Europe and North Africa. The new conservative governments throughout Central America have established contacts with the Spanish Popular Party while the defeated parties in Nicaragua and Costa Rica maintain their links with the socialists. Spain's role as broker was requested by Central American leaders and supported by major political parties as well as public opinion in Spain. With relatively little cost to itself Spain played a useful role in the pacification process, thereby gaining more influence as a middle power in the international system.

Although important gains have been made in the pacification process to which Spain has contributed, much yet remains to be done. Spain could continue to play a role in facilitating talks and agreements between government and opposition leaders. However, political peace will be impossible to achieve without assistance in solving the critical economic problems. Although annual meetings with the European Community achieved less in aid and concrete measures than many in Central America had hoped, they helped to diversify the region's foreign relations and encouraged peace and economic integration by linking it to aid programs. While these programs are limited, at a time when the United States has turned its attention and its financing towards the Persian Gulf, any assistance is welcome.

Bibliography

Agencia Española de Cooperación Internacional (AECI). *Análisis de las actividades de cooperación técnica de las administraciones públicas con Iberoamérica. 1983-1986*, n.p.

Arahuetes, Alfredo y Alfonso Gama. *Aproximación a la realidad de las ONG en España*. Madrid: CEDEAL, March, 1989.

Bayo, Francesc. "Las relaciones entre España y América Central (1976-82)" in *Las relaciones entre España y América Central (1976-1989)*. Barcelona: CIDOB & AETI, 1989.

Centro de Investigaciones Sociológicas (CIS). "Banco de Datos." *Política Exterior*, January 1984, n.p.;*Barómetro*, November, 1986, n.p.

Commission des Communautes Europeennes (CEC) *Document de Travail de la 4ème Commission Mixte CE/Amérique Centrale*, Tegucigalpa, July 17-18, 1990, n.p.

Fernández, Damian J. *Central America & the Middle East, the Internationalization of the Crises*. Miami: Florida International University Press, 1990.

Mujal-León, Eusebio. *European Socialism and the Conflict in Central America*. New York: Praeger, 1989.

Plan Anual de Cooperación Internactional (PACI). *Previsiones para 1989 y 1990*. Madrid: Ministerio de Asuntos Exteriores.

Pérez Herrero, Pedro, coord. *América Latina vista por los partidos políticos y los sindicatos españoles*. Madrid: OEI, 1990.

Piñol i Rull, Joan. "Las relaciones españolas con Centroamérica: el período de los gobiernos socialistas (1982-1988)." *Afers Internacionals*, Barcelona, 14 i 15, 1988, p 5-40.

______. "Las relaciones españolas con Centroamérica: El período de los gobiernos socialistas (1982-1989)," in *Las relaciones entre España y América Central (1976-1989)*. Barcelona: CIDOB & AETI, 1989.

Puig, Juan Carlos. "La Comunidad Europea y los conflictos centroamericanos." *Mundo Nuevo*, Caracas: April-September 1987, p. 270-295.

Vanderlaan, Mary. *Revolution and Foreign Policy in Nicaragua*. Boulder, Colorado: Westview Press, 1986.

THE CHANGING LATIN AMERICAN TRADE ENVIRONMENT: OPPORTUNITIES AND CHALLENGES FOR CENTRAL AMERICA

Mark B. Rosenberg

Florida International University

The Emergent Trade Environment

Following a decade of lost opportunities in Central America as a result of the continuing debt crisis and excessive superpower competition, there is a new surge of optimism, hope, and uncertainty throughout the hemisphere. Critical issues such as democracy, environmental protection, and the development of more effective justice systems continue to grow in importance. As a result, the agenda of inter-American concerns is being transformed.[1]

There is much evidence to support this assertion. One of the best examples, however, is an opinion-page article that appeared early in 1990 in *The Wall Street Journal* (March 20, 1990). Suggesting that "Latin America needs trade and not aid" from the U.S., the article calls for new U.S. attention to the region. Such attention is justified because it will help restore Latin markets for U.S. exports, thus helping to reduce, significantly, the American trade deficit. The author of the article? Peter Drucker, the foremost U.S. management consultant.

A major factor accounting for this transformation is the decline of hostilities between the U.S. and the Soviet

---

[1]See *The Americas in a New World: The 1990 Report of the Inter-American Dialogue* (The Aspen Institute: The Inter-American Dialogue, 1991).

Union and the movement toward a single European market (SEM) in 1992. Despite President George Bush's efforts to promote a "new world order" in the post-Persian Gulf era, there are no guarantees that anti-communism as a policy will be replaced by a clear set of new directions in U.S. foreign policy. Anti-communism in the U.S. has not only been a policy, but a basic value of American life. As a result, the issues emerging in the wake of anticommunism are a "mixed bag of incomplete and sometimes incompatible ideas."[2]

Nowhere is this "mixed-bag" clearer than in the area of trade policy. As Professor Henry Nau has commented, "International trade is mostly a matter of domestic politics..." and "the future of the trading system depends on the domestic choices" that industrial and developing countries will make over the next few years.[3] In the post-Cold War era escalating conflict in the trade arena will clearly demonstrate the inherent contradictions of competing interests in public policy during the 1990s. A clear example of the political ambiguities engendered around trade is best illustrated by examining the changing positions of Florida Senators Bob Graham and Connie Mack. Both have traditionally been freetraders and outspoken advocates for open markets, deregulation, and privatization.

However, in the face of the realities of free trade, Senator Graham now speaks about "fair trade"[4] and Senator Mack has been subject to withering pressure from agricultural interests in Florida, which will be immediate short-

---

[2]Norman Ornstein and Mark Schmitt, "Post-Cold War Politics," *Foreign Policy*, No. 79 (Summer 1990), 174.

[3]Henry Nau, "Domestic Trade Politics and the Uruguay Round: An Overview," in Henry Nau, ed. *Domestic Trade Politics and the Uruguay Round* (New York: Columbia University Press, 1989), p. xiii.

[4]Bob Graham, "Trade-offs? The U.S. and the Caribbean," *Hemisphere* Vol. 3, No. 1 (Fall 1990), p. 2.

term losers in free trade agreements with neighboring countries.

Thus, the trade terrain will be a singularly important arena for world conflict during the 1990s. In the Western Hemisphere, there are a range of new forces and developments that present unprecedented challenges and opportunities for Central America. The nature of hemispheric trade relations will be dramatically altered during this decade.

What are these new developments and what will be their impact on Central America?

* The emergence of enhanced regional trade relations, including the Enterprise for the Americas Initiative (EAI), the U.S.-Canada and U.S.-Mexico Free Trade agreements, and the emergence of a Single European Market in 1992;

* The emergence of Japan as a world economic power and its potential to alter the course of traditional hemispheric trade relations;

* The Uruguay Round of the General Agreement on Tariffs and Trade (GATT).

The Bush Initiative

Following nearly a decade of economic experimentation there seems to be a general consensus throughout Latin America and the Caribbean that structural adjustment and enhanced support for free markets offer potent alternatives to previous economic development efforts. In this view international trade and development of the external sector are key elements of renewed economic growth.

President George Bush's proposal to create a hemispheric free trade zone with the Enterprise for the America's Initiative (EAI) opens the door to serious discussions throughout Latin America and the Caribbean about the region's destiny. The Bush plan, based upon a call for open markets, new debt measures and enhanced investment support, offers an unprecedented opportunity for the region to gain predictable and stable access to the U.S. market and to new investment capital.

On the heels of the agreement between the U.S. and Mexico to initiate negotiations for a free trade agreement, the Bush plan has been motivated by a genuine U.S. concern for the specter of global trading blocs and the possible exclusion of the U.S. In general, the response from Latin America and the Caribbean has been positive in terms of rhetoric and action.[5] In the Caribbean, assertive leadership is now moving the 13 countries there toward a single regional market and economy by 1993.[6] Andean countries are now reexamining their regional trade arrangements and have set forth a bold new effort to reduce trade barriers; Southern Cone countries have concrete plans to open their borders to products from their respective neighbors. Central America has taken some steps to invigorate regional trade but civil turmoil there and the absence of strong leadership continue to hamper collective state action.

Most dramatically, Mexico has moved rapidly to end its traditional diplomatic and commercial isolation.[7] In response to Latin American concerns about the potential trade and investment diversion impact of privileged access for Mexico to the U.S. market, Mexico has mounted an aggressive campaign to cooperate with Caribbean, Central and South American neighbors. It now views itself as a commercial intermediary for Caribbean rim countries anxiously worried about Mexico's potential preferential access to the U.S. market.

---

[5]"Five Latin Ministers Embrace Free Trade," *The Wall Street Journal*, September 13, 1990.

[6]See Anthony P. Gonzalez, "The View from the Caribbean," *Hemisphere*, Vol. 3, No. 1 (Fall, 1990), pp. 26-29; "Caribbean Initiative," (Editorial) *Journal of Commerce*, March 7, 1991.

[7]See George Grayson, "Mexico-Bashing in Washington," *Hemisphere*, Vol. 1, No. 2 (Winter 1989), pp. 45-48.

Flexibility is the hallmark of the trade dimension of the Enterprise for the Americas Initiative. At this point, there are more questions than answers. Will the prospect of free trade with the U.S. promote enhanced bilateralism in the region or will it foster greater regional cohesiveness among groups of countries with similar levels of resource endowments? Will free trade with the U.S. reduce even further intra-regional trade? How will free trade with the U.S. reinforce or undermine the understandings fostered through the General Agreement on Tariffs and Trade? How will countries maximize their bargaining leverage with the U.S. in trade negotiations?

If Central America is to benefit and protect its own interests during this decade, it will need to develop an expanded base of knowledge about the changing nature of the global economy, new production styles, and enhancements and impediments to international trade. Further, since the U.S. and Canada will offer a huge new market, there will need to be greater awareness about these markets and consumer preferences there. Finally, a potentially frenzied rush to restructure local economies can not come at the cost of diminished rights and protection for labor and the working class in Latin America. There will inevitably be great tension between the economic demands of free trade and the pressure to reduce rather than expand political freedom.

The Mexican case is important because it will be the first Latin American country to negotiate a free trade agreement with the United States. Many important lessons can be learned from the Mexican experience that will guide trade negotiators from throughout the region.

U.S.-Mexico Trade

Following years of mutual hostilities and tensions, there is a new tone to U.S.-Mexican relations as both attempt to sort out common mutual interests in the new trade environment. The primary ingredient for this new phase of harmony has been the political will of the leadership of both countries. President Salinas has willingly tempered the most strident anti-U.S. aspects of Mexican nationalism to seek a new high ground in bilateral relations. Moreover, he has led a process of restructuring the Mexican economy that has had high short-term costs, especially for Mexican labor. A critical ingredient to this process has been the growing receptivity of key segments of the country's private sector, traditionally one of the most protected and privileged in the Western Hemisphere.

United States President Bush has continually demonstrated his interest in improving relations with Mexico and shows a firm commitment to the deepening of trade relations with that country. However, the Bush Administration has clearly underestimated the political potency of the forces unleashed against the pact with Mexico. An unholy alliance, including environmentalists, human rights promoters, labor unions and Mexico-phobes are ganging up to stop the U.S.-Mexico proposal.[8]

If they occur, free trade negotiations will have several dimensions:

Tariff reduction for the exports of both countries, which may be specified through the development of a timetable in accordance with specific sectoral interests. The average tariff for imports from the U.S. is about 13 percent. U.S. imports from Mexico have an average tariff of 5 percent. However, some Mexican products such as brooms, glass, melons, and footwear have tariffs that vary between 38-35 percent.

Reduction of Non-Tariff Barriers (NTBs) will be a critical dimension of the forthcoming trade talks. The arbitrary nature of NTBs promotes uncertainties that hamper long-term investment plans and strategies. For instance, about 20 percent of Mexican imports from the

---

[8]See for instance "California Firms Air Concerns Over a Mexico Trade Pact," and "U.S. Labor Fights Mexico Trade Pact," *Journal of Commerce*, February 6, 1991; "Group Seeks Reforms in Maquiladora Plants," *Journal of Commerce*, February 13, 1991.

U.S. are subject to licensing, including agriculture, livestock and forestry, oil and derivatives, and automotive products. The U.S. maintains restrictions for the import of textiles, steel, and agricultural products (see List 1).

List 1

U.S. Non-Tariff Barriers on Mexican Products

* Textiles: wool suits, trousers, skirts, shirts, acrylic fibers, cotton webs

* Steel: tubes, wires, metal sheets, and special steels

* Agricultural Products: avocados, potatoes, milk, and sugar products

Dispute resolution is an important component of free trade. Both countries signed a "Bilateral Understanding on Subsidies and Countervailing Duties" in 1985 that has been periodically renewed. This mechanism is designed to promote the resolution of differences that could lead to the application of unilateral measures. Mexico views the understanding as particularly useful because it perceives that U.S. legislation and rules on subsidies and countervailing duties are often more severe than GATT rules.

Complementarity is a concern of both parties. Can there be compatibility between a post-industrial economy and one that is highly segmented such as Mexico's? One positive approach to this question is that the disparities can actually promote complementarity. The best example is the *maquiladora* industry, which now plays a leading role in the generation of foreign exchange and employment in Mexico.

Assessments of risks and benefits to both parties are numerous. However, one early analysis by the *Journal of Commerce* (August 24, 1990, p. 1) points to the unique views on the issue taken by the private sectors in both countries.

In the U.S., the primary advantage to free trade is the opening of the Mexican market and the investment possibilities there.[9] For the Mexican private sector predictable and stable access to the U.S. market is a powerful rationale. But even more compelling is the access to new sources of finance in the context of the country's capital shortage. After eight years of capital flight, heavy debt, devaluation, and reduced productivity, new investment capital is in short supply.

But Mexicans also understand that an open trade system will not only alter the structure of trade and finance. It will likely accelerate the transition from family owned companies to those with diversified shareholder ownership and professional management. For small and medium sized business that do not have access to capital markets, the transition may be more abrupt unless they can find joint venture partners to infuse new levels of capital and technology. Nonetheless, it is important to note that the emergent free trade relationship between the U.S. and Mexico will have an array of costs and benefits that will vary across the production spectrum.

The Canada-U.S. Free Trade Agreement will offer important lessons and guideposts for Mexico and other Latin American countries. An early assessment of the agreement suggests that its impact has been mixed—perhaps more positive for the U.S. than Canada. For instance, the Canadian Labor Congress states that 36 companies have closed facilities in Canada since the U.S.-Canada Free Trade Agreement was signed. A total of 11,064 jobs have been lost as a result. U.S. firms are apparently using the liberalized foreign investment code to transform them into subsidiaries of existing Canadian-owned firms. In the process, little new productive capacity has been created in

---

[9]United States International Trade Commission, *The Likely Impact on the United States of a Free Trade Agreement with Mexico* (Washington, D.C.: United States International Trade Commission, Feb. 1991), p. vii.

Canada.[10] However, Canadian and U.S. industrialists have requested accelerated tariff phase-outs for more than 400 products that account for about $6 billion in bilateral trade. Subsidies still are to be negotiated (*International Business Chronicle*, July 23-August 5, 1990).[11] Canada's economy is far more advanced than Mexico's—there are major structural differences between the two countries. Thus, while lessons can be learned from the Canadian-U.S. negotiations, they have their limits.

Canada's interest in joining the pending U.S.-Mexico talks is motivated by its effort to avoid a "hub-and-spoke" model of hemispheric trade. In such a scenario, the U.S. hub would have a separate arrangement for each participating country or group of countries. Canada would risk losing Mexican trade to U.S. based companies. It could also lose investment to the U.S.—because only U.S. based companies would enjoy tariff-free access to all three markets.[12]

Although there is optimism in both the U.S. and Mexico about the forthcoming negotiations, there are many obstacles to successful discussions. In the U.S., President Bush may not have the political capital to fight protectionist interests throughout the country who will point to the large wage differentials between Mexican and U.S. labor and who are focusing on other issues such as environment as a means to slow talks.[13] Pro-free trade interests in the private

---

[10]Some analysts argue that the major problem in Canada has been of a macroeconomic nature, thus accelerating or being independent of the agreement with the U.S. For more information, see *Hemisphere*, Vol. 3, No. 2 (Winter/Spring 1991) on lessons of the U.S.-Canada Free Trade Agreement for the forthcoming U.S.-Mexico-Canada free trade negotiations.

[11]*International Business Chronicle*, July 23-August 5, 1990.

[12]Leo Ryan, "Trade Talk from Canada," *Journal of Commerce*, February 8, 1991.

[13]John Maggs, "Gephardt: Mexico Pact Must Cover Such Topics as Labor, Environment," *Journal of Commerce*, March 6, 1991.

sector may not have the leadership and cohesion necessary to mount a successful campaign to support the president. Congress's tendency to micro-manage foreign affairs and its appetite for Mexico-bashing could reverse the current era of good-will between the two countries. In Mexico, continuing problems with that country's political opening and mounting evidence of widespread human rights abuses could undermine the government's capacity to continue its progress in structural adjustment, a key element underlying its free trade interests.

Mexico's involvement in a new North American trade arrangement has caused concern within Central America and the Caribbean. Leaders from both regions have publicly suggested that any U.S.-Mexico agreement would be a major step in eroding preferential market access provided by the Caribbean Basin Initiative, which allows 28 countries to ship a range of products duty free to the U.S.[14] The general argument is that trade diversion would be possible because of Mexico's many advantages, including lower production costs, proximity to the U.S. market and therefore cheaper transportation and communication costs, abundant natural resources, and a large domestic market.[15]

---

[14]See Dory Owens, "Other Nations Fret Over Free-Trade Pact," *The Miami Herald*, October 24, 1990; Canute James, "Central America, Caribbean Fear Free-Trade Impact," *Journal of Commerce*, December 11, 1990.

[15]In response to concerns that CBI countries might be early losers from any U.S.-Mexico agreement, a number of proposals have been offered. First, Mexico could be required to open up its market to Caribbean products on a tariff-free basis under which these goods can then enter the U.S. Second, rules-of-origin in any U.S.-Mexican agreement could permit Caribbean goods to be treated as if they originated in Mexico. Third, that Mexico could permit Caribbean countries to transship their goods freely through Mexico, without administrative delays. See *Review of Trade and Investment Liberalization Measures by Mexico and Prospects for Future United States Mexican Relations: Phase II: Summary of Views on Prospects for Future United States Mexican Relations* (Washington, D.C.: United States International Trade Commission, October 1990), pp. 1-29.

Versions abound concerning the impact of a U.S.-Mexico agreement. Estimates suggest that the elimination of U.S. tariffs on Mexican products will increase Mexican exports to the U.S. by about $1.4 billion in the short run. The elimination of both tariff and non-tariff barriers will increase Mexican exports by about $2.8 billion. The trade diversion impact on Central and South America is estimated at about $250 million over a five year period. However, this figure could rise if sector-specific arrangements on non-tariff barriers come at the expense of third countries.[16]

Mexico and the countries of Central America have taken some steps to reorganize their trade relations in preparation for an eventual U.S.-Mexico agreement. At a January 10-11, 1991, meeting in Tuxtla Gutiérrez, a framework agreement was signed that calls for sectoral agreements leading to free trade in a range of products that will expand over the next six years.[17] In the context of this agreement, Mexico emerges as an intermediary, developing its own role as a "hub" with numerous other spokes—Central America, Venezuela, and Colombia and at some point in the future, the Caribbean.

In practice, the Mexico-Central America agreement has only symbolic importance at this point. In relative terms, Central American exports to Mexico were only 2

---

[16]Gary Clyde Hufbauer and Jeffrey Schott, "Options for a Hemispheric Trade Order," in Mark B. Rosenberg, ed. *The Changing Hemispheric Trade Environment: Options and Obstacles* (Miami: Florida International University, Latin American and Caribbean Center), 1991 p. 15.

[17]The trade agreement has three major components. The first is known as "asymmetrical reciprocity," which allows for a more rapid opening of the Mexican economy to Central American products. The second component stresses "multilateralism," which assures that products will move about through Central America free of barriers. A third component focuses on the general nature of the agreement, broadly encompassing all sectors of the economy. See *Centroamerica Hoy*, No. 51 (January 15, 1991), p. 17.

percent of Mexico's total imports, and Mexican exports to Central America totaled about 1.5 percent of total Mexican exports. Guatemala is Mexico's leading trade partner, with a total trade exceeding $130 million in 1987.[18]

Early concerns expressed about this agreement include fears that Central America's import and export costs will rise, since those countries will not be trading directly with the U.S., and that the renewed Central American integration efforts will be put at risk.[19]

The New Europe and Latin America[20]

The fast-paced changes in Eastern Europe during 1989 and the pending unification of the Western European market in 1992 give Europe a new and central role in the emerging global economy. Transformation of the Soviet economy into a free-market system will give added weight to Europe's emerging leadership role.

For the foreseeable future, it is clear that Europe will be preoccupied with Europe, particularly in economic, trade and political considerations. In general, "asymmetry"

---

[18]See Jorge Salazar-Carrillo and Irma Alonso, *Mexico as a Potential Market for Central American and Caribbean Products*, (Miami: Florida International University, 1990), pp. 9-12.

[19]See "Mexico—Key Player in Regional Trade Bloc," *Central America Report*, Vol. XVIII, No. 2 (January 18, 1991) and "Framework Trade Accord Strengthens Mexico's Role as U.S. Intermediary," *Mexico and Central America Report*, February 21, 1991.

[20]Alberto van Klaveren, "European-Latin American Relations in a World in Flux: From Optimism to Fatalism to Realism," prepared for a Workshop of the Inter-American Dialogue, Airlie House, May 23-25, 1990; and Henry S. Gill, "Economic Implications for Latin America and the Caribbean of Changes in Eastern Europe," paper presented to the Conference on The Crisis in Eastern Europe: The Emerging New World Order and Its Implications for the Third World (Institute of International Relations, The University of the West Indies, St. Augustine, May 9-10, 1990).

tends to characterize Latin American trade with the European Community. First, unlike other areas of the developing world, Latin America does not benefit from specific EC policies of preferences except for the General System of Preferences (GSP), which applies to all developing countries. Second, about three quarters of Latin American exports to the EC are primary products, for which a relatively lower demand elasticity exists. Finally, there is a lack of diversification of Latin American exports to the EC, especially with regard to semi-manufactured or manufactured goods.

What are some of the most recent trends in European-Latin American trade relations?

The structure of trade between the European Community and Latin America has a more typical North-South quality. Trade revolves around Latin American fuel, primary goods, and agricultural products in exchange for European industrial products. Indeed, Latin America has had a declining impact on European commercial markets during the last two decades. In 1970, Latin America accounted for 8.1 percent of the imports and received 7.2 percent of the exports of the European Community; in 1988 there had been a drop to 6 percent and 3.8 percent respectively. More dramatically, in 1979 the EC had provided 27.3 percent of the imports and received 31.3 percent of the exports from Latin America. By 1988, these percentages had declined to 17.7 percent and 21.1 percent.

With some notable exceptions, Latin America has encountered increasing difficulty in exporting to the European market. The EC's Common Agricultural Policy (CAP) has served as an important barrier to many Latin American agricultural products and to a loss of third markets because of highly competitive prices resulting from subsidies.

Although two new Caribbean countries (Haiti and the Dominican Republic) have recently been given preferential access to the EC through the Lomé (IV) Convention, their entry carried explicit conditions to prohibit the entry of other low development countries. Central America was an obvious target of this restriction. One trade analyst has suggested that the purpose of the recent Lomé negotiations was to "prepare the Caribbean countries for life without preferences...as the EC seeks to globalize its relationship with the developing world and carve out its special trading relationship with Eastern Europe and the Mediterranean."[21]

Thus, Latin America's role in European priorities is secondary. However, there are instances in several Latin American countries where the European presence is as important as the U.S. presence and more significant than Japan's.

What will be the impact of the Single European Market on these relations?

Little concrete information is yet available to answer this question. Several general conclusions can be drawn:

> * The initiation of the SEM will be accompanied by a new diversion of trade from other markets. While some traditional Latin American exports may be hurt, dramatic effects are not expected given the complementarity of the markets.
>
> * The increase in European demand may offset the negative impact on traditional exports from the region, particularly in some product areas such as bananas.
>
> * Pending the outcome of the Uruguay Round of GATT, a slow reduction in subsidies for agricultural production can be predicted.

In this context, the SEM's effects on commercial relations with Latin America are of less importance than with those regions of East Asia or traditionally developed countries where manufactured goods dominate trade relations. The SEM's effects on Latin America, either positive or negative, are likely to be marginal since the SEM will have less impact on primary products than on manufactured goods.

---

[21]Anthony P. González, "The Implications of Changes in the International System for the Caribbean Region: A Focus on Trade Policy," loc. cit., p. 6.

The SEM will have an impact on U.S.-Latin American trade within a context of growing Latin dependence on commercial relations with the U.S. It is likely that the growing income effect brought about by the SEM in EC countries will affect positively aggregate import demand, including imports from the U.S. and Latin America.[22] Thus, although Latin Americans had seen Europe as an important "third option" during this same period, there is a new sense among many that the region is now marginal to European interests and concerns.

The transition in Eastern Europe to open markets presents special challenges to Latin America and the Caribbean. Not counting the Soviet Union (population of 288 million people), the Eastern European market has some 137 million eager consumers. The economic conversion of these countries has clearly captured the interest of the industrial world, particularly Western European countries.

Eastern Europe has several distinct advantages for the foreign investor. First, it has both an industrial infrastructure and an industrial culture. Second, Eastern Europe's labor force is skilled and wages are low. Indeed, the average Eastern European worker makes about one-fifth or one-sixth the salary of a Western European counterpart. Third, geography and ethnicity favors intensified Western European interest in the new economies of the region. Finally, a number of Eastern European countries are adopting policies and legislation to encourage foreign investment. Privatization has been embraced and joint ventures are aggressively solicited. One observer has stated that "for the European investor, Eastern Europe today is like having his 'Asian NIC' of the future next door."[23]

However, the early optimism about the region's rapid transition to market-based economies has been replaced by

---

[22]Wolf Grabendorff, "The Single European Market and its Impact on U.S.-Latin American Trade Relations," in Rosenberg, op. cit.

[23]Henry S. Gill, "Economic Implications for Latin America and the Caribbean of Changes in Eastern Europe," loc. cit., p. 17.

the sober recognition of the difficult process of transition. One analyst has stated that "while communism has been roundly defeated in Central Europe...its residual impact is hardly negligible. No magic wand can suddenly erase the habits and customs of four decades of communist rule..."[24] In general, Eastern Europe's tendency to open markets can facilitate trade relations with Latin America. However, Latin America has no specific advantage with the newly emerging market.

The fears of fortress Europe may well be exaggerated. In such a scenario, the trade loss to Latin America would not have a major impact on either partner. However, the specter of a giant European market may function to siphon foreign investment as a result of the productivity gains to be made by these firms.[25]

Japan's Role: Cooperation or Rivalry with the United States

Japan's impressive economic development during the last two decades has led many Latin American leaders to consider a "Pacific Rim" strategy as a means to diversify trade and investment opportunities for their countries. Japan's potential importance for Latin America will become more apparent as the 1990s crystallize the co-equal status of Europe and Japan with the United States. What is the Japanese trade relation with Latin America? What are the implications for the United States?

---

[24]Charles Gati, "East-Central Europe," *Foreign Affairs*, Vol. 69, No. 5 (Winter 1990-91), pp. 132-133.

[25]Winston Fritsch, "Domestic Trade Reform and Policies Toward the Trade System: Is there a Common Latin American Agenda?" (Prepared for the Working Group on Economics of the Inter-American Dialogue), May 1990, p. 13.

Is Japan Interested in Latin America?

Although Latin America's attention toward Japan has grown in the 1980s, Japan's interests during the past decade have been focused elsewhere—on relations with the United States and with the booming Asian market. Japan views itself as being part of two triangles—one composed of Japan, the United States, and Europe; the other of Japan, Asia Pacific, and the United States. While Japan's aid efforts now make it the largest aid donor in the world in absolute terms, its program tends to respond to pressure from other developed countries.[26]

Latin America's share of Japan's economic transactions has fallen, but the absolute value has been constant or increased slightly. Trade has tended to be the lagging sector in Japanese-Latin American relations. Japan's relations with the region have tended to be investment and finance dominated. It is estimated that Japan is now Latin America's leading creditor for medium- and long-term private bank loans. Japanese banks hold about $46 billion of debt from Latin America compared to about $36 billion held by U.S. banks.

Total trade between Latin America and Japan amounted to $16.5 billion in 1989, about 3.6 percent of Japan's total trade. The high point in trade relations was in 1955, when Latin America accounted for about 9 percent of Japan's trade. Trade between Latin America and Japan tends to follow a traditional "colonial pattern." Raw materials are imported by Japan. Latin America receives industrial products.[27] Some key Latin exports to Japan include food products and raw materials. The most important items

---

[26]Charlotte Elton, "The New Japanese Presence in Central America: Challenges and Opportunities," (Washington, D.C.: XVI LASA Congress, April 4-6, 1991), pp. 9-10.

[27]About 41 percent of Latin America's exports to Japan were manufactured products with almost 75 percent of these listed as semi-processed metals.

include iron ore, coffee, unwrought copper, ferroalloys, silver, pig iron, emeralds, forage, and salt. Japan is more significant as an export market (10 percent of Latin American exports are sold there) than as a provider of imports (about 7 percent of imports originate in Japan.)

Brazil is Japan's largest Latin American trade partner after Panama.[28] With a surplus in its trade with Japan, Brazil accounted for 25 percent of Japan's total trade in 1989. Mexico follows as a leading trade partner with Japan (about 21 percent of Japan's Latin American trade), followed by Chile (11 percent), Colombia (4.5 percent), Venezuela (4.3 percent), Argentina (3.4 percent), Peru (3.3 percent), Ecuador (1.3 percent), and Honduras (1.1 percent).

In 1989, Japan was the second largest export market for five Latin American countries including Chile, Brazil, Peru, Honduras, and Mexico. Chile in particular has been able to increase its non-traditional product trade with Japan, especially in fish, fruits, and forestry products. Mexico's non-oil exports to Japan have also increased by about 14 percent per annum in the late 1980s. For imports, Japan is the second largest source for six countries, including Ecuador, Colombia, Panama, Honduras, Haiti, and Mexico.

Although Latin America has had success in trading raw materials and semi-manufactured goods with Japan, the prospects for manufactured goods are not high. A major impediment is price competitiveness. The "tyranny of distance" plays against Latin American products as a result of longer shipping distances from most Latin American cities to Japan than to other major markets (i.e., in the United States). Other factors such as lower product quality, punctuality and stability of product delivery, aftercare

---

[28]Panama has been used by the Japanese as a registry for its shipping fleet. Sales of ships to Panamanian-based Japanese companies inflate trade figures for Latin America. Without the large Japanese trade surplus with Panama, its trade with Latin America would be in deficit. See Stallings, op. cit.

service, and specialized consumer tastes are other impediments.[29]

A key element in the evolving Japanese-Latin American trade relation is the role of Japanese trading companies, which have emerged as key promoters. They are involved in transaction intermediation, purchasing goods worldwide and selling them in Japan (and increasingly to third country parties); they act as bankers—financing trade and in some instances providing equity capital; and they gather and process information that is used for company decision-making. Six of the nine major Japanese trading companies have offices in 13 or 14 Latin American countries, including Cuba. Nine trading companies move about one-half of Japanese-Latin American trade and about 10 percent of all Latin American trade is moved by these companies. The trading companies have been especially important for small and medium-sized firms in Japan and Latin America. These trading companies could be the major beneficiaries of enhanced trade in the Americas. During the 1980s their third country efforts spiraled as Japanese domestic market demand for imports slowed.

What are the Implications for the U.S?

Alternative scenarios for U.S.-Latin American-Japanese trade relations in the 1990s have been advanced: a Western Hemisphere trade bloc with little role of the Japanese, a Japanese "headquarters strategy" in which Japan replaces the United States, and a "cooperative" option in which the U.S. and Japan do not compete for markets in Latin America.

What appears likely at this point is the third scenario. One knowledgeable observer has suggested the following:

---

[29]Tetsuro Iino, "Comment," in Rosenberg, op. cit.

> My own interviews in Japan over the past three years find little interest in Latin America. Most of Japan's official activity in the region is to protect its relationship with the United States. As far as the private sector is concerned, I have met no one who expects a return to the level of activity in the 1970s. The banks have opted out; non-financial investors are retaining their holdings but not expanding except in very special circumstances: Mexico (the maquiladoras) and Chile (natural resources).[30]

In such a situation, the United States will remain with the main responsibility and opportunities for trade and investment in Latin America. The Japanese government will probably continue to show a willingness to help the United States, if for no other reason than because an improved trade balance with Latin America may take pressure off the Japanese.[31] However, Latin American hopes that Japan can help in economic recovery and enhanced trade vigor are misplaced.

The Uruguay Round

The General Agreement on Tariffs and Trade is the principal multilateral body concerned with international trade. It comprises some 100 member countries. GATT is credited with promoting a tenfold growth in the volume of international trade since World War II.

A new round of trade negotiations with 15 groups initiated in 1986 was scheduled to end in December 1990. The intent was to further liberalize world trade and to go

---

[30]Stallings, op. cit., p. 15.

[31]Although maquiladoras are an exception, there has been little interest by either private sectors in Latin America. As one specialist has suggested, "the irony is that U.S. stimulated liberalization in Japan has made it more difficult for the Japanese government to influence its private sector...thus making rivalry more likely and U.S. benefit from Japanese activity less." See Barbara Stallings, "Japan and Latin America: New Opportunities in the 1990s?" (Prepared for a Workshop of the Inter-American Dialogue, Airlie House, May 23-25,1990), p. 10.

beyond GATT's traditional focus on tariffs. A major U.S. objective in the discussions was to extend GATT coverage to new and previously unregulated areas of the global economy: agriculture, services,[32] trade related to intellectual property and investment, which may account for up to one-third of the world's four trillion dollars in trade. As a corollary, the hope for the Uruguay Round was to examine and regulate other types of trade barriers that have increased in importance as tariff barriers have diminished. Of particular U.S. interest has been the elimination of agricultural subsidies, which contribute to much of the estimated $94 million a year in the costs of agricultural protectionism on world trade.[33]

From the Latin American viewpoint, the Round's importance revolved around two critical issues. First, a successful Round could provide a multilateral framework within which Latin America could protect itself from unilateral U.S. impositions through the Enterprise for the Americas Initiative. In the same vein, it could constitute a forum from which negotiations for privileged access to the U.S. market for Latin America could be arranged in key sectors such as textiles, apparel, and tropical products. It would have also provided for measures to diminish non-tariff barriers to Latin American products.[34]

A second issue of importance for Latin America revolves around agriculture, where such exporting countries as Brazil, Argentina, Australia, and Canada, among others, united to form the Cairns Group. The objective of the

---

[32]The role of banking, insurance, information, transportation, and other services in the U.S. economy and in international trade has expanded significantly in the last three decades. Services account for 70 percent of the US Gross National Product and 75 percent of employment.

[33]*Times of the Americas*, August 22, 1990, p. 9.

[34]Acuerdo de Cartagena, *La iniciativa para las Américas del Presidente Bush: Un desafío para América Latina y el Caribe* (Lima: September 1990), p. 9.

group was reform of farm trade, particularly the EC's Common Agricultural Policy (CAP). Stating that the reduction of farm subsidies would be a pre-condition for progress in such areas as trade in services and intellectual property, the developing countries led by Brazil made clear their opposition to any agreement unless the EC initiated farm subsidy reforms. In the face of EC opposition to such reforms, the talks collapsed in December 1990.

In general, there has been greater cooperation and harmony between U.S. and Latin American negotiators than in most previous "rounds." The most important explanation for this harmony is the Latin American embrace of economic restructuring and open markets. President Bush's Enterprise Initiative is an added sweetener that has enhanced Latin America's cooperation on a range of Round issues. However, some European cynics have suggested that the U.S. initiative is really a tactic to force the EC to modify its protectionist CAP.

Central American countries have had little participation in past GATT trade rounds, in part because few countries of the region participated in the organization. Prior to the initiation of the Round, only Nicaragua belonged. Now Costa Rica has already been admitted, and Guatemala, Honduras, and El Salvador have requested entry. A major item of concern to Central American countries during the final stages of the Round focused on improved market access for Central American exports such as tropical and forestry products, as well as agriculture and textiles. However, like other smaller countries engaged in Round politics, Central America's delegates had little advance preparation or sufficient quantity to participate in the many discussions that informed the multiple meetings that have taken place since 1986.[35]

---

[35]"Comunicación de los paises miembros del Mercado Comun Centroamericano (Guatemala, El Salvador, Honduras, Nicaragua y Costa Rica)," Uruguay Round of Multilateral Trade Negotiations, Geneva, November 7, 1990.

The failure of the talks in December reflects the new global economic and political realities. Europe no longer has the specter of Soviet power hanging over it. The United States' bargaining leverage has been reduced as a result. Despite its economic global reach, Japan gave little leadership in the final December GATT negotiations, in part because of its desire to protect its agricultural sector, especially rice. Developing countries showed unexpected resolve, insisting that no agreement would be possible without fundamental agricultural reforms. Finally, for many senior U.S. officials, a bad GATT agreement would be worse than none at all. Given the absence of good will by the key players, it is not surprising that the talks collapsed.

The matter is further complicated by the U.S. Congress' reluctance to renew the president's "fast-track" negotiating authority. U.S. trade officials have repeatedly and correctly asserted that without such authority, they will have little credibility in their continuing negotiations at GATT or with major trade partners such as Canada and Mexico.

Implications for Central America

Continuing participation in the emerging global economic order for Central America will present unprecedented challenges to the region's leadership. In the future, less reliance will have to be placed on geopolitical status, historical commitments and third world solidarity. Rather, there is little choice but to find meaningful spaces or niches in the international economy and compete as heartily as possible.

The likelihood of a U.S.-Mexico-Canada Free Trade Agreement has already diminished investor interest in Central America.[36] Although early analysis suggests that trade and investment diversion should not be that great, any

---

[36]Interviews with knowledgeable specialists in the public and private sector.

diversion away from Central America can be ill-afforded at this critical point in the region's history.

Lessons from the Caribbean Basin Initiative are instructive. One of the major reasons that it has not had the anticipated impact is that market access for Caribbean products has been insecure. But there are other reasons. Serious international investors in search of joint venture opportunities are conscious of the capacity and commitment of local private sectors to the national development of their respective countries. If the local private sector has little confidence in its own business environment, this is quickly captured by potential new investors. The Central American private sector's willingness to accept the new reality of open markets has been mixed at best. While the idea of export processing zones seems to have been enthusiastically embraced, other measures of a fiscal and monetary nature have been rejected, perhaps with good reason. Although there are exceptions,[37] few Central American firms can compete in the international market place, even with the privileged one-way nature of the CBI.

Sweeping transformations in communications technology and the resultant changes in international commercial law cannot be ignored by Central America's leaders. Strategies must be found to understand and keep pace with the new infrastructure of global economic discourse. Ten years of infrastructure damage in Central America during the 1980s coupled with antiquated state ownership of the communications sector in the region puts it at a competitive disadvantage in the cellular age. Countries such as Guatemala, which otherwise offer some attractive conditions for foreign investors, are at a major competitive disadvantage with a phone system that simply does not work.

Central America will need to move rapidly in its effort to promote regional integration as a means to in-

---

[37]"Central American Firm Builds Solid Local Base," *Caribbean Action*, December 1990; Duncan Robinson, "Guatemalan Textile Sector Gains Yardage in U.S. Market," *The Journal of Commerce*, March 4, 1991.

crease intra-regional trade. Such a move would almost be a necessary prelude to entry into a North American Free Trade area. Given the course of events and the new forces in the global economy, the longer Central America remains outside of a trading relation with North America, the greater will be the effects of trade and investment diversion.

Thus, the post-Cold War era offers important new trade opportunities for Central America. However, even if such opportunities are seized through a combination of aggressive public and private sector leadership, other critical issues on the Central America agenda will need attention: debt restructuring or forgiveness, the expansion of democratic rule, the reduction of urban and rural poverty and income inequality, and environmental protection. Expanded free trade in Central America can be a means to a larger end; it cannot be an end in and of itself.

TOWARD RECONCILIATION AND DEMOCRACY IN CENTRAL AMERICA: POSSIBLE ROLES FOR EXTERNAL ASSISTANCE

John A. Booth

University of North Texas

The consolidation and stabilization of democracy in Central America are difficult and complex but probably obtainable objectives. Democracy is defined in terms compatible with those set forth in the Esquipulas Accords: public participation in rule within a constitutional regime of fundamental political and human rights.

This paper assumes that negotiated settlements of the guerrilla insurgencies in Guatemala and El Salvador are both essential and possible for the eventual consolidation of democracy. It further assumes that national reconciliation and elite settlement—an accord among the leaders of most political forces to accommodate each other and play by the same rules—is necessary to achieve political stability in Central America.

Stable democracy, it is argued, requires an elite settlement that involves the widest possible group of social forces and that establishes democratic political norms and institutions. Steps needed for such reconciliation are outlined, and roles for external actors are spelled out, including the promotion of national reconciliation dialogues, the continuing development of inter-elite accords, and the improvement of human rights.

In order to pursue such objectives, the paper proposes that Central American and external donor nations jointly establish an International Fund for Reconciliation and Democracy (IFCARD), financed over six years with $2 billion. The purpose of the IFCARD would be to 1) create strong economic incentives (in the form of development assistance grants) to encourage Central American nations to pursue reconciliation and democratization; and 2) to provide technical assistance, verification, and other support for these processes.

Introduction

Pessimism dominated speculation about Latin American democracy from the mid-1960s through the 1970s,[1] but renewed hope has developed with the emergence of numerous civilian regimes in the region in the 1970s and 1980s.[2]

---

[1]See, for instance, Glen Dealy, "The Tradition of Monistic Democracy in Latin America," and Howard J. Wiarda, "Social Change and Political Development in Latin America: Summary," both in Howard J. Wiarda, ed., *Politics and Social Change in Latin America: The Distinct Tradition* (Amherst: University of Massachusetts Press, 1974); James M. Malloy, "The Politics of Transition in Latin America," in James M. Malloy and Mitchell A. Seligson, eds., *Authoritarians and Democrats: Regime Transition in Latin America* (Pittsburgh: University of Pittsburgh Press, 1987, p. 235). Examples of enduring pessimism in the 1980s may be found in Juan J. Linz and Alfred Stepan, eds., *The Breakdown of Democratic Regimes* (Baltimore: Johns Hopkins Press, 1978); Russell Fitzgibbon and Julio A. Fernández in *Latin America: Political Culture and Development* (Englewood Cliffs, NJ: Prentice-Hall, 1981 ed.), chapters 1 and 17; and Howard J. Wiarda, *The Democratic Revolution in Latin America: History, Politics, and U.S. Policy* (New York: Holmes and Meier, 1990).

[2]See Instituto Interamericano de Derechos Humanos (IIDH) - Centro de Asesoría y Promoción Electoral (CAPEL), *Agenda para la consolidación de la democracia en América Latina* (San José, Costa Rica: IIDH-CAPEL, 1990); Malloy and Seligson, eds., *Authoritarians and Democrats*; Guillermo O'Donnell, Philippe C. Schmitter, and Laurence Whitehead, eds., *Transitions from Authoritarian Rule* (Baltimore: Johns Hopkins Press, 1986); Paul Drake and Eduardo Silva, eds., *Elections and Democratization in Latin America, 1980-1985* (La Jolla: Center for Iberian and Latin American Studies—Center for U.S.-Mexican Studies, University of California San Diego, 1986); John A. Peeler, *Latin American Democracies* (Chapel Hill: University of North Carolina Press, 1985); Larry Diamond, Juan Linz, and Seymour Martin Lipset, eds., *Democracy in*

There nevertheless remains considerable caution among those who write on elections and the chances for democratization in the region, and in particular among students of Central America.[3]

In Central America itself, great hopes were raised by the Esquipulas Accord of August 1987, its reaffirmation at subsequent Central American presidential summits, and the settlement of Nicaragua's Contra war and transition to a new regime. Yet there remain two guerrilla wars in the region, and seemingly perpetual internecine political conflict afflicts four of five isthmian nations. Combat and political terror still take thousands of lives, and refugees from conflict and repression abound. In four countries, military forces play a role in politics that retards or threatens democratization.

Such difficulties notwithstanding, there has indeed been tangible progress in one of the region's worst conflicts. The very Esquipulas process and actions of the United Nations (U.N.) and Organization of American States (O.A.S.) helped reduce conflict in Nicaragua and facilitated the 1990 election and transfer of power. Such progress strongly suggests that conflict need not be perpetual and that democratization is possible. This paper explores what must happen for Central American nations to advance toward the political reconciliation and democracy that will permit stability, social peace, and economic recovery. It also speculates about possible roles in the process for such

---

Developing Countries, Vol. 4: Latin America (Boulder, Colo., Lynne Rienner Publications, 1989).

[3]See, for example, John A. Booth and Mitchell A. Seligson, eds., *Elections and Democracy in Central America* (Chapel Hill: University of North Carolina Press, 1989); and Terry Karl, "Imposing Consent? Electoralism vs. Democratization in El Salvador," in Drake and Silva, eds., *Elections and Democratization in Latin America*, pp. 9-36; John A. Booth, "Toward Democracy in Nicaragua? Elites, Political Culture, and the 1990 Election," paper presented at the International Symposium on Transitions to Democracy in Europe and Latin America, Guadalajara, Jalisco, Mexico, February 21-25, 1991.

external actors as the European Community. It proposes the creation of an externally funded regional nongovernmental institution to encourage and foment, using substantial economic incentives, political reconciliation and democratization within Central American nations.

Democracy

The essence of democracy, as defined in the 1987 Esquipulas Accord, is the participation in the rule of each society by its general populace.[4] This approach is consistent with classical conceptions of democracy and with the practice of Western nations, but is sufficiently flexible to admit considerable variety on specific details of particular systems. Even with its specificity, the Esquipulas Accord implicitly accommodated systems as diverse as those of Costa Rica and revolutionary Nicaragua.

This approach to democracy has several implications. First, democracy involves public participation in decision making and administration, which can vary in amount and quality. Democracy, therefore, is not a constant but a variable. There may be more or less democracy, depending upon the amount and quality of public participation in decision making and rule in any particular system. Because democracy is variable it can be evaluated on the amount and quality of political participation in the following terms: its *breadth* (the fraction of the citizenry participating in the

---

[4]The accord, the "Procedure for the Establishment of a Strong and Lasting Peace in Central America," was signed on August 7, 1987, in Guatemala City. In it the governments commit themselves to "promote an authentic democratic, pluralist and participatory process that includes...respect for human rights,...the improvement of representative and pluralist democratic systems which would provide guarantees for the organization of political parties, effective popular participation in the decision making process,...complete freedom of the press, television, and radio ... without prior censorship,...full exercise of the right of association and the right to manifest publicly the exercise of their right to free speech, ...[and the elimination of any] state of exception, siege, or emergency."

making and carrying out of decisions), its *range* (the array of issues and decisions over which the public exercises decisions, e.g., leader selection, areas subject to legislation, dispute resolution), and its *depth* (how effective is popular participation).[5]

Second, certain rights are essential to democracy, especially the right to participate in choosing leaders, policy decisions, and the implementation of decisions. The principal condition under which the rights of one individual to participate should be limited is to protect the fundamental right of other citizens to take part. Third, there must be a constitution—an agreement among citizens on the rules of the political game—that establishes and protects the right to participate for both majorities and minorities. In practical terms, essential democratic rights include the right to speak freely and to publish political opinions, the right to safely oppose incumbents in office, the right to associate and assemble freely, the right to petition the government, and the right to seek and win redress from abuses of authority.[6]

In order to move the four more conflict-ridden Central American countries toward greater and more stable democracy, several essential things must occur: the fighting must end in El Salvador and Guatemala, and in both of the former and in Nicaragua and Honduras there must be reconciliation among national elites, adoption of democratic rules for the political game, and the stabilization and reinforcement of the democratic regime.

---

[5]John A. Booth, "Elections and Democracy in Central America: A Framework for Analysis," in Booth and Seligson, eds., *Elections and Democracy in Central America,* pp. 7-39. For an alternative formulation of democracy that has similar implications, see Juan Carlos Rey, "Problemas de transición democrática y de la consolidación de la democracia en América Latina," in IIDH-CAPEL, *Agenda para la consolidación de la democracia en América Latina*, pp. 343-370.

[6]See José Zalaquett, "Democracia y derechos humanos," pp. 447-477, and Pedro Nikken, "La cooperación internacional para la promoción y defense de la democracia," pp. 500-503, both in IIDH—CAPEL, *Agenda.*

For reasons of length I will not discuss the question of ending the fighting in El Salvador and Guatemala, but will merely assume that the wars there can indeed be stopped as in Nicaragua. I will then list certain practical steps toward democratization and propose policies and programs external actors might adopt to assist in that process. Once the fundamental institutional frameworks are negotiated, these proposals should be implemented on a case by case basis as soon as possible.[7]

National Reconciliation and Elite Settlement

Much more than just an agreement among combatants to stop shooting each other, there must be an elite settlement in each country. An elite settlement is an accord among the leaders of significant sociopolitical forces to accommodate each other in politics and to play the political game by the same rules.[8] An elite settlement that is sufficiently broad (i.e., includes a very wide array of the most significant sociopolitical forces) has a good chance of being stable because it is less likely to be challenged by disgruntled, excluded elites. Historically, such regime-defining

---

[7]That is, the programs and benefits set out below should be instituted where feasible without waiting for an end to conflicts elsewhere in the isthmus. Indeed, thus to proceed would provide at least some additional incentive for the reconciliation of violent conflicts.

[8]John Higley and Michael G. Burton, "The Elite Variable in Democratic Transitions and Breakdowns," *American Sociological Review*, 54: 17-32; John Higley, Richard Gunther, and Michael Burton, "Preface," and John Peeler, "Elite Settlements and Democratic Consolidation in Latin America: Colombia, Costa Rica, and Venezuela," both in John Higley, Richard Gunther, and Michael Burton, eds., *Elites and Democracy in Latin America and Southern Europe* (forthcoming 1990). See also John Peeler, *Latin American Democracies: Colombia, Costa Rica, Venezuela* (Chapel Hill: University of North Carolina Press, 1985). See also Raúl Alfonsín, "Necesidad de una convergencia política," in IIDH—CAPEL, *Agenda*, pp. 529-548.

settlements have sometimes taken the form of pacts among the leaders of critical political and economic groups. The adoption of formal political constitutions may embody important aspects of such accords and the agreed-upon political rules.

The drafting and ratification of the U.S. Constitution (1787-1789) is a familiar example of an elite settlement. Latin American examples are the 1958 National Front constitutional accord between Colombia's liberals and conservatives that eventually subdued the decade-long *violencia*, the Venezuelan three-party accord of the late 1950s, and the 1948 and 1972 Nicaraguan power-sharing arrangements between the ruling Somozas and the Conservative party. The Venezuelan and Colombian settlements broadly included many social forces and settled upon liberal democratic political rules. They have proved to be quite stable. In contrast, the Nicaraguan accords were narrowly based agreements between the dictator, an important opposition faction, and certain powerful economic interests; democratic political rules were not adopted. The Nicaraguan settlements both proved unstable.

Elite settlements may also develop slowly and much less dramatically than in previous examples. In Costa Rica an inter-elite accord among national party and economic leaders emerged during roughly a decade after the 1948 civil war. It was forged from a series of unilateral decisions by the social democratic victors in the war to accommodate other groups and from reciprocal accommodation by other factions when they won power.

There is a possibility that the series of (partly externally facilitated) agreements in Nicaragua from 1987 to 1990 may constitute the initial basis of an elite settlement. The Esquipulas Accord of August 7, 1987, led to reconciliation mechanisms and cease-fire talks that greatly curtailed the Contra war. The August 4, 1989, Central American presidential summit in Honduras brought a commitment to set forward Nicaragua's 1990 election by several months. That agreement in turn facilitated Nicaragua's August 1989 21-party accord on electoral rules and media. External observation by the U.N., O.A.S., and numerous other groups and nations boosted popular and opposition confidence in the 1990 election.[9] The Sandinista National Liberation Front (FSLN) accepted the voters' mandate and then relinquished power to the victorious United Nicaraguan Opposition (UNO) coalition following procedures elaborated in transition negotiations in February and March of 1990. The new government of Violeta Barrios de Chamorro has encouraged a policy of moderation and reconciliation and has avoided anti-Sandinista revanchism. Negotiations with the Contras by the outgoing FSLN and new UNO government resulted in the definitive end of the Contra war and the Contras' demobilization, repatriation, and political rehabilitation. Negotiations with FSLN-led unions in July 1990 brought an economic accord (*concertación económica*) that ended widespread strikes and labor unrest. A *de facto* coalition between Mrs. Chamorro's moderate UNO faction and the FSLN-in-opposition developed in late 1990 and continues to function on key National Assembly votes.[10] There remain many obstacles to a full and politically stabilizing elite settlement in Nicaragua, but such arrangements—facilitated in general by external encouragement and assistance—clearly demonstrate the capacity of once-warring parties to work together and of external actors to contribute constructively to national reconciliation in the region.

Why do such settlements or accords among rival elites occur? What motivates parties to them to acquiesce to or cooperate with enemies or rivals for power whom they

---

[9]Latin American Studies Association (LASA), *Electoral Democracy under International Pressure*, report of the Latin American Studies Association Commission to Observe the 1990 Nicaraguan Election, Pittsburgh, LASA, March 15, 1990.

[10]John A. Booth, "Toward Democracy in Nicaragua? Elites, Political Culture, and the 1990 Election," paper presented at the International Symposium on Transitions to Democracy in Europe and Latin America, Guadalajara, Jalisco, Mexico, February 21-25, 1991.

previously would not tolerate? The answer is that fundamental interests of the elites (and their constituencies) must be served. Ultimately, acquiescing parties must believe that the balance of what they stand to gain and lose (in safety, security rights and privileges, status, wealth) from agreeing with competitors is more favorable to them than what would be gained/lost by giving up their previous autonomy in conflict. Obviously, the more inclusive the prospective accord (i.e., the greater the number of parties involved) and the greater the perceived imbalances in outcomes among participants, the more complex will be the accord and the more difficult the forging of it will be.

The promotion of national reconciliation in these four Central American states at a minimum requires that political elites, civilian and military, Ladino and Indian, of parties across the ideological spectrum, develop a consensus on the political game that includes mutual tolerance under fair rules and involvement in political life by ordinary citizens. In this situation there are several important needs to be met:

* Parties to reconciliation dialogue and negotiations must be willing to give up something in exchange for peace and for freedom from repression. Everyone involved must want or need an accord, should gain something from it, and should give something up in a negotiating process—an absolutely minimal concession would be for each party to the accord to agree to tolerate and accommodate each of the other parties.

* Incumbent elites (particularly the governments and the armed forces) must accept self-restraint in exercise of power, and their opponents must accept self-restraint in opposition in exchange for security, protection of interests, and inclusion in the political game.

External Actors

The process of reaching elite settlement in situations like those in Central America is fundamentally an internal political matter to be negotiated among national political actors and not one that can or should be substantively shaped by outside actors.[11] When an external actor has sufficient power to dictate the positions of a key domestic elite in a negotiation, the risk is very great that a resultant accord will not satisfy the true preferences of the manipulated party (parties) and will therefore be unstable. Powerful outsiders, especially if they control vital resources of parties to negotiations, may be able to veto or disrupt a prospective inter-elite settlement.[12]

Outside actors such as the European Community, the United States, Costa Rica, the Contadora and Support groups, the United Nations, Organization of American States, Inter-American Court of Human Rights, regional organizations, and such non-governmental organizations as the international Catholic Church may play constructive or facilitating roles in moving national conflicts[13] toward elite settlement in several ways:

> * Interested intergovernmental organizations (the O.A.S., the U.N., and Contadora and Support Group) and governmental actors—especially the European Community but also if possible the United States and Cuba[14]—should work jointly to develop a common framework and strategy for promoting reconciliation and

---

[11]I would exclude from this generalization cases like occupied Japan and Germany or the American South during Reconstruction, in which the actual presence of an occupying power gives virtually complete control of the situation to outside actors.

[12]An example of such influence occurred when U.S. pressure on the Nicaraguan Resistance leadership in mid-1988 resulted in suspension of the talks.

[13]Nikken's "La cooperación internacional..." pp. 491-516, discusses the constitutional, legal, and historical dimensions of such international cooperation to promote democratization.

[14]If the United States or Cuba should be reluctant to cooperate in this process, the intergovernmental organizations and Europe should consider moving ahead without them.

democracy in Central America, and to develop specific proposals for carrying out the following steps.

* External actors, especially suppliers of vital economic and military aid, must then actively employ diplomacy to press parties to conflict to take part in discussions or dialogues aimed at national reconciliation.

* External actors (especially intergovernmental organizations like the O.A.S. or Contadora group) should provide diplomatic good offices to promote reconciliation dialogues among parties to national conflicts, and should offer venues for discussions abroad if not possible domestically.

* The O.A.S., U.N., and Contadora/Support Group should make available international verification teams to monitor the separation of military forces, movement of arms and troops, and compliance not only with cease-fire provisions, where applicable, but with concrete steps taken to carry out terms of inter-elite accords. The Esquipulas Accord set up an International Commission for Verification and Follow-up (CIVS) that toured Central America in late 1987 to assess compliance with the agreement. The recommendation here is to broaden the potential international verification role to include more permanent detachments in situ in the isthmus.[15]

* There should be established and funded (by the European Community and/or intergovernmental organizations in conjunction with the Central American nations and/or the United States, if willing) an International Fund for Central American Reconciliation and Democracy (IFCARD). The IFCARD should be established in addition to any other specific economic recovery programs that might develop.

* The IFCARD should establish a six-year, two-phase program of promotion of reconciliation and democratization for the five Central American nations.[16]

---

[15]The achievements of international facilitators and observers, especially the UN and OAS, in the Nicaraguan reconciliation, election, and contra demobilization were exemplary.

[16]It could, of course, be expanded to include Belize and Panama. The principal five are singled out in this discussion largely because of their tradition of regional integration and common historical roots in the

* The IFCARD should probably be set up as a multilaterally financed nongovernmental organization administered by a governing board consisting of representatives of major donor nations (as proposed here the European Community), the recipient nations, and the United Nations and Organization of American States. This board would establish an administrative directorate to 1) oversee the various programs spelled out below, and 2) oversee several proposed dependent service entities.

* The IFCARD should establish strong, conditioned economic incentives in the form of development grants to encourage national elites in conflict to move quickly to negotiate settlements among themselves. To advance these goals, the IFCARD's functions would be:

> * To provide a significant, two-year program —Phase I— of debt relief or development grants (in proportion to a country's population) from a $400 million fund,[17] to be made available to individual nations upon certification that an effective national dialogue among governments and national political forces was under way within a particular nation.[18]
>
> * To monitor Phase I compliance with provisions that facilitate the conduct and advancement of national inter-elite dialogue, such as fundamental civil liberties. IFCARD monitoring should be conducted in con-

---

Central American Federation.

[17]The total aid level recommended ($400 million for Phase I and $1,600 million for Phase II—a four year period) is somewhat arbitrary and could be increased. Regional GDP for 1988 was $31 billion (Inter-American Development Bank, *Economic and Social Progress in Latin America: 1989 Report,* Washington D.C., 1989, p. 463), so that the $2 billion total amount recommended over four years would equal roughly 1.6 percent of regional GDP, a significant incentive to potential beneficiary nations.

[18]The aid program should be sufficiently flexible so that it would enter into operation in a country when a dialogue for reconciliation begins there, irrespective of progress elsewhere in the isthmus. Costa Rica or Honduras, for example, might begin receiving funds almost immediately, whereas in the cases of Guatemala or El Salvador it could take a longer period to set up a dialogue.

junction with extant international verification and monitoring mechanisms.

* To underwrite the organizational and operational cost of inter-elite negotiations and dialogues in Phase I, and to finance the diplomatic and representational costs of reconciliation dialogue participants.[19] IFCARD support to insurgent groups should be made contingent upon verification of sharp reductions of their human rights abuses.[20]

Summary

This section has recommended that external actors, led by the European Community, establish an International Fund for Central American Reconciliation and Democracy (IFCARD), as well as employ diplomacy to encourage and promote reconciliation dialogue within Central American nations. The IFCARD would provide the incentive of economic assistance (recommended $400 million total in Phase I) to nations undertaking such dialogue.

Democratization

An elite settlement to constitute a new political regime does not per se assure democracy, for elites may or may not adopt democratic rules. The successful establishment of an electoral, constitutional regime can be judged only superficially at first. For example, in certain recent elections such as those held in Nicaragua (1984, 1990), Guatemala (1985, 1990), and El Salvador (various), the

---

[19]The IFCARD should avoid subsidizing salaries for participating groups' representatives in order to prevent the institutionalization of negotiation as a permanent career, a development which could delay accords.

[20]See below for recommendations for human rights performance for regimes.

meeting of obvious procedural standards for election quality were necessary but by no means sufficient conditions for democratization. While the absence of open and fair campaigning and a free and fairly counted election would surely signal that a procedurally democratic regime was lacking, the mere presence of such conditions might not mean real movement toward democracy. Authoritarian regimes can—without relinquishing a tight grip on power, accommodating other political forces, or accepting democratic norms—liberalize election procedures. External pressures can also temporarily coerce warring elite factions into temporary and unstable cooperation around democratic procedural norms.

For a settlement to contribute to democratization, it must be broad, establish democratic rules, accommodate public participation in politics, and respect fundamental participatory rights. The definition of democracy employed under the Esquipulas process admits a wide variety of models that might be adopted, but any scheme should probably contain at least these essential elements:

> * The accord must be broadly inclusive—i.e., involve the widest possible spectrum of significant military, economic, political, social, and major interest group elites (including not only those representing capital, but labor as well). Narrowly based inter-elite accords involving few significant groups are much more prone than broad ones to disregard the interests and participation of those not included.
>
> * Recognizing that there are a variety of political arrangements and structures that provide for democratic participation, and that the establishment of institutions, practices, and cultural norms of stable governance requires both time and much adjustment, it is, nevertheless, possible to identify certain standards and practices most likely to advance and establish democratic rule:
>
> > Formal constitutions that provide limitations upon the power of rulers and means for redress of grievances and that establish political rules that include
> > free and fair elections,
> > political pluralism,
> > and press freedom.

External actors, especially the European Community, might play some very constructive roles in encouraging democratization, in particular via the International Fund for Central American Reconciliation and Democracy:

> * In a second stage of aid (Phase II) the IFCARD would provide an additional and larger debt relief or reconstruction financing package of grants (to be allocated in proportion to each recipient country's population) from a $1.6 billion fund, to be made available to individual nations for a period of four years after Phase I upon certification, by appropriate verification bodies to be established by IFCARD's members, that an explicit inter-elite accord consistent with democratic principles set out in the Esquipulas agreement had been reached.[21]
>
> * In Phase II the IFCARD would monitor compliance with provisions that facilitate the implementation of national elite settlements, such as protection of fundamental civil liberties and compliance with provisions of new or amended constitutions, subject to appropriate verification.
>
> * Legal and technical advice on elections could be provided or underwritten by the IFCARD. One recent example of such aid is the provision by Spain, Costa Rica, the United States, and the Scandinavian nations of assistance on various technical issues in recent elections in Nicaragua, El Salvador, and Guatemala. Another example comes from the Inter-American Institute of Human Rights, which sponsors the Inter-American Center for Electoral Promotion and Assistance (CAPEL). CAPEL has for several years studied elections, election laws, and electoral procedures in Latin America and given technical advice on electoral matters. The IFCARD could underwrite CAPEL's continued assistance to Central American nations in electoral affairs at a very modest cost.
>
> * The IFCARD could facilitate legal and technical advice on formal constitutional structures via the creation of an Inter-American Center for Constitutional Research (Centro Inter-

---

[21]Given Costa Rica's advanced state of inter-elite agreement, one might reasonably propose that Costa Rica might immediately and simultaneously begin to receive aid under Phase I, and that Phase II could run coterminously with Phase I there.

Americano de Investigación Constitucional [CIAIC]). The CIAIC would take advantage of similarities in Latin American legal traditions and the common practice in the region of borrowing constitutional features. The IFCARD should finance and establish at CIAIC a data bank on constitutional norms and a technical staff of legal experts (primarily Central Americans) to advise constituent assemblies, legislatures, and national reconciliation dialogues on specific constitutional matters.

* The IFCARD should avoid direct subsidization of political parties in Central America (including the underwriting of election campaign costs) because such aid would have a high probability of encouraging external dependencies rather than developing integral, autonomous, solidly grounded parties in touch with their local constituents.

* European political parties (such as the Christian Democrats, Social Democrats, Liberals) should continue to provide financial assistance and training to their ideological brethren in Central America in order to strengthen them and increase their vitality, viability, and adherence to democratic norms and practices.

* The IFCARD should establish and finance programs of technical assistance and advice to Central American police forces and courts to improve due process of law in the handling, tracking, and case disposition of persons arrested by the security forces.

Because certain direct U.S. bilateral aid programs (e.g., the Contra war, aid to political parties in the 1990 Nicaraguan election, military assistance to Honduras and El Salvador) have aroused such controversy, they suggest certain norms that all donors of external assistance might wish to follow:

* There should be a ten-year moratorium on direct, governmental bilateral aid to incumbent or opposition political parties or groups in Central America. During this moratorium, all governmental aid to domestic political actors in Central America should be channelled through multilateral programs like the IFCARD.

* All other bilateral aid programs could be structured and conditioned to encourage sharp improvements in human rights performance and encourage civilian rule. Good examples of this are the reported 1983 linking by the United States of the continuance of U.S. military aid to El Salvador to a curtailment of death squad

killings and the 1990 linkage of U.S. military assistance to improved human rights performance. In this regard, future military assistance to Honduras, Guatemala, and El Salvador from whatever source should be made contingent upon two principal conditions:

> 1) The military must remain in its barracks (i.e., discharge its security functions without intervening in civilian politics).
>
> 2) The security forces (military and police) should curtail human rights abuses (measured in terms of extrajudicial political killings and disappearances) by at least 50 percent below the previous year's level in each of five successive years.[22] Certification of compliance should be jointly made by the Interamerican Institute of Human Rights and other extant verification agencies.

Stabilization of a Democratic Regime

In addition to adopting democratic rules and establishing an inclusive political game, it is necessary to promote the stabilization or survival of democratic practice. While an elite settlement is mainly an agreement among elites, democratic stabilization involves the development of structural supports for the regime and democratic practice. A strong cultural commitment of both elites and populace to democratic norms must be developed and reinforced. It is generally believed that such commitment will grow with time, with increased political participation and civic education, and as the operation of the system con-

[22]This provision could, if implemented, reduce extrajudicial killings by 97 percent in a span of five years. To those who argue that the security forces are not responsible for all such abuses, one should note that such a policy would encourage security forces to curtail the human rights abuses of other actors as well. It could also possibly reduce the motivation of insurgent groups to engage in acts of terrorism.

tinues to serve the interests of parties to the agreement.[23] Regimes must also be flexible enough to accommodate significant new social forces as they develop. The failure to accommodate significant new forces runs the risk of breakdown, as in the case of Lebanon or of Chile in the 1970s. It must be emphasized that the stabilization of democratic regimes in Central America is a process that could require decades, especially in the face of countervailing cultural traditions among elites and general publics of the region. Several means might help reinforce elite and mass democratic culture and practice over the longer run:

> * Central American governments should consider deepening and broadening democratic practice by creating new venues for popular participation in policy-making and implementation. For example, Costa Rica has had extensive and successful experience with the promotion by government of community self-help programs (in health, housing, and infrastructure development) in rural areas and among the urban poor, which reinforce democratic values by increasing participation at the community level. Nicaragua under the FSLN government implemented popular and interest-group consultation systems in different policy arenas that actually permitted citizens and interest groups to shape the formulation and implementation of agrarian policy. Nicaragua also made extensive and successful use of citizen participation in health and sanitation matters. Such experiments should be implemented widely both for their intrinsic developmental worth and for their utility as laboratories in participation and democratic values.
>
> * Actors already participating in the systems must accommodate within the system new sociopolitical forces that may emerge after the elite settlement in order to prevent the development of discontented rivals for power. In successfully functioning democratic regimes there is usually a middle ground between institu-

---

[23]Indeed, Mitchell A. Seligson and John A. Booth ("Political Culture and Democratization: Alternate Paths in Nicaragua and Costa Rica," paper presented at the meeting of the American Political Science Association, San Francisco, CA, September 1990) report that as early as August 1989, urban Nicaraguans manifested a high degree of support for civil liberties—comparable to that in Costa Rica. They speculate that such public norms could help stabilize democracy in Nicaragua.

tions that are so flexible that they themselves destabilize by rapidly changing rules and expectations, and institutions not flexible enough to adjust to important social changes. In the writing of constitutions, provisions should be made for adjustments in political structure.

* Elites that are parties to democratic settlement agreements should monitor and consider adjustments to their informal and formal arrangements through periodic "encounters" or renewed dialogues.

* The maintenance of good human rights climates that provide extensive organizational and press freedom will help assure that new social forces are recognized and their needs known. Central American governments should establish agencies or ombudsmen to promote and monitor their own human rights performance. Central American nations should also permit international human rights groups to operate freely in their countries.

* One of the most difficult problems for democratic stabilization will come from military institutions, which have traditions of intervention in politics and considerable autonomy from civilian government.[24] What is needed is the development of a military ethos of loyalty to democratic norms and subordination to civilian control. This might be promoted in Central American armies in three ways:

> 1) Civilian-dominated political institutions must not threaten military corporate self-interest by sudden reductions in military budgets.[25]
>
> 2) Militaries should explicitly educate their officer trainees to respect democracy, human rights, and constitutional civilian rule.

---

[24]Military professionalization in Latin America has often increased, not reduced, armies' penchants for intervention in politics, so more training in military skills seems unlikely to be helpful.

[25]The dramatic reduction in military force and budget in Nicaragua in 1990-1991 represents a good example of what may be accomplished in this regard.

3) In the middle run, military violators of human rights and constitutional norms should be sanctioned.[26]

External actors might be able to play a significant and constructive role in the stabilization of democratic regimes through diplomatic exhortation, the use of technical assistance, and through the provision of conditioned aid:

* Diplomatic pressure by the European Community, the United States, and other nations should continue to insist on the importance of the continuation of civilian, constitutional government in Central America.

* The IFCARD could be funded beyond its initial six-year life span (encompassing Phases I and II) in order to continue the encouragement and facilitation of ongoing reconciliation dialogues within nations.

* International party organizations, the IFCARD, and other multilateral actors should continue advice and technical assistance (training programs in political organization) to enhance the participatory skills and democratic commitment of Central American parties, interest groups, and unions.

* The IFCARD and other external actors should encourage, facilitate, sponsor, and help finance periodic encounters where national elites can discuss national problems and consider necessary adjustments to settlements and formal institutions.

* International aid programs aimed at popular economic and infrastructure development should build in, wherever possible, self-help and citizen participation features.

* All suppliers of military assistance to Central America must consistently condition aid on (a) compliance with stringent human

---

[26]Short-run campaigns to punish human rights abusers in the Guatemalan, Salvadoran, or Honduran armed forces, while just, might threaten the elite settlement itself by arousing military hostility. Such sanctions must be implemented very carefully, very gradually, and probably with the cooperation of the armed forces. Although morally repugnant, an agreement not to punish past human rights abuses may be the price civilian elites must pay Central American militaries for agreements to permit civilian rule and curtail future human rights abuses.

rights provisions and (b) continued military deference to constitutional civilian rule.

Conclusion

Democracy in Central America requires an end to wars in Guatemala and El Salvador. Assuming, however, that the fighting will stop, reconciliation among key elites is needed. Even in Honduras where there is no war, reconciliation of elites is key to the stabilization of democracy. Considerable progress has been made in Nicaragua, but the situation in the country still remains volatile and the road to democratic stabilization remains long.[27] For democracy to emerge, the settlement among elites must be broad rather than narrow and must result in democratic rules.

One picture that emerges from the foregoing discussion is the enormity of the requisites for democratization and the many obstacles in democracy's path in Central America. However, there are concrete conditions and actions by domestic and external actors that can improve the odds for democracy. The discussion of internal steps toward democracy is not very specific because the actors, problems, and details of specific arrangements must vary from nation to nation and must be hammered out among local actors rather than prescribed from outside.

Some of the above recommendations for external actors, however, are fairly specific. The call for the creation of an International Fund for Central American Reconciliation and Democratization sets out clear and practical incentives and promotes technical assistance for reconciliation, human rights, and democratic practice. Such steps appear easily within the capacity of important international

---

[27]See Booth, "Toward Democracy in Nicaragua?" for further discussion. What may prove to be a particularly perturbing event in the process was the assassination in Managua in February 1991 of former contra leader Enrique Bermúdez and the remobilization of contra elements (the "re-contras).

actors on the Central America scene. Many of the recommendations for external actors are designed to enhance the will of local actors to work toward democratization. It should be emphasized that, even if the proposal to establish the IFCARD proves too ambitious or politically infeasible, many of its specific provisions could be implemented through already extant multilateral entities such as the O.A.S.

It is possible that elite settlements might emerge gradually (over a decade or more) in Central America even without formal inter-elite pacts. However, it seems much more likely that failure to progress toward elite reconciliation and settlement will assure that new democracies will not be consolidated in Central America in the foreseeable future.

RETHINKING SPHERES OF INFLUENCE: THE UNITED STATES, WESTERN EUROPE, AND CENTRAL AMERICA

Mark Falcoff

American Enterprise Institute

Whatever may now happen in the Soviet Union, one of the undeniable outcomes of the Gorbachev presidency is bound to be an end to the Cold War in what used to be called the Third World. To be sure, in such countries there will still be forces that appeal to either Washington or Moscow for support; which embrace what they regard as the ideologies of one or the other superpower; and which seek to improve their own situation by leveraging the support of outsiders. Nonetheless, their ability to inflate local conflicts into world-wide confrontations will be much diminished, particularly if they do not possess a vital national resource like oil.

Central America happens to be one of those regions. Though its political life will continue to be somewhat conflictive, its strategic relevance will be greatly reduced. This is both good news and bad news for the Central Americans. Their leverage vis-à-vis the great powers will diminish considerably; on the other hand, they can look forward to reduced inputs of arms and ideology, as well as an enhanced potential for cooperative assistance, particularly on the part of the developed democracies of the United States and Western Europe.

The United States and Central America

While the United States has been the principal outside influence in the region for more than a century, the dramatic events of the last decade and a half have tended to exaggerate Central America's importance both economically and strategically. To be sure, in the nineteenth century it was the United States' only important area of foreign policy concern, and as late as 1914 it accounted (together with Mexico and Cuba) for 90 percent of its overseas investment. Nonetheless, since the Second World War, U.S. economic interests have been concentrated in Western Europe, Canada, Asia, and other parts of Latin America; the Central American share has dropped drastically both in absolute and relative terms.

In addition, the U.S. decision to withdraw from Panama, embodied by the Carter-Torrijos treaties (1978), has undercut the strategic importance of the region. At one time the mere existence of the Canal and the Zone under U.S. control tended to render intolerable any unusual or unfriendly developments in any of the Central American republics. Indeed, even before the Canal was built, the United States viewed the potential for a trans-isthmian route as a strategic *causus belli*—witness the decision to undercut the regime of José Santos Zelaya (1893-1910) in Nicaragua, which was thought to be contemplating granting access to a rival seapower. Certainly the Canal itself was frequently invoked by U.S. policymakers to justify concern over political developments in the individual Central American republics; it was, for example, one of the reasons why the United States became involved in the coup that toppled the Arbenz regime in Guatemala in 1954.[1]

---

[1]An internal State Department memorandum in May 1954 explained to the secretary that Moscow had "chose[n] Guatemala as a testing ground" because, among other reasons, of its proximity to the Panama Canal. For this reason, it added, domination of any Central American Republic "would give Russia an important military gain." *Foreign Relations of the United States 1952-54: V: The American Republics* (Washington:

If the Central Americans themselves tended to overrate their importance to the United States in recent years, this was surely not their fault: both the Carter and Reagan Administrations regarded Nicaragua and El Salvador as major theaters of foreign policy concern, and both countries have occupied far more space in the American press (and more debate time in the U.S. Congress) than their size or geopolitical importance would seem to suggest. Indeed, for some years El Salvador was the fifth or sixth largest country in the world—if one were to judge these things solely by the size of the annual U.S. appropriation for overseas assistance.

Evidently, Carter and Reagan approached the region differently: Carter saw it as a laboratory for his human rights policies and the willingness of the United States to accept and work with forces for political change; Reagan tended to view it through the prism of traditional Cold War geopolitics. Nonetheless, the differences between the two policies have been somewhat exaggerated. For both were operating from the traditional security presumption—merely pursuing it with different ("soft" versus "hard") instruments. Moreover, both Carter and Reagan policies evolved over time; towards the end of his presidency Carter was more sympathetic to military instruments, and Reagan very early on discovered that anti-Communism without a commitment to democratization and human rights held out little prospect of success, both in Central America and at home.

However one may feel about either Carter or Reagan policies, they cannot be understood outside the context of the Cold War and the U.S.-Soviet rivalry. Surely the United States did not involve itself in Nicaraguan politics because it was worried about the threat of nationalization of American property, or in El Salvador because it had some vested interest in the survival of that country's traditional business and military classes. Of course, both

---

GPO, 1983), pp. 1,108-09.

administrations may have been wrong in their perception of the Soviet (and Cuban) threat to the region—but their policies were based on genuine conviction, not the crass pursuit of economic gain. Far from it: Salvador was a net loss for the U.S. exchequer.

The European Perspective

Evidently, Central America has not been a major theater of concern for most Western European countries, although Spain, Germany, Britain, and France have each in their own way sustained a quiet if rather low-level interest in the area for many decades. The degree of involvement rose considerably during the 1980s, particularly with regard to the Nordic countries, a departure which can probably be explained by the acute distaste of these countries (particularly Sweden, but also Norway) for the Reagan Administration and all its works. Indeed, from some points of view the accelerated European interest in the last decade could be studied as a branch of U.S.-European relations, with a hidden cultural dimension far stronger than political or economic rivalries.

In some ways the U.S.-European disagreement over Central America has been part of a differing approach to Third World issues generally. The Europeans tended to see conflict as an extension of situations of structural injustice, and to downplay or deny altogether the role of deliberate intervention by outsiders (in this case, the Soviets or Cubans); the Americans were willing to concede the motivating force of hunger, unemployment, or denial of basic human rights, but refused to build their entire policy around that fact. Both sides did in fact contribute very significantly to aid levels in the region in the '80s, though U.S. aid tended to be centered in El Salvador (and to some extent Honduras), while the privileged recipients for

European aid were Nicaragua (and to some extent Costa Rica).[2]

The end of the Cold War now offers for the first time the opportunity for a depoliticized approach to the area by both trans-Atlantic communities. Whether such cooperation does in fact occur will depend largely, however, on the degree of interest that each can bring to the area at a time when both are beset by new demands for resources. At any rate, there is no deep-seated ideological or political reason why the two cannot work together cooperatively, and there is no government in Central America that would not welcome the participation of both.

The U.S. in Central America: Influence Flowing in Both Directions

Though Central America has been declining in importance to the United States over many years, the reverse is hardly true. Indeed, never has the region been closer to the North American continent. Jet air travel, FAX, and cable television has brought the United States into Central America's metaphoric living room. English is more widely spoken than ever before, and all of the more affluent areas of Central American capitals are trying to resemble parts of Miami or Coral Gables both physically and in terms of consumer trends. (Indeed, young people dress as much like their American counterparts as their finances permit.) Without even trying the United States is exercising

---

[2]The domestic critics of the Reagan Administration in the United States—in this case, Democrats in Congress—tended to share the European perspective, at least rhetorically. But if they really believed that the problem in Central America was (to quote Senator Gary Hart) "not communism but poverty," they showed no particular interest in alleviating poverty to the extent of championing new and extensive aid policies. Rather their approach was purely negative—either to deny the administration funds for El Salvador, or support in its paramilitary campaign against the Sandinista government in Nicaragua.

a strong cultural influence that seriously endangers indigenous Central American identity.

At the same time, several million Central Americans are now resident in the United States, legally or illegally, and their financial remissions are vital to the survival of their families and the solvency of the countries from which they have come.[3] There is considerable movement back and forth; many American cities (notably Miami, Los Angeles, and Washington, D.C.) now have television and radio programs, groceries, churches, and other services especially designed for Central American migrants. Although at some future date the U.S. political community may attempt to stem the flow by tightening up the rules governing entry of undocumented (or semi-documented) nationals, as the system is presently constituted one can expect that over time some American cities—particularly Los Angeles—will simply become Central American suburbs in the same way that Marseilles has become a North African city.

It is not clear how this Central American presence in the United States will come to affect U.S. policy towards the parent countries. Though nearly one million Salvadorans resident in the United States is a great deal for El Salvador, it is less so for the United States. Moreover, most immigrants are at a point in their history as a community where larger political agendas are premature. Meanwhile, unlike North Africa for the French, Central America for the United States is not a potential economic asset (it has neither oil nor natural gas nor any other strategic commodity) in significant amounts. Quite the contrary: in recent years all five Republics (as well as Panama) have asserted strong claims for financial assistance, and in many cases have received it.

---

[3]In the case of El Salvador, it is estimated that remissions from migrants to the United States amounts to at least $1 billion, which is several times the current U. S. government aid appropriation.

Is Europe an Alternative?

The answer is both yes and no. Evidently, it is an alternative to the extent that it is the only other part of the developed world that has shown any serious interest in the region, and possesses the resources to make a meaningful contribution. At the same time, most of the elites of Central America (but particularly in Guatemala and Costa Rica) would wish to diversify their dependence on outside sources of aid and trade and would consider Europe much the most desirable alternative.

It is also true that strictly at the level of elites, the political culture of Western Europe is much more attractive than that of the United States. The existence of large, well-organized Christian Democratic parties in Italy and Germany; the successful socialist parties (and governments) of Spain, France, and Portugal; the evident European preference for a "middle way" between public and private sectors; even the fact that most of Western Europe is simply a nicer place to travel and spend time than Miami, Los Angeles, or even Washington, D.C. all conspire to attract Central American politicians, clergymen, and intellectuals. Certainly there are many more genuine interlocutors in Western Europe for this particular group of Central Americans.

On the other hand, it is doubtful that Europe could or will replace the United States as the principal outside source of foreign assistance or influence. It is not merely a question of geographical fatalism: Europe has too many other agendas on its plate, particularly the new democracies of Czechoslovakia, Hungary, and Poland, combined with the demands of the less developed members of the Community (Portugal and Greece).

What makes the U.S.-European relationship particularly interesting at this time, however, is that in the present context a more balanced approach to Central America is possible. European interest in the region is growing, while American interest is moderating or declining. This context offers the European Community an opportunity to influence events to a much greater degree than would have been true in decades past. Moreover, the United States would probably welcome a strong European involvement as a way of relieving it of sole responsibility for a region having shown itself capable of absorbing as much money as the U.S. Congress was willing to appropriate—that, and more.

What is perhaps crucial is the fact that for the first time in many years there are no conflicting U.S.-European agendas for the region. All five republics (as well as Panama) are ruled by elected governments, and there is no significant external (that is, extra-hemispheric) involvement to provoke U.S. concern. It is true that the Cubans continue to connive at revolution in El Salvador, and presumably have some influence over the violent left in other countries. On the other hand, deprived of heavy subsidies from what used to be called the Soviet bloc, Castro is not likely to constitute a serious threat to his neighbors for the foreseeable future.

How Would the Division of Labor Work?

The European-American agenda for Central America has yet to be worked out, and in any event would have to include adequate participation by the Central American governments themselves. Indeed, what is probably needed now are triangular discussions in a neutral venue (say, Spain or Jamaica). It may well be that there will be no prearranged division of labor, but a more systematic approach would have many advantages.

Certainly it is clear that major changes in aid policy are on the way, at least for the United States. In the past, the bulk of Washington's money has gone for balance-of-payments assistance, followed by military aid. Balance-of-payments assistance can hardly continue, at least at the levels of the recent past, since budgetary stringencies, new obligations elsewhere in the world, and a declining geopolitical interest can hardly encourage the U.S. Congress to take on what is virtually an open-ended commitment for all five countries.

A more productive approach for the United States would be to adopt the European practice of individual project assistance. This has always been an aspect of American aid policy, but might now be more profitably expanded with the Europeans considering taking over some of the balance-of-payments assistance that the United States offered in the past. Such assistance would necessarily carry with it a greater degree of political neutrality; Central American governments would feel less conditioned by it, and Europeans would also have fewer inhibitions about imposing strict compliance with human rights and other criteria.

Roles might also be profitably reversed in the area of military aid. This has always been a controversial item in the United States, and in the present context no administration will wish to spend much domestic political capital obtaining it. As things stand now, the United States has been steadily reducing its military assistance to El Salvador and has suspended it with Guatemala. Given the changed geopolitical situation and the continued egregious human rights violations in both countries, it is not unthinkable that military relations between the two countries and the United States might well end before the middle of the 1990s. Of course, the Europeans might have no particular interest in replacing the United States as a source of military aid, in which case either the Central Americans would have to do without external sources of arms and training or resort to extremely nontraditional providers.[4]

In sum, what we can anticipate is less American involvement, and (relatively) more European involvement; less American balance-of-payments assistance and more project assistance; less American military aid (or perhaps

---

[4]It is by no means unthinkable that some Western European countries might replace the United States in providing military and police assistance; during the Carter Administration, for example, Guatemala was able to obtain both from Italy and Spain.

none at all). If the Europeans do not step in to replace some of these categories, then the entire range of international aid will drop qualitatively as well as quantitatively. Certainly Central America will not be in much of a position to "play off" Europe and the United States, but it is possible that a nonconfrontational and cooperative mutual effort, however diminished in scale, is in the works for the rest of the century and beyond.

Two Caveats: Cuba and Panama

U.S. policy towards Central America cannot be fully disentangled from its posture towards Cuba and Panama, since both countries in quite different ways have a strong impact on the region. In the case of Panama, the United States is scheduled to withdraw its troops and bases from the Zone in the year 2000 and return the territory to the Republic. At that point, Panama will cease to have a common "border" with the United States, or a resident U.S. community whose safety requires Washington to be concerned with the quality of its local political life. Presumably Panama will continue to be stable without the presence of an American garrison, but even if it is not, Washington is not likely to step in to restore authority. If it were merely a matter of the Canal, that is not a problem: it is not likely to be closed, and as Vice-President Ricardo Arias Calderón has insisted, Panama's national police are fully capable of maintaining the normal order and security the facility requires. For Central America, the disappearance of Panama as a major geostrategic factor for the United States is bound to devalue the importance of their own countries. On the other hand, it will also incline the United States far less towards intervention in the internal affairs of the five republics.

Geostrategic changes have also affected the role of Cuba in the region. While Castro is no longer in a position to assert a major military or ideological influence in the region, he is still capable of assisting some insurgent elements with arms and training. It may be, of course, that the United States would not regard this as a serious problem for itself (particularly since the Soviet-Cuban connection is far less relevant and threatening than in the past), but most of the Central American governments probably would not view the matter quite so calmly. On the other hand, probably no guerrilla movement in Central America is anywhere near assuming power, and if a peace settlement is reached in El Salvador, the entire guerrilla mystique will suffer a serious decline in appeal.

For the United States, one of the larger questions of the 1990s is what Cuba will represent—if anything—in the absence of a credible Soviet threat. It is certainly not an important country in and of itself, and according to the economic indicators, it is becoming less so. On the other hand, the United States is under no particular obligation to normalize relations with a country whose entire organizing principle of existence is hatred of the United States. The Europeans obviously would prefer to see Cuba integrated as a "normal" country in the region, but as long as Castro himself is at the helm, this seems unlikely. (The last thing in the world Castro wants is for Cuba to be a "normal" country.) Nonetheless, the Cuban issue is bound to be one of the last really contentious issues between the United States and Europe—and perhaps also, eventually, between the United States and the Central Americans.

Concluding Remarks

It is easy to plot war and conflict; nothing is more difficult than to imagine peace and normality. The Central American states have been pawns in the Cold War for so long that it may take some time for outsiders to decide upon the intrinsic value of these countries and the proper role of outsiders toward them. At a minimum, however, the Central American republics are bound to profit from the new order of things—at least to the extent that the presence of the United States is less asphyxiating, the interest of the Western Europeans more profound, and the distorting priorities of geopolitics dispensed with once and for all. Where this will leave the Central American states remains to be seen, but for the first time in many decades they will have the opportunity to build on the basis of their own priorities, rather than responding to those of someone else.

As for Western Europe, Central America will be its great test to see whether it is capable of forging a constructive relationship with an area in which it has little or no traditional economic interest, and for which there is no important constituency at home. It will also test the role of the European Community, to establish whether, once and for all, this supra-national agency can play a recognizable international role. Central America is one area where the United States would gladly share the obligations and burdens of assistance; there is plenty to do, and every new hand will be welcome.

UNITED STATES STRATEGY AFTER THE COLD WAR: CENTRAL AMERICAN POLICY

Ambler H. Moss, Jr.

University of Miami

Despite the unresolved internal problems in the Soviet Union today, historians will probably agree that the Cold War really ended around 1989. Even if an authoritarian regime were to replace the Gorbachev opening, relations between East and West would not be as before. Germany is united; the Warsaw Pact is dead. The Soviet economy is unable to sustain prolonged superpower status.

In the present circumstance, the assumptions that have governed the behavior of nations for more than 40 years must necessarily change. At the same time, no replacement paradigm has been found, other than that which is vaguely called multipolarity. President George Bush's reference to a "new world order" is more a hope for the future than a specific formula.

For a decade, most of United States' policy toward Latin America consisted of a Central American policy deeply rooted in Cold War, East-West thinking. Even foreign assistance was ruled largely by the political and ideological agenda.

For more than a century before the Cold War even began, however, Latin America was considered by the United States to be a region of strategic importance. It was, in fact, the first such area of the world to be so identified by the young republic, in the administration of James Monroe. By the mid-nineteenth century, a permanent interest in the isthmus of Panama had been clearly identified.

There is ample reason to argue that, for the United States, Latin America remains strategically important today.

To think and act otherwise could prove to be dangerously shortsighted. We must recognize that since World War II, U.S. strategic interest has been equated almost exclusively with a latter-day variant of the Monroe Doctrine, i.e., keeping Soviet hands off the Western Hemisphere. Now, with the evident internal focus of the Soviet Union and what looks like detente for the foreseeable future, what strategic interests remain? Should we define strategic interests in a different way?

Events in the Middle East beginning early August 1990 won consensus on a second point—the era of bipolarity as the world order—but this does not mean the dawn of permanent peace and harmony. Even if the ultimate threat of a nuclear war by the superpowers has receded, there may be an abundance of threats to United States interests, perhaps vital interests in some cases, from points around the globe. Iraq, for example, never posed a threat against our national territory or our sea lanes, but President Bush stated that its actions threatened "our way of life."

In Latin America, specific United States national security objectives of the present and of the immediate future may well be defined more by the development of events within the region than by the traditional fear of incursions by extra-hemispheric powers. In both cases, however, political, economic, and defense strategies will aim at creating or enhancing a positive orientation of Latin American countries toward the United States as well as reinforcing stable conditions within countries. It may be a wise investment. The Good Neighbor Policy of President Franklin D. Roosevelt was developed long before most Americans understood that this country would soon be at war with Germany and Japan. The immediate alignment of almost all of Latin America with the United States at the war's outset was a benefit that came from that policy.

Today, we still are challenged to understand the difference between stability and the needs of security. The *National Security Strategy of the United States* (White House, March, 1990) recognized that the security of this country "is inextricably linked to the hemisphere's collective security, social peace, and economic progress" (p. 12). That document celebrates the resurgence of democracy in the Americas and speaks of the need for a "mature partnership." What is missing, however, is a sense of urgency to the issues at hand. Social peace and economic progress may not follow automatically from the swing of the pendulum in democracy's direction.

There is a complex set of tough issues on the agenda with all of Latin America, not just Central America. Every one of them bears upon the protection of U.S. strategic interests. Successful negotiation on an equitable basis with Latin American countries, in pursuit of common objectives, is the task of the 1990s. Briefly listed, the issues are:

> * External debt as a continuing obstacle to development. The debt overhang remains as a major impediment to most countries' economic development strategies, however enlightened these may be.
>
> * Investment; the search for sources of capital for development; competition for capital is intense, and Latin America has been losing capital for more than a decade.
>
> * Trade and the increase of markets for Latin America and the U.S.; this is an area in which great hope is placed but where considerable obstacles remain.
>
> * Drugs; appropriate ways to shut down illegal trafficking; there are clear divergences between the U.S. and Latin American perspectives.
>
> * Democracy and its consolidation; the fragility of democratic institutions and structures should be of high concern, especially since democracy might be identified with poor economic performance in the near future.
>
> * Environmental issues, which no longer can be considered purely questions of national sovereignty, but issues of global scale.

The importance of all of these issues tends to vary according to the distance of any given country from the United States. All of them loom large with respect to Mexico, for example, as does the issue of immigration. Still important, although somewhat to a lesser extent, immigration is an important issue with respect to Central America. Apart from those rather special cases, the debate will be whether this agenda can command enough attention in Washington to be given any appreciable importance by policymakers. Conversely, we must ask whether U.S. policy is headed for a period of neglect, interrupted only by specific irritations such as one or another country's failed performance under Washington's particular approach to the war on drugs or a worsening of the war in El Salvador.

On June 27, 1990, proper recognition was given to these issues in a speech by President George Bush at the White House in which he called for a new initiative in the Hemisphere, focusing upon trade, investment, and debt as the "three pillars" of the proposal. This "Bush Initiative", properly known as the "Enterprise for the Americas Initiative" (EAI) does not call for more than a very modest amount of official investment aid. It did, for the first time, offer the possibility of reducing or eliminating debt representing U.S. aid, which had been given on concessional term. Such debt reduction is significant for some Central American and Caribbean countries and amounts to $7 billion.

Since its announcement, few details have been filled in to complete the concept of the new initiative. It is important, nonetheless, as a starting point for Latin American countries to use as an agenda with the United States. It was the centerpiece of discussions at meetings of the Latin American Economic System (SELA) and the Rio Group in late 1990. The initiative has clearly captured Latin America's attention.

The principal risk of the Bush Initiative does not lie in conceptual weakness but in the doubt that either Washington or Latin America will give sufficient urgency to its completion and implementation. It is not, as were the Marshall Plan and the Alliance for Progress, portrayed as an emergency plan designed to "jump-start" ailing economies with an infusion of capital. Although it faithfully reflects consensus economics—privatization, market-governed systems, and free trade and investment, it is not clear that early results can be expected from its adoption. Fragile political and social systems may not endure. It is, in many ways, a race against the clock.

Since the Enterprise for the Americas Initiative was announced, other important events have taken place. Several heads of state meetings among Central American Presidents (all of whom are different now from the signers of "Esquipulas II"), from the Antigua meeting in June to the Puntarenas meeting in December 1990, have emphasized economic integration and the building of market economies.

Among other things, the Puntarenas meeting ratified support for a new multilateral effort begun at a meeting in Washington on November 20, 1990, known as the Partnership for Development and Democracy in Central America (PDD). The PDD is clearly an outreach to the 24 countries of the OECD to join forces in supporting the economic progress which will be necessary if democratization is to be allowed to advance.

The PDD reflects an underlying fact of U.S. politics that it will be increasingly difficult to commit resources to Central America, important as that region is to U.S. policy.

The question therefore remains: can Washington, given its other priorities today and in the absence of the traditional setting of the Cold War, recognize sufficient importance in the North-South issues of our hemisphere to pursue a dynamic agenda? Let us first examine the main features of the U.S. approach to Latin America for the past 45 years.

The Post–World War II Setting

Although the Cold War was the basic framework for U.S. policy in the region since World War II, (and even that fact not always explicitly acknowledged by some administrations), there were nonetheless numerous inconsistencies and discontinuities in that policy.

Confusion, both on the sending and receiving ends of policy, often arose from the three distinct ways that different political actors in the United States have tended to see Latin America: as a strategic battleground in the East-West struggle, as an area characterized by acute but typical North-South economic issues, and (mainly for the political left) as an area whose main problems are caused by a repressive military and greedy oligarchy. An underlying factor has been the tendency of Washington to look upon the exercise of hegemony in Latin America as the normal state of affairs, the maintenance of which is dependent only upon the assertion of Washington's political will.

In the aftermath of World War II, Washington essentially got what it wanted from Latin America in the form of the Charter of the Organization of American States and the Rio Treaty. From the beginning, however, these institutions were deficient in that they did not respond to Latin America's main concern, which was economic relations and development. In 1953, Dr. Milton Eisenhower recommended to the president that economic cooperation was the key to better relations with Latin America. The anti-communist emphasis of the O.A.S. Foreign Ministers meeting in Caracas in 1954 followed by the U.S. intervention to oust the Arbenz regime in Guatemala was more typical of the direction of U.S. policy of that decade, however.

Two rude shocks at the end of the 1950's told Washington that all was not well in its relations with the hemisphere. During Vice President Richard M. Nixon's trip to Latin America in 1958, he was attacked and nearly killed by a mob in Caracas. In January 1959, Castro's revolution took over Cuba; an anti-United States policy soon became its dominant feature. The response from the United States was the hugely ambitious Alliance for Progress, as well as a very active diplomatic and military strategy designed to contain communist expansion in the Western Hemisphere. Formally launched in August 1961, the Alliance was to continue for most of the decade. The Alliance promised the transfer of $20 billion from the United States to Latin America in ten years, half to come from official aid programs of the U.S. Government and the international financial institutions.

The Alliance for Progress produced some notable economic growth and also some economic and social dislocations. It certainly failed to produce democracy as a way of life in Latin America. By the 1970s, most of Latin America was in the hands of dictators, all repressive to varying degrees. Incidentally, despite the help they received from the United States for security reasons, they were not grateful. General Augusto Pinochet brought his terror to the streets of Washington in 1976 with the assassination of former Chilean ambassador Orlando Letelier and the U.S. citizen who accompanied him. By the end of the Ford Administration, the Congress had reacted by imposing human rights standards as a condition of foreign aid and required annual country reports to be compiled by the Department of State. Emphasis on human rights became one of the salient features of the Carter Administration.

The guerrilla war in El Salvador and the Nicaraguan revolution set the stage for attention by the Reagan Administration to Central America practically to the exclusion or issues involving the rest of Latin America. As President Ronald Reagan put it to a joint session of Congress in April 1983:

> The national security of all of the Americas is at stake in Central America. If we cannot defend ourselves there, we cannot expect to prevail elsewhere. Our credibility would collapse, our alliances would crumble, and the safety of our homeland put in jeopardy.

Three years later, in a televised address on March 19, 1986, he said:

> Using Nicaragua as a base, the Soviets and Cubans can become the dominant power in the crucial corridor between North and South America. Established there, they will be in a position to threaten the Panama Canal, interdict our vital Caribbean sea lanes, and, ultimately, move against Mexico. Should that happen, desperate Latin peoples by the millions would begin fleeing north into the cities of the southern United States or to wherever some hope of freedom remained.

This apocalyptic vision was not shared in its entirety even within the administration, much less by a Congress, which often denied it the means to implement the Contra war legally, and little at all by Latin America. Public opinion polls in this country were never favorable either to the Contra policy or to aid to the Salvadoran army.

By 1990, however, a great deal had changed. The Central American Peace Accord, Esquipulas II, signed August 7, 1987, came to replace United States initiatives, especially the Contra policy, by 1988. The bipartisan accords in the Congress on Contra aid in early 1989 virtually nullified the Contra policy, but the Soviets had also given indications by then that they had stopped military aid shipments to the Sandinistas. The Nicaraguan elections of February 1990 replaced the Sandinista government in that country s first-ever democratic, peaceful transition of power. Meanwhile, Cuba had declined economically, was no longer in a position to threaten any Latin American country and was like a museum of the former communist world.

While Washington's gaze was fixed on Central America for so many years, however, events of great importance were happening elsewhere in Latin America. Except for Cuba, the dictatorships are gone; participatory democracy is the prevailing norm in most of the region. Market economics has become the prevailing standard; central direction of economics and state-owned enterprise have become discredited. Mexico has sought a free-trade agreement with the United States. The countries of the

Southern Cone are working seriously toward an economic integration plan. Yet all of these positive developments exist precariously within a fragile framework, and the continuation of positive trends is far from certain.

Even if the attention of the United States were to be diverted from Latin America to other parts of the world in this age of change, Latin America may ultimately become an area of greater interest than it is today to the new economic superpowers, Europe and Japan, and possibly to the Soviet economy. Japan's financial and investment interests in Latin America are not far behind those of the United States even today. The "Bush Initiative" may be based in part on the notion that the United States may need Latin America in the future if part of the new economic order of the world is to involve the formation of regional trading blocs. In other words, the United States may need a trading bloc to call its own.

Lessons of Iraq

It is not too early to derive a few tentative conclusions from the Persian Gulf war that relate to our thinking about future Latin American policy.

First, it is clear that in regional conflicts of the future, even an unprecedented level of cooperation between the United States, the U.S.S.R., and a clear majority in the United Nations, will not necessarily be able to force a favorable outcome, at least early during the problem.

Second, there should be no doubters left on the question of the globalization of the world economy and the impact of events everywhere throughout all the financial centers of the world. Among the major nations, autarky is dead.

Third, international mechanisms are unable to control events of vital interest to most of the world's nations. The United Nations has emerged from the Iraqi crisis as being perhaps the best forum to develop a system of world order, as it was originally designed. It had already proved its merit, in fact, in practical ways such as the functioning of U.N. peacekeeping forces and as the observer team, which includes military representatives called in to supervise the Central American peace process (ONUCA) under "Esquipulas II." President Mikhail Gorbachev has, for several years, been speaking in favor of giving greater scope to the functions of the United Nations. President Bush, in his address to a joint session of Congress on September 11, 1990, hinted that it could be the centerpiece of the new world order.

Fourth, differences, principally economic, will emerge among the major areas of the world—the United States, Europe, and Asia. Their divisive capability cannot yet be foreseen if heavy sacrifices must be made over time. The day is clearly past, for instance, for the United States to be able to underwrite the expenses of an operation such as that in the Persian Gulf.

Fifth, issues of a global nature have been neglected the search for energy alternatives, environmental issues, problems of poverty and its causes, and others. They must be addressed on a more urgent basis. The continuation of such neglect will lead to unacceptable costs in the future. Even in a small region such as Central America, long of particular interest to the United States, solutions cannot come from Washington alone.

Above all, we are moving into an era into which the somewhat comfortable certainties of the Cold War framework have already given way to uncertainties. It is a time calling for leadership and a vision of the future.

Consolidating Democracy In the Hemisphere

During the past few years, the trend toward democratization in the Western hemisphere has been so strong that the hope arises that democracy will become the permanent norm, that the Americas will become like Western Europe. Optimists even hasten to include Central America into this happy framework.

Old Latin America hands must be forgiven a certain measure of skepticism; the swings between dictatorship and democracy have occurred before. Even the words chosen by President Bush in his June 21 speech on the EAI are somewhat contingent when he speaks of the "resurgence of democratic rule, a rising tide of democracy..." Tides can rise and fall.

Fortunately, support for democracy is so strong today that it has already withstood difficult tests in certain countries in which, arguably, such would not have been the case in years past. But the threat to nascent democracy is enormous everywhere, from many sources—the weak economies, tremendous social problems of poverty and inequality, and the weakness of civilian institutions. Above all, in several Central American countries, it is the holding of disproportionate power by the military establishment and unstable electoral politics where there is at best a shaky consensus among political forces as to how the system should function.

A good, short working definition of democracy in developed countries is that of Robert Dahl: "public contestation (by a political opposition) in elections and the right to participate." This view looks, of course, only to process and not to other objectives assumed in developed-country democracies such as some reasonable measure of equality and concern for social objectives, including distribution of income. But a strictly "process" test seems to have been that largely used by the State Department when coloring its map to show the democracies.

It is true that the process has been greatly improved through election techniques, opinion polling, and international observation. The fault lies in a policy that puts unique emphasis on elections alone. In many cases, elections may be contested and public but may not reflect at all where the real power lies. Guatemala and El Salvador are two cases in point: civilian governments have been impotent to stop the killing of civilians by military units and associated death squads. One can scarcely apply the term "democracy" to these countries without very serious qualifications.

Still, after a long period of military dictatorships and authoritarian rule of both left and right, there seems to be a new awareness in Latin America of the value of participatory system as a means of achieving social ends, as opposed to the extremism once espoused from each end of the political spectrum. Equally important is the adoption of a system to move countries toward national reconciliation. More than just a few Latin American intellectuals have reached the conclusion of the Mexican writer Octavio Paz:

> Latin American democracy arrived late and has been disfigured and betrayed over and over again. It has been weak, indecisive, rebellious, its own enemy, subject to the flattery of demagogues, corrupted by money, corroded by favoritism and nepotism. Nevertheless, almost all the good that has been done in Latin America for a century and a half has been under a regime of democracy, or, in the case of Mexico, one moving toward democracy.[1]

It is also disquieting that there can be widespread violations of human rights in what appears otherwise to be a working democracy, Peru being a good example. In the sectors in which the army is carrying out counterinsurgency operations against the Sendero Luminoso, the dead and missing exceed those of Chile under Pinochet—another reason for the United States to be cautious about becoming involved.

Former President Jimmy Carter echoes the prevailing U.S. attitude when he says that human rights and democracy are intimately related and that: "Human rights have become a standard by which the world judges individual governments." Without the Cold War excuse that a particular tyrant is friendly to the United States and a staunch anti-communist, the Carter standard will become more universally shared in this country.

---

[1]Octavio Paz, *Tiempo nublado* (Barcelona: Editorial Seix Barral, 1986), p. 188.

Economists who specialize in Latin America warn that democracies will not necessarily be able to produce a more equitable system of distribution within high rates of economic growth. Paradoxically, Chile under Pinochet was the South American country that had the greatest measure of economic recovery, even though it was achieved at tremendous social cost. Whatever the rates of growth in coming years, however, populist demands for redistribution will threaten the new democracies. Central America, as well as Brazil and Argentina, are all excellent cases in point.

The survival of existing democracies and the persistence of democratic trends in Latin America are clearly in the U.S. national interest. Understanding the threats to democracy must be taken into account in any U.S. policy objective, and helping its consolidation should be a high priority. All U.S. programs, including military assistance and training, should be specifically tailored to this objective.

It is important that this objective not be subordinated to other policy objectives, as has happened in the past, for reasons of expediency. Past reasons for violating this principle largely involved Cold War objectives; today they may involve the "war on drugs" or an economic objective. In this context, United States policy should look very carefully at the social impact of demands being made in Brady Plan negotiations as well as debt-waiver offers under the Bush Initiative, which will principally benefit Central America and the Caribbean.

There will be ways to include those Latin American nations that have set a decisive course of political and economic liberalization in becoming members of a system of like-minded countries. It was necessary for Spain to become a democratic state before it could be considered for membership in the European Communities; that membership in itself reinforces democracy. Perhaps this is what Octavio Paz had in mind when he advocated a political as well as an economic dimension to the new relationship between Mexico and the United States.

President Bush's proposal for a free trade zone of the Americas should presume an arrangement among like-minded democratic states, both as the morally correct position and the only one that will assure long-run stability to such a plan. Central Americans are undoubtedly watching and waiting to see how the proposed North American Free Trade area will shape up. If it does and is significant, they will want to joint.

Conclusions—A Time of Unparalleled Opportunity

President Bush's proposal could not have been more timely. Latin America has been undergoing a profound transformation of the way its leaders see their future. If the political and economic liberalization taking place today can be consolidated, if it is more than simply a "high tide" that could again recede, the advantages to this country's economy and security should be obvious. The success of the trend is not automatic or guaranteed however; there are immense obstacles to be faced.

In view of the many demands upon Washington's attention, it will be primarily up to Latin America to come forward with an early and comprehensive response to the initiative. This is the first time in 30 years that the United States has come forward on its own with a major economic proposal. Yet, the details of the initiative have to be filled in.

The proposal for the Alliance for Progress was first unveiled in much the same manner as the Bush Initiative, a White House announcement on March 13, 1961. By August of that year, at Punta del Este, however, it was formally launched in great detail at a meeting of the Organization of American States. The U.S. fielded a formidable team of area experts and economists to work on the program, and the major Latin American countries did the same.

This time, no such elaborate followup seems to have been programmed. Moreover, as we have seen all too often, the constituency for a comprehensive Latin American policy in this country has always been extremely weak. There is no stimulus such as Castro's takeover of Cuba to give it strength. In the long run, however, this initiative could achieve as much or even more than the Alliance for Progress. It could become Latin America's initiative, based on the consensus formula of both North and South, democracy, and economic liberalization. Latin America is today, better equipped to meet that challenge than it was in 1961. Ever since the Latin American nations came together to draw up the Consensus of Viña del Mar in 1969, they have had years of experience in close economic consultation on economic matters. Already the Bush proposal has been discussed in a meeting of the Latin American Economic System (ECLA). There has been political evolution, too, within the region. The PDD begun in November 1990, the Puntarenas Heads of State Meeting the following month, and the interest shown by the European Communities in the future of Central America are all important factors.

European involvement, on a scale well beyond that known in the past, is important for two reasons. First, politically, it is important to balance what has been historically the overarching U.S. presence in the area. Secondly, assistance is needed well beyond what the United States will be able to provide.

The fact is that Central America stands at a crucial junction. The threat of regional war is past, and it is no longer the battleground between the two superpowers of the 1980s. Yet, paradoxically, its internal problems are as great as ever, and, above all, its economic needs are enormous. A successful outcome, in favor of national reconciliation, democratization, and accelerated economic progress are attainable. The right formula of partnership and a sustained commitment are the keys to that success.

DEMOCRACY AND DEVELOPMENT IN CENTRAL AMERICA: OPPORTUNITIES FOR U.S./EC COOPERATION

James H. Michel

Agency for International Development

I will not be the first speaker here, and I hope I will not be the last, to observe that what Enrique Iglesias has called "the silent revolution" in Latin America has a special vigor in Central America. The elected civilian governments that are in office in all the capitals of the isthmus all came to power through elections in which they defeated incumbent governments. All are implementing economic reforms that hold the promise of opening their societies to broad participation in the benefits of economic growth. And the process of collaboration within the region begun at Esquipulas has become institutionalized at Puntarenas. There is reason for optimism that the 1990s will be a decade of hope and a decade of progress in deepening the roots of political and economic freedom in each of the countries of Central America and in the region as a whole.

In addition to favorable trends within the region, the 1990s offer new opportunities for international collaboration in support of the efforts of the Central Americans. When President Bush said last June in presenting the Enterprise for the Americas Initiative that the future of Latin America lies with free governments and free markets, his words and his initiative were hailed in Central America and in Europe. The policy of the United States was seen not as a challenge but as a contribution to the consensus in support of that silent revolution that is taking place.

This atmosphere of consensus is important—albeit, of course, the Central Americans bear the responsibility for shaping their own destiny, and it is they who must make the primary effort. But they face enormous problems in consolidating still fragile democratic gains, in overcoming structural impediments to the alleviation of still widespread poverty, in building an institutional base for protecting human rights and assuring that justice is accessible for all, in safeguarding the region's natural resource base, and in achieving national reconciliation and mutually beneficial regional collaboration. They seek and deserve international support for their efforts. And where that support is based on common interests and shared values, there is an increased likelihood that it will be forthcoming and effective.

U.S. Support for Central America

Support by the United States for the ongoing efforts of the Central Americans toward democracy and development takes many forms. The vision of the Enterprise for the Americas Initiative—a democratic hemisphere enjoying the benefits of free trade, increased investment, reduced debt, and a clean environment—establishes the basic framework. To support that vision, the Agency for International Development has devised a new U.S. economic assistance strategy for the 1990s. Our point of departure is support for the broad goals identified by the Central American presidents in their Declarations of Antigua and Puntarenas. Our economic assistance programs, thus reflecting a convergence of views, will be specifically focused on three objectives: 1) the development of stable democratic societies; 2) the achievement of broad-based, sustainable economic growth; and 3) the attainment of effective regional cooperation.

To enhance democracy, we will increase support for democratic institutions, especially to broaden and deepen participation in democratic processes. Local governments need to be strengthened in order to better deliver services and to broaden citizen participation in government. Judicial, legislative, and electoral systems need to be independent, professional, and effective in order to consolidate democratic gains. Public finances must be managed with the competence and integrity necessary to merit public confidence. Democratic values need to be promoted to develop stronger, more effective citizen participation.

To stimulate economic growth, we will help Central America eliminate obstacles to private investment, trade, and employment generation. U.S. assistance programs will encourage the adoption of policies, incentives, regulatory frameworks, and management practices that protect the natural resource base as well as facilitate greater participation in the economy by the disadvantaged. Our assistance to governments and non-governmental organizations will also support their efforts to improve the effectiveness, efficiency, financing, and local control of basic social services.

To foster regional cooperation, the United States will place greater emphasis on implementing initiatives identified by the Central Americans within a regional framework. We will encourage policy, legal, and other reforms to further liberalize trade within Central America, to strengthen democracy and protect human rights, and to safeguard the region's natural resource base. We anticipate that much of the effort will be made within the framework of the Partnership for Democracy and Development, working with key regional institutions while at the same time helping them to achieve greater self-sufficiency and reduce their dependence on donor resources.

Aid levels are not, in themselves, a very reliable barometer. The extraordinary levels of U.S. economic assistance provided in the mid-1980s supported economic reforms that have helped Central American countries regain access to the international financial institutions. As positive resource flows are resumed from the International Monetary Fund, the World Bank, and the Inter-American Development Bank, and as the region's economies begin to recover, it would seem unreasonable to expect a continuation of the same unprecedented levels of U.S. aid that we provided at a time of crisis when the international financial institutions were not so deeply engaged as they are now. Moreover, our aid levels for Central America actually were higher in 1990 and 1991 than in 1989 due to supplemental funding approved for Nicaragua and Panama. When compared to the more "normal" 1989 level of $690,000,000, the $685,000,000 budgeted for 1992 hardly suggests a loss of interest in Central America.

United States and European Community Programs are Compatible

The United States welcomes the European Community's continued involvement in the development of Central America. The Community has demonstrated its interest in the region through increased assistance as well as its ongoing support for key integration institutions. As a result of the San José meetings, the Community has successfully implemented an intra-regional trade facility agreement, established refugee aid programs, assisted in social, as well as in the agricultural and food security areas, and promoted democracy.

The recent emphasis on reactivation of economic integration in the region and improved trade relations is particularly important. Central Americans agree that they need not only to revitalize the Central American Common Market, but to revamp it so that it is more outward oriented focusing on both intra-regional trade and participation in global markets. Based on European experience and the aspiration to achieve a single market in 1992, the European Community's expertise will be invaluable to Central Americans.

Opportunities for U.S./EC Cooperation

As the global market place becomes larger, the need for interaction between Central Americans and the rest of the industrial world becomes greater. As regional approaches are utilized, the Central American countries can take advantage of economies of scale and can maximize their comparative advantages. In order for the Central American countries to engage effectively in the global market place, both the United States and the European Community not only need to continue to provide assistance, but more importantly need to increase interaction and coordination of efforts in furtherance of increased self-sufficiency within the region.

The spirit of the Partnership for Democracy and Development, which Ford Cooper will address, is to mobilize support for Central America and to ensure that international efforts are coordinated. The goal is to achieve a greater coherence and consistency among international donors so that the combined effort is greater than the sum of the individual contributions. In light of budget constraints worldwide, as well as competing demands in other regions of the world, programs in Central America need to be complementary and not duplicate.

Already the United States and the European Community have been working well together through a variety of international meetings, such as the International Conference on Refugees in Central America (CIREFCA) in June of 1990 and the Rome Donors' Conference for Nicaragua held in May 1990. There has been an increase in the number of meetings between U.S. and EC officials at all levels. There has been useful dialogue and exchange of information both in Washington and Brussels, as well as in Central America.

However, there is room for improvement. A more regular and formal exchange of information could ensure that the effective use of funds is maximized and that our respective programs are complementary instead of duplicating, or worse, working against each other.

The United States and the European Community can combine their efforts in expanding trade opportunities. The Central American Trade Facility, supported by the European Community, is a positive step toward the reactivation of intra-regional trade. The Enterprise for the Americas

Initiative has set in motion talk of establishing free trade throughout the region. It is important to underscore that the Enterprise for the Americas is not an initiative for a trading bloc for the United States—it is a vision for a free trade area within a global trading system.

Another area where the entire donor community should focus more resources over the next few years is in promoting democracy. Because of the rich experience that both the European Community and the United States have had in building democratic institutions for the sustained and stable evolution of democratic societies, a coordinated effort of assistance offering a variety of models and experience would be welcome and useful to Central Americans.

Unfortunately, the donor community, including the United States, has in the past focused on fostering "economic development" per se and given too little attention to fostering democratic institutions within which and through which economic development policy and decisions should be formulated and executed.

Economic development occurs in the political context of a society faced with making choices among competing demands, inevitably in a world of scarce resources. Experience has repeatedly demonstrated that development can best be sustained over the long term in a political environment in which the people can participate because democratic institutions are strong, individual liberty is protected, and human rights are respected. The United States and the European Community both offer examples that support the conclusion that political freedom and economic freedom are mutually reinforcing in support of the well being of a nation's citizens.

A third important area where the combined efforts of the United States and the European Community can effectively contribute is in the area of regional institutions that foster regional integration based on an outward-oriented model. Because many of the problems facing Central Americans are common, the countries need to work together as a region to solve them. The Central American presidents have clearly signaled their intent to work on regional solutions. Through support for key regional institutions, both public and private, the United States and the European Community can help further the movement towards integration.

Conclusion

We are living at a time of unprecedented opportunity because of the convergence of interests and values in Central America and also in the United States and in Europe. This does not mean that all differences will disappear or that success is assured. It does mean that there is a sufficiently broad community of interests so that we can all work together in some areas, and that there is a foundation of incentives for seeking to overcome those differences that constitute obstacles to achieving mutual objectives.

We can, out of fear, stand back from collaboration. We can allow events at home or elsewhere in the world to distract our attention. Or we can seek to follow the path of collaboration, seizing the opportunities and acting on our hopes rather than our fears. I believe this conference is providing an excellent opportunity for all of us to examine the terrain and better understand the implications of the policy choices that lie before us. I am confident that it will help us to choose the right path.

CURRENT STATUS AND ISSUES

Ford Cooper

Partnership for Democracy and Development in Central America

I can think of no forum more appropriate or more relevant to my responsibilities than a panel on cooperation between the European Community and the United States in the reconstruction of Central America. The United States government considers such cooperation, and cooperation with other countries interested in the future well-being of Central America, to be absolutely essential if, working together, we are to help Central America seize the historic opportunity that now exists to break out of old patterns and to move forward towards the goals set out in the Esquipulas process.

We strongly believe that the current situation in Central America presents us with a unique challenge to help Central America change the course of its history. After many years of national and regional conflict, with a near total breakdown of social, economic, and political systems, Central America is now poised to recover and move forward, ready to consolidate recent advances to region-wide democracy, and to break the chains of economic and social underdevelopment.

For those who have been long-time observers of the Central American scene, it is difficult to believe—and maybe at the same time, too easy to forget—how far the area has moved compared to just a few years ago. Who could have predicted that the bleak political landscape that was once Central America would have given way to six democratically elected governments and that the presidents of these democratic governments would have embarked upon an ambitious and evolving joint program now commonly referred to as the Esquipulas process? And who could have predicted that these democratic leaders would set as the goals of this increasingly institutionalized process the deepening of democracy, peace and demobilization, respect for human rights, more open market economies, and a Central American economic community?

However, for all the promise of recent developments, the road ahead for the democracies of Central America will not be an easy one. The fact of the matter is that all of these countries continue to be saddled with the legacy of underdevelopment that proved such fertile ground for violence and instability in the past. No one, surely, will dispute that democracy is key to development in Central America, as elsewhere in the world, but democracy—especially in its embryonic form—will not have the opportunity to succeed unless it enjoys a breathing space of social and economic stability. None of us would, I am sure, want to see a return to the divisiveness and instability of the 1970s and 1980s with its poisonous spillover effects on the climate of international relations. And the globalized economy, on which all of us increasingly depend, requires the successful integration of Central America into the world market, no less so than in the case of Eastern Europe and other regions of the world that have embraced reform and are seeking our help.

Just as in their own context, Poland, Hungary, and the other countries of Eastern Europe needed, and still require, an extra measure of support, so it is with Central America. It is that extra measure of support that is going to make the difference between success and failure in Central America's effort to build a region of peace and justice, to develop economically, and to stabilize politically under a democratic banner.

It was with that need for broad support in mind, as well as the earlier example of the advanced democracies of the world working together in support of Eastern Europe, that Secretary of State James Baker proposed the creation of a Partnership for Democracy and Development in Central America (PDD). The purpose of such a partnership would be, above all, to focus the attention of the world on the importance and on the needs of this region at a time in which there are an increasing number of claimants requiring attention and support. We seek a partnership that would share information, lead to better coordination of our individual assistance efforts, and stimulate progress toward and provide support for the goals set by the Central Americans themselves in the areas of democracy, peace, and economic development.

On November 20, 1990, the Department of State hosted an exploratory meeting in Washington to discuss the proposal for a PDD. Invited to the meeting were government representatives from the 24 OECD countries, the six Central American countries (including in this context Panama), and Central America's three closest neighbors (Colombia, Mexico, and Venezuela), as well as participants and observers from international organizations. The Washington meeting revealed widespread agreement that an unprecedented and historic opportunity now exists in Central America and demonstrated broad interest among the invitees in forming a partnership to support Central America's goals.

The December 17, 1990, Puntarenas Summit Declaration issued by the Central American presidents contained a strong endorsement of the PDD, which they see as a forum to strengthen peace and democracy and to contribute to the economic development of Central America.

As U.S. special coordinator for our PDD efforts, I visited Central America in December 1990 and was able to confirm that in each country there exists strong support for the PDD as a means for periodic dialogue with the world's key players on the broad range of Central American political, economic, and social issues. They hope the forum will improve understanding for what they are trying to achieve through the Esquipulas process, as well as bring support in addressing the problems and obstacles that stand in the way.

Similarly, in a January 1991 visit to several countries in Europe I encountered positive interest in the potential value of the PDD as a periodic forum for close examination of developments in Central America with a view to encouraging them in the positive direction set forth in the documents of the Esquipulas process. Subsequent consultations with embassies in Washington and by our embassies abroad with host governments of a number of other countries have resulted in indications of positive interest as well, although discussions continue among all parties regarding specific features that might characterize the proposed partnership.

Encouraged by the generally positive attitudes toward the idea of a Partnership for Democracy and Development in Central America, the government of Costa Rica has issued invitations to the governments and institutions that participated in the November 1990 Washington meeting to attend a meeting on the PDD in San José, Costa Rica, April 9-10, 1991, with the intention of defining the organization, structure, and operational characteristics of the partnership and to formally establish it. Broad participation at next month's San José meeting is expected and preparations for the meeting are actively underway.

The United States delegation will be headed by Assistant Secretary of State for Inter-American Affairs, Bernard W. Aronson. We are looking forward to the meeting with great anticipation. We hope and expect that there will be full consensus that a Partnership for Democracy and Development in Central America is an idea whose time has come and that we cannot turn our back on Central America at this critical juncture in that troubled region's history.

MEXICAN-CENTRAL AMERICAN COOPERATION MODEL

Renato Iturriaga

Mexican Foreign Relations Secretariat

Before beginning with substantive matters, a semantic precision: reconstruction signifies to build again; the term implies rebuilding material things. Thus, our vision differs from the diagnosis implicit in the title of the conference, for to propose the reconstruction of Central America would assume, on the one hand, that its infrastructure was destroyed or is obsolete, and on the other hand, that the question is to build things, and not to develop persons. Central America has never had the opportunity to enjoy a significant material infrastructure. The problem is not limited to constructing such an infrastructure, but fundamentally concerns developing conditions that improve the population's quality of life. Thus, we visualize a cooperation for *development*, and not for reconstruction.

Commitment

In October 1990, Mexican President Carlos Salinas de Gortari, during his state visit to the Republic of Honduras, offered the support of Mexico to contribute to the development of the Central American region. With this began a very accelerated process to give form and content to the commitment Mexico assumed.

In January 1991, in the Mexican city of Tuxtla Gutiérrez, a summit was held with the presidents of Mexico and the five Central American republics in which the commitment was reiterated while the extent of the cooperation program was clarified with the signing of a framework agreement.

Mexico's Interest

Central America has a priority place in Mexico's foreign policy agenda because:

*its near geographical location makes it naturally convenient to strengthen reciprocal economic and trade ties;

*important historical and cultural ties unite us;

*it is Mexico's geographic port to the southern continent;

*the instability that has characterized the region in the last decade (armed confrontation, migration problems, militarization, political instability) constitutes a national security problem for Mexico in its neighboring zone.

New Central American Context

Since mid-1990, Central America has undergone important changes: democratic institutionalization processes have been strengthened in the countries of the region; there have been important advances in peace negotiations in El Salvador and Guatemala; the Central American countries have demonstrated their decided political will to consolidate the peace process and begin sustained development.

Mexico's Intermediate Development

My country is in a peculiar position, which we may illustrate as a glass half-full or half-empty. This means that regarding international cooperation, we have as much potential to receive as we have to give. There are still many shortages, and we will demand various forms of cooperation. But we will achieve them, and the experiences are significant, for because of them we can offer cooperation in various economic, technical, or cultural areas.

Objectives of Mexico's Cooperation with Central America

*Consolidate the mutual ties of friendship and cooperation between Mexico and Central America;

*Contribute to the economic and social development of the Central American countries;

*Collaborate with the maintenance of peace in the region, based on the accords adopted by the Central American countries themselves;

*Support the Central American integration process.

Cooperation Criteria

Mexico, in its international cooperation relations, strictly abides by the principles of international law: self-determination, nonintervention, and international cooperation for development. In this sense, Mexico's cooperation relations with the Central American countries are sustained by the following:

*Abstaining from any type of political conditions;

*Respect for their institutions, as well as for their reconciliation mechanisms;

*Strict attachment to their self-determination and sovereignty;

*Establishment of programs in accord with their priorities.

The Organization of Cooperation

For Mexico, the pivot of cooperation is the *Mexican Commission for Cooperation with Central America*, which was recently established by the executive and, in the first stage, has 11 state secretariats who have important cooperation ties with Central America. Other branches, including the private and academic sectors, will be incorporated as needed.

In the inner circle of the Foreign Relations Secretariat a coordinating "Special Group," or "task force," has been formed in which various general directorates participate. It is what keeps these activities going.

Areas of Cooperation

Mexico's cooperation activities with Central America have been divided into three large areas: economic, technical/scientific, and educational/cultural. These areas have specific cooperation titles that result as much from the needs mentioned by the Central American countries as from Mexico's ability to respond to them.

Forms of Cooperation

Mexico's cooperation relations with Central America are broad and diversified. For this reason there are numerous forms and modes that these cooperation relations assume.

Several economic cooperation mechanisms have been established. Among the outstanding ones are:

* The San José Accord that supplies hydrocarbons to the Central American countries at preferential rates;

* Partial-reaching accords that grant unilateral tariff preferences to the Central American countries, as well as equally preferential

mechanisms for incoming Central American products along our country's border area.

Concerning what is referred to under the scope of education/cultural and technical/scientific cooperation, cooperation takes place through:

*Mexican missions to Central America;

*Central Americans staying in Mexico;
*Exchange missions;

*Short training courses;

*Graduate scholarships;

*Meetings of counterparts;

*Document and information exchanges;

*Organization of seminars and conferences;

*Exchange of materials, among other things.

The First Results

Recently an "Inventory of Mexico's Cooperation Activities with Central America" was compiled. It designated 760 actions at various levels of evolution (highlighted ones, in execution, or completed) covering a variety of sectors: agriculture, energy, education, health, trade, tourism, etc.

President Salinas has ordered quarterly evaluations. To do this, definite goals have been established by commitment, fulfillment period, Mexican and Central American institutions involved, mode of cooperation, etc.

Conclusions

Mexico-Central American cooperation relations are in their initial phase. Together we are learning to coordinate our efforts.

Mexico's cooperation model is based upon clearly defined objectives and principles from which there have been numerous actions done in agreement with the recipient countries. First has been the effort to act and realize, leaving to one side designs based one earlier theoretical schemes. Theory will come later when the experiences have been organized systematically.

THE WORLD BANK'S ROLE IN CENTRAL AMERICA'S RECONSTRUCTION AND RECOVERY

Marko Voljc

The World Bank

After more than a decade of economic deterioration, political unrest and civil war, the countries of Central America are making major progress toward reestablishing peace in the region and reforming their political and economic structures. At various summit meetings the presidents of the six countries of Central America have stated their strong commitment to the process of peace, economic adjustment, and poverty alleviation. Many donors have also expressed their strong interest in supporting Central American efforts as a group. Although this process is far from complete, the changes already underway inspire new hope and improve prospects for sustained economic recovery and growth in the region.

These changes have also opened the way for a much more active World Bank effort to support the region's economic recovery and reconstruction. Indeed, for the first time in over a decade, the bank is actively working with all six them in the region—Costa Rica, El Salvador, Guatemala, Honduras, Nicaragua, and Panama—to help these countries prepare and implement major adjustment and debt workout programs.

This paper briefly reviews the Central American region's political and economic trends as well as principal development challenges, assesses prospects for the region in the short to medium and longer term, describes the Bank's expanding role in the region, and stresses the need for a coordinated regional approach among key donors to build effectively on the momentum for adjustment and change.

Political and Economic Background

Central America has long suffered from the lack of stable and effective political structures, from serious social and economic inequalities that have left the large majority of its population in extreme poverty, and from heavy reliance on a few basic export commodities—with variable prices and market prospects—that have resulted in uneven growth and periodic fiscal and balance of payments crises. Since the late 1970s and early 1980s, the region has been struggling with the worst political and economic crisis in its history, marked by declines in economic growth and per capita incomes in most of the countries and by political violence and civil war in El Salvador, Nicaragua, and Guatemala.

The region's economic difficulties have been compounded by the failure to develop participatory political structures able to resolve conflicts peacefully, protect human rights, and ensure a more equitable distribution of the benefits of economic growth. These political constraints exacerbated the region's economic collapse by restricting the capacity of governments to respond to major economic challenges. More importantly, the sharp disparity in economic and political power between the privileged upper and emerging middle classes and the poverty stricken majority helped fuel the region's political crisis and resulting violence and civil war. The only country able to avoid serious political problems in recent years has been Costa Rica with its well established democratic political institutions, absence of an army, high levels of education and literacy, and strong commitment to solving social issues.

The economic and human cost of ten years of economic decline and civil war has been enormous. About 70 percent of the region's population lives in poverty, with extreme poverty affecting as much as 50 percent of the population. Real per capita incomes are currently at the same levels as prevailed in the early 1970s in Costa Rica, Honduras, Guatemala, and Panama. In El Salvador and Nicaragua, incomes have receded to the levels of the early

1960s and 1950s. Moreover, given the region's pervasive poverty and extreme inequalities in income distribution, these per capita calculations significantly overstate the actual income levels received by the bulk of the population. Savings and investment ratios have fallen in all of the countries except Costa Rica. More than 160,000 people have died in wars or unrest during the 1980s. Estimates of thc number of displaced persons vary from 1.8 to 2.8 million, or almost 10 percent of the region's total population. Unemployment estimates of more than 20 percent in all countries except Costa Rica, underscore the poor state of the region's economic situation.

Economic Adjustment Strategy and Principal Development Needs

Although economic circumstances and development needs vary from country to country, all of the Central American economies need improvements in resource allocation and expansion of external trade. This requires removing unnecessary public sector controls that limit private sector investment, mcasurcs to promote diversification of exports and accelerated export growth; public sector reforms to reestablish fiscal balance and improve resource mobilization; actions to strengthen the financial sector and access to credit; and more attention to human resource development and poverty alleviation.

In the short term, the emphasis for most countries has to be on reestablishing and maintaining a stable macroeconomic environment; recovering external balance while simultaneously eliminating foreign payment arrears to official creditors and in some countries reducing heavy debt service burdens through rescheduling and debt reduction; meeting the urgent needs of repatriated and resettled refugees; and initiating actions to repair and rehabilitate basic infrastructure, which has been damaged by years of neglect and civil war.

Over the medium term, the countries of the region must develop new sources of economic growth. To do so, they must encourage more rapid export growth of goods and services. The emphasis should be on penetrating new markets and expanding nontraditional exports so as to reduce over time the region's dependence on a few primary commodities. Such export diversification should be encouraged, however, by offering adequate incentives to all potential producers and not through discriminatory policies that harm the traditional sectors. This strategy requires a stable macro-economic framework, with appropriate fiscal and monetary policies, and also changes in the incentive structure to encourage exports, including tariff reform and maintenance of competitive exchange rates. The emphasis on export-led growth will have to be based on an expanding role for the private sector. This in turn implies a major effort to eliminate unnecessary public sector controls and bottlenecks, revise tax and investment regulations, and ensure the liberalization and efficiency of financial institutions (both public and private) to facilitate increased private sector savings and investment. This would also create a more favorable business climate for private foreign investment.

Along with the emphasis on liberalizing the economy and enhancing the private sector's contribution is a need to resolve serious public sector management and resource allocation issues. For most countries, the principal focus is on creating more efficient public sectors that can adequately meet basic social, investment, and other public service requirements. Increased resource mobilization is important, especially in Guatemala. However, in most countries the first priority is to reallocate expenditures toward basic health and education, ensuring adequate spending for agriculture research and extension, and maintaining adequate funding for maintenance and operation of public infrastructure that complements private investment. It also means increasing expenditures and services in rural areas to ensure a fairer distribution of public resources. For some countries, decentralization of management and financing of public services is important to enhance public sector efficiency and responsiveness to local needs. Public enterprise reform and privatization are also key elements of the public sector agenda.

A further critical goal for the 1990s is action to alleviate widespread poverty. Reestablishing sustained economic growth may not, by itself, improve the living conditions of the very poor, especially in the short and medium term, unless governments take specific actions to increase the poor's access to education and health services and to the technical and financial support needed to improve productivity and incomes. This requires not only increased public spending in health and education, with improved efficiency and targeting, but also steps to encourage and facilitate local community development efforts, including self-help programs and programs directed specifically at women. Equally important is the need to support expanded family planning and other social and economic development programs that encourage formation of smaller families, which is essential for bringing down the region's very high population growth rate.

Another important item in the development agenda for the 1990s is the environment. All of the countries face increasingly serious environmental issues, including rapid deforestation, water and air pollution, inadequate handling of contaminated waste, and soil erosion. Economic and social policies should take into account their potential effect on the environment. Designing a proper incentive system will be the most effective way of changing behavior on a broad scale to stop environmental degradation and eventually reversing this process.

Regional Concerns and Approach

The region's ability to tackle satisfactorily its principal economic development challenges depends primarily on the extent to which individual country adjustment efforts succeed. Nevertheless, the existence of regional institutions and a regional framework for strengthening coordination and cooperation among Central American countries provide additional instruments for complementing and reinforcing individual country reform efforts. In addition to well established regional technical institutions, such as those concerned with agricultural research and strengthening public administration, as well as other regional institutions established as part of the Central American Common Market arrangements, new vehicles for regional consultation and coordination have been organized in recent years in connection with the peace process and efforts to promote democracy in the area. These include steps to establish a Central American Parliament as well as numerous summit meetings of Central American presidents. Although these summits focused initially on actions to reestablish peace in the region, the most recent summits—attended by all six presidents—concentrated on economic matters, including agreement on a Plan of Economic Action for Central America. This plan seeks to strengthen regional integration through actions aimed at removing obstacles to regional trade, better coordinating macro-economic policies, and improving cooperation in matters related to agriculture, science and technology, export promotion, and programs to minimize the social adjustment costs.

As part of efforts to strengthen intra-regional cooperation, the five Central American countries need to address a number of institutional issues at the regional level, namely how to restructure the Central American Common Market (CACM) and what to do with a number of existing regional institutions, especially the Central American Bank for Economic Integration (CABEI) and the regional payments clearing house. Efforts to reform the common market by reducing the high levels of effective protection prevailing earlier were initiated in the mid-1980s. Since then, considerable progress has been made in lowering external tariffs on an individual country basis. During the early 1990s several countries are expected to continue the tariff reform process and to remove existing intra-regional trade barriers. The decline of intra-regional trade during the 1980s has been a continuing source of concern, prompting calls for action to revive the Common Market. On that issue, the World Bank has recommended that the Central American countries strive to achieve an economically integrated region with low trade barriers toward third countries.

To help reactivate intra-regional trade, the Central American countries must take steps to restructure the regional trade clearing house mechanism and resolve existing trade payment arrears. A proposed EEC initiative to support reform of the regional payment system and finance a revolving fund to facilitate trade related payments will help in reactivating regional trade, provided it is accompanied by policy changes in individual countries that improve their trade financing capacity. Progress in reestablishing peace and economic recovery also opens the way for a revitalization of CABEI. But the five member countries must first agree on the role CABEI should play in a region that has changed considerably since CABEI was first established. They must also follow through with plans for clearing existing arrears to CABEI as well as taking actions to strengthen the institution's financial viability. CABEI needs clear signals and a strong commitment from its member countries to improve its finances, management, and technical capacity before it becomes viable as a major channel for donor assistance and can play an important role in the region's recovery.

These regional institutions—properly strengthened—along with other instruments for regional consultation and cooperation, can be utilized to facilitate reconstruction and recovery in the region. Enhanced regional coordination can help improve the consistency and effectiveness of policies and programs in a number of areas, some of which can have an impact on more than one country at a time. Policies and programs related to the environment, trade, foreign investment, health, and nutrition, for example, can all benefit from enhanced regional coordination, both in terms of strengthening program development through the exchange of information and experiences, as well as by ensuring more consistency in policy initiatives.

Prospects for the 1990s

The success of Central American governments in accelerating adjustment and economic recovery in the region will depend to a large extent on how well the region is able to strengthen new political structures and institutions; overcome serious human resource constraints and institutional bottlenecks, especially in the public sector; reduce the region's high debt burden; and attract adequate and sustained external financing. Even with strong and successful adjustment efforts, the economies of most of the countries will remain vulnerable to sharp changes in the external environment, such as the latest oil shock, fluctuations in prices for major export commodities, and slower growth in principal market countries, especially the United States.

The existence of weak and/or newly established political structures and in some countries continued sharp social divisions and lingering political violence presents a difficult political environment in which to implement major structural reforms. With the exception of Costa Rica, all of the governments in the region are operating within fragile or uncertain political environments that could lead to serious delays in moving ahead with key adjustment measures.

In addition to underlying political constraints, the complexity and seriousness of existing economic constraints and debt problems—which vary from country to country—further increase uncertainties and risks as to the speed and viability of economic reform. The three countries currently in non-accrual, Nicaragua, Panama, and Guatemala, must not only implement rigorous adjustment programs, but also simultaneously pay off very large multilateral arrears, while remaining current on new debt service. This severely limits the amount of external resources available to support new investment and economic recovery. It also makes it indispensable that Nicaragua and Panama seek large reductions in public debt, including buy backs of commercial debt at steep discounts. Although both Panama and Guatemala have reasonably strong economies upon which to base their recovery—assuming good policies—Nicaragua's economic situation is close to desperate, with continued rampant inflation, huge fiscal imbalances, and a total external debt in excess of U.S.$10 billion (close to nine times GDP).

Honduras, on the other hand, having successfully initiated its adjustment program and paid off its arrears to multilaterals, now faces the even more difficult task of keeping up the momentum of reform (including maintaining debt service current), even though economic gains from the program will be minimal during the initial years of the program. For El Salvador, improved economic management is making a clear difference; nevertheless, sustainability remains clouded by continuing civil strife. In Costa Rica, prospects for sustaining the adjustment effort remain strong, although short-term economic management has deteriorated and continuing fiscal constraints reflect problems in the size and structure of the public sector that have yet to be effectively tackled as part of the adjustment process.

In addition to political uncertainties, the impact of sharp variations in economic prospects and potential and the continued vulnerability to changing external economic conditions, there are two other factors that affect the sustainability of the reform process. One is the existence of weak public sector institutions and the lack of sufficient high level technical staff and advisors to provide essential support to key policy makers. This undermines the capacity of many governments to implement effective policy adjustment and carry out urgently needed rehabilitation and reconstruction activities. Human resource constraints and institutional bottlenecks—which can only be remedied over the medium term—therefore add further uncertainties and risks to country efforts to adjust. A second factor is the large size of the region's external financing requirements—estimated at between U.S.$2.5 and U.S.$3 billion per year for the next five years—and the fact that resources of this magnitude may not be forthcoming as donor priorities shift away from Central America to meet pressing needs in other parts of the world, such as in Eastern Europe or Persian Gulf reconstruction.

The World Bank's Role in Central America in the 1990s

Recognizing the region's uncertain political and economic environment, but taking into account the growing commitment of Central American countries to put in place significant structural reforms, the World Bank's principal objectives in the region are to: 1) support the implementation of sound country economic stabilization and growth oriented adjustment programs through both IBRD/IDA lending as well as the continued provision of economic analysis and advice; 2) support the establishment of an aid coordination framework for the region as a whole—in partnership with the IMF, IDB, the UNDP, and major bilateral donors—which can offer the region an efficient and flexible mechanism for providing sustained high levels of financial and technical support over the medium to long term, help maintain consistency in the policy dialogue with the region, and help ensure overall coordination and division of labor between various donors; and 3) help the region— through our support of country and regional initiatives—to liberalize its trade with the rest of the world, improve the private investment climate, and more fully integrate the region into global markets, while also reducing barriers to intra-regional trade. In pursuing these broad objectives, the bank attempts to follow an integrated regional approach that combines both support for individual country programs and projects with support for region-wide initiatives that would strengthen the focus on key adjustment and sector priorities, enhance prospects for mobilizing additional external resources, and ensure adequate attention to major region-wide issues, such as in respect to trade and the environment.

The United States and the IDB are expected to continue to provide the bulk of resources to the region, with the bank maintaining its current share as the third largest contributor. The composition of the bank's share, however, is shifting to allow 1) greater access to IDA funding for those countries that qualify, and 2) a moderate increase in IBRD lending to strengthen the bank's role as a credible partner in the adjustment process and to attract co-financing. Given the expected constraints on new resources from bilateral sources and the limitations on multilateral lending if debt service constraints are taken into account, the Bank's objective is to play a catalytic role in securing both additional concessional resources and encouraging higher levels of foreign private investment.

Within the context of the broad objectives cited above, the World Bank's expanded effort in the region focuses on six policy issues or development tasks that are critical to the success of the recovery effort.

The first task is to help the countries accelerate growth through the design and implementation of comprehensive adjustment and recovery programs. Although each of the Central American countries must tailor its adjustment program to fit its particular economic and political circumstances, there are several essential requirements for a successful adjustment that apply to all. These include strong political commitment, adequate preparation and design of key measures, and sufficient arrangements to implement and monitor the adjustment programs. In addition to structural and sectoral adjustment lending, coupled with an expanded economic and sectoral analysis program, particularly in Nicaragua and Panama where economic work has not been carried out for some time, there is also the need to expand technical assistance. Enhanced technical assistance provided through a coordinated effort of various other aid agencies (UNDP, IDB, IMF) could provide the region with a further source of economic and sector advice and further strengthen country efforts to undertake urgent adjustment and development tasks.

The second task is to resolve current arrears problems and find ways to reduce the region's substantial debt burden. During the 1980s the region's medium and long term debt burden more than tripled, from US $8.7 billion to U.S.$27 billion in 1989. Although the size of the debt burden varies substantially from country to country, it constitutes a major constraint on growth. With three countries in non-accrual (Nicaragua, Guatemala, and Panama) and one country (Honduras) only recently out of non-accrual status, resolving arrears problems and preventing new debt servicing problems, is clearly critical to future bank involvement in the region.

To address the debt issue the bank, together with the other international financial institutions (IFIs), must consider new approaches to eliminate arrears and keep overall external debt service at manageable levels. This will require finding a way to lower the existing burden of non-concessional debt—through debt service reduction agreements with commercial creditors and the refinancing of official debt with concessional funds—while mobilizing new money at concessional rates, including increased use of IDA during the initial adjustment period for qualifying countries. The recent initiatives on debt announced by the U.S. and the expected bigger participation of EEC and Japan in these efforts are a welcome step in finding new ways to approach debt problems. Availability of increased concessional funds for Central America's adjustment and development policies would boost resource flows and give the international donor community added leverage in supporting strong country performance.

The third task is to facilitate and encourage a much more substantive and larger role for the private sector in the process of economic recovery and in meeting medium-term development goals. This requires steps to eliminate excessive regulatory controls and government intervention in the economy as well as actions to strengthen incentives to promote increased private sector investment, including the return of flight capital and the inflow of private foreign investment. It will also require actions to facilitate increased investment in the agricultural sector, which remains the principal and most important productive sector in the region. Central America's recovery will depend heavily on the private sector's willingness to invest and provide the new jobs urgently needed to meet basic economic and social goals. Bank supported adjustment operations, with their focus on macro economic and public sector management issues, trade reform and export promotion, agriculture sector pricing, marketing, and technical support, and financial sector reforms aim at restoring private sector confidence and opening the way for expanded private sector investment.

During the initial years of the adjustment effort, foreign private investment in Central America is likely to remain relatively low but should pick up when the adjustment and recovery efforts show success and political stability improves. Continued strong bilateral support in ensuring access to markets and facilitating foreign investment as well as the transfer of technology is also essential.

The fourth task is the sharp expansion of country efforts to alleviate poverty and improve social indicators. Progress in this area is critical, both to the welfare of the poor and to the region's political stability. With the exception of Costa Rica and Panama, all Central American countries confront serious deficiencies in health care coverage and problems of malnutrition. Alleviating poverty by only emphasizing aggregate growth is not sufficient, given the enormity of the problem and the sharp social inequalities in the region. If progress is to be made, governments must increase the coverage of basic social services with well targeted programs and offer better access to credit and technical assistance, particularly in rural areas.

Increased support for programs and projects carried out by local communities and local nongovernmental organizations (NGOs) is also important, including the establishment of social investment funds, which is being tried in Honduras, El Salvador, Guatemala, and Nicaragua with the World Bank, IDB, and other donor support. Given the difficulty of rapidly improving public sector management, reinforcing local community efforts and self-help programs may prove to be the more effective approach in the short term. Programs that target women can also be important, particularly since civil war and political violence in a number of countries has left many women as heads of households.

The fifth task is to help improve the mobilization, allocation, and management of public resources. Public sector financing and management issues are complex, and their resolution politically difficult. Resource mobilization in many countries has been handicapped by inadequate and poorly designed tax regimes, as well as by difficulties in implementing timely adjustments in public utility tariffs. At the same time poor or inadequate tax administration has further weakened revenue collections. Country efforts to improve resource allocation have been frustrated by ineffective planning and budgeting. Heavy military spending, especially in El Salvador, Nicaragua, and to a lesser extent in Honduras, has further reduced flexibility in the allocation of limited public resources. Finally, most Central American countries also confront serious problems in the financing and management of social security systems.

On the management side, many countries have used the public sector as an employer of last resort, thus burdening it with unnecessary staff. Bureaucracies are overly centralized, slow, and often operate with inadequately trained staff. Austerity programs have required drastic cuts in funding. As a result, investment budgets have been slashed, routine maintenance expenditures neglected, and materials, supplies, and operating budgets cut to the bone. Generally low pay scales, reduced even more by years of fiscal austerity, leave little room to reward good performers, exacerbating these problems.

To address these serious public sector issues, country adjustment programs must include measures to 1) strengthen public finances, including implementation of comprehensive tax reforms and steps to improve tax administration; 2) begin overhauling of needed social security systems to ensure future viability; 3) modify the resource allocation process (including planning and budgeting procedures and management) in a way that gives governments the capacity to ensure adequate funding for key programs and core investments (such as maintenance expenditures and social sectors programs), as well as the flexibility and control needed to manage revenue shortfalls (as the economic situation deteriorates) or large increases (windfall gains from export price increases or from the "peace dividend" as military expenditures decline) in a manner consistent with sound expenditure management; and 4) improve public sector efficiency through actions to streamline the decision-making process, including decentralization in some countries, as well as steps to improve pay and incentives and programs to facilitate retraining or personnel reductions as appropriate.

The sixth task is protecting the environment. Central America confronts serious and accelerating environmental degradation, which threatens medium- and long-term development prospects. The region's problems include rapid loss of forest resources (with most of the primary forest expected to disappear by the turn of the century) severe soil erosion, particularly in hilly and fragile tropical forest areas, as well as serious water pollution and watershed protection issues.

While there is increasing awareness in the region of the seriousness of environmental issues, efforts to tackle these issues are handicapped by weak public institutions, insufficient attention to environmental education, a tendency to adopt new technology without the accompanying actions needed to minimize harm to the environment, and the fact that short-term measures to spur growth and meet pressures from rapidly growing populations tend to conflict with efforts to ensure a more balanced use of natural resources over the medium term. Environmental degradation is also linked to the region's high poverty levels, since the poor must maximize their limited incomes without concern for utilizing land and forests in a more sustainable manner.

The region's environmental problems require increased attention by the bank and the donor community at large. As part of this effort, the Bank has increased its effort to do more to ensure that environmental issues are incorporated directly into the planning and preparation of country adjustment programs. As part of this effort, the bank has initiated additional economic work on environmental issues and has started preparation of free-standing environmental projects in a few countries. Nevertheless, additional efforts are still needed, including further work in developing practical and financially viable schemes for addressing environmental problems. In this regard, the ongoing USAID regional environmental initiative should help countries in the region to address these issues better.

BIOGRAPHICAL NOTES ON THE CONTRIBUTORS

Abel Matutes. Member of the Commission of the European Communities responsible for Mediterranean policy and Latin American, Asian, and North-South relations. Born in Ibiza, Spain, he received degrees in law and economic sciences from the University of Barcelona. He was mayor of Ibiza, senator for Ibiza and Formentera, and member of the Chamber of Deputies. He is a member of the Spanish Academy of Economic and Financial Sciences and honorary professor at the University of Buenos Aires, Argentina.

Joaquín Roy. Director of the Iberian Studies Institute and professor of International Studies at the University of Miami. Born in Barcelona, Spain, he received a law degree from the University of Barcelona and a Ph.D. from Georgetown University. His most recent books are *Cuba y España: Relaciones y percepciones* (1988), and *El pensamiento demócrata-cristiano en América Latina* (1991). He is also the editor of the *Ideas '92* journal.

Roy H. Ginsberg. Professor of International and Comparative Politics at Skidmore College in Saratoga Springs, New York and chairman of the European Community Studies Association of the United States. He received his Ph.D.in political science from George Washington University and is the author of *Foreign Policy Actions of the European Community: The Politics of Scale* (Lynne Rienner, 1989) and co-author of *The United States and the European Community in the 1990s: Partners in Peril* (Macmillan, 1992).

Angel Viñas. Ambassador of the Commission of the European Communities to the United Nations and Professor of Economics at the University of Madrid. Born in Madrid, Spain, Viñas was adviser to the Spanish Foreign Relations Ministry and director of the Commission of the European Communities for Latin America. He is the author of *Los pactos secretos de Franco con Estados Unidos* and *La Alemania Nazi y el 18 de julio.*

Fernando Cardesa. Ambassador and head of the Delegation of the Commission of the European Communities in Central America. Born in Spain, he received a law degree from the University of Zaragoza and a diploma in financial analysis from the University of Madrid. He was economic adviser at the embassies of Spain in Bolivia, Peru, and Indonesia and professor of political economy at the University of Madrid.

Wolf Grabendorff. Director of the Instituto de Relaciones Europeo-Latinoamericanas (IRELA), Madrid, Spain. Born in Germany, he studied in Frankfurt, Berlin, and the United States. He was a visiting professor at Johns Hopkins University, Washington, D.C. and is the author of *¿A dónde Latinoamérica?* and co-author with Manfred Nitsch of *Brasilien: Entwicklungsmodell und Aussenpolitik*.

Rafael Menjívar Larín. Academic Coordinator at the Secretaría General de la Facultad Latinoamericana de Ciencias Sociales–FLACSO, Costa Rica. Born in El Salvador, he studied in San Salvador, Mexico, and Chile. He was the president of the University of El Salvador 1971-72, and is the author of *La Pobreza en América Central* (FLACSO, 1990) and co-author of *Informalidad urbana en Centroamérica: Entre acumulación y la subsistencia*.

Rafael de Juan y Peñalosa. Professor of international economics at the University of the Basque Country. Born in Guipúzcoa, Spain, he has degrees in philosophy (1963), theology (1969), and economics (1973). He finished his doctoral dissertation at the Instituto Brasileiro de Desenvolvimiento (IBRADES), Rio de Janeiro, Brazil. Among his publications is "La CEE y Centroamérica: Un ensayo de cooperación global integradora" (1988).

Laurence Whitehead. Chairman of Oxford University, Social Studies Faculty and Official Fellow at Nuffield College, Oxford University. He is the editor of the *Journal of Latin American Studies* by the Cambridge University Press and was acting program director at the Center for U.S.-Mexico Studies at the University of California, San Diego. He co-authored *Transitions from Authoritarian Rule* with Guillermo O'Donnell and Philippe Schmitter.

Pierre-Henri Laurent. Professor of history at Tufts University, Medford, Massachusetts, and adjunct professor of diplomatic history at the Fletcher School of Law and Diplomacy at Tufts University. He received a Ph.D. degree from Boston University and has lectured at the College d'Europe, University of Freiburg, Université Libre de Bruxelles, and the University of Amsterdam. He is a contributor to *The Reshaping of Europe, 1944-1949* (1984) and *Making the New Europe* (1991).

Albert Galinsoga Jordà. Professor at the Law School of the University of Barcelona. He recieved a Ph.D. degree at the Autonomous University of Barcelona and won the "Maspons Anglsell" award from the Catalan government for the best dissertation concerning the European Communities. He is the author of "Entropía y Coalescencia en las relaciones CE-América Latina," in *Afers Internacionales*, No. 14-15, 1988 and *España y la política centroamericana de la CE*, Working Paper, IRELA, 1991.

Mitchell A. Seligson. Director of the Center for Latin American Studies and Professor of Political Science at the University of Pittsburgh. He received a Ph.D. degree from the University of Pittsburgh and co-edited *Authoritarians and Democrats: Regime Transition in Latin America* (1987) and *Elections and Democracy in Central America* (1989). Dr. Seligson has written several articles on rural studies and democratization.

Ricardo Córdova Macías. Ph.D. student in political science at the University of Pittsburgh. Born in San Salvador, El Salvador, he has published various articles on Central America. He is the author of "El Salvador: Análisis de las elecciones presidenciales y perspectivas políticas" (1989) and co-author of "Reflexiones en torno al estado en Centroamérica" (1990).

Gabriel Aguilera Peralta. Professor of political science at the University of San Carlos and of the International Relations Program at FLACSO, Guatemala. Born in Guatemala, he was a public official in Guatemala's Foreign Relations Ministry and director of the Central American Program on Social Sciences of the Superior University Council of Central America (CSUCA). Among his publications is *La dialéctica del terror en Guatemala* (1981).

Guillermo Molina Chocano. Professor of urban sociology and social theory at the Autonomous University of Honduras. Born in Honduras, he was a visiting professor at the Free University of Berlin and Florida International University. He is the author of various publications on Central America and researcher at the Centro de Estudios y Promoción del Desarrollo (CEPROD).

René Herrera Zúñiga. Professor of Latin American Studies and researcher at the Center for International Studies of El Colegio de Mexico. He is the author of *Centroamérica en Crisis* (El Colegio de Mexico, 1981), *La política exterior de México hacia Centroamérica* (1984), and *Relaciones internacionales y poder político en Nicaragua*, 1979-1991 (El Colegio de Mexico, 1991).

Victor Bulmer-Thomas. Professor of economics at Queen Mary and Westfield College, London University. He is the author of *The Political Economy of Central America since 1920*, (Cambridge University Press, 1987), *Studies in the Economics of Central America* (Macmillan, 1988), and editor of *Britain and Latin America: A Changing Relationship* (Cambridge University Press, 1989). He is also co-editor ,with Laurence Whitehead, of the *Journal of Latin American Studies*.

Cristina Eguizábal. Professor at the University of Costa Rica. Born in Costa Rica, she studied political science at Burdeos and Paris. She was a visiting professor at the University of Burdeos, Florida International University, and researcher at the Superior University Council of Central America (CSUCA). Dr. Eguizábal was the compiler of *América Latina y la crisis centroamericana: En busca de una solución regional.*

JoAnn Fagot Aviel. Professor of international relations at San Francisco State University. She received a Ph.D. degree from the Fletcher School of Law and Diplomacy, Tufts University. She was a visiting professor at Peru's Diplo matic Academy and has published numerous articles including "Nicaragua and the United Nations" (1988) and "The Enemy of my Enemy...the Arab-Israeli Conflict in Nicaragua", *Central America and the Middle East* (U. of Florida Press, 1990).

Mark Rosenberg. Director of the Latin American and Caribbean Center and professor of political science at Florida International University. He received a Ph.D. in political science from the University of Pittsburgh and has published numerous articles on Central America. Dr. Rosenberg is the author of "Central America: Toward a New Research Agenda" (1984), and is co-editor, with Philip Shepherd, of *Honduras Confronts its Future: Obstacles and Opportunities* (Lynne Rienner Publications, 1986).

John Booth. Professor of political science at the University of North Texas. He is a member of the editorial board of the *Latin American Research Review* and has served on election observer delegations in Nicaragua (1984, 1990) and Guatemala (1985). He is co-editor of *Political Participation in Latin America*, Vols. 1 and 2 (1978, 1979), author of *The End and the Beginning: The Nicaraguan Revolution* (revised ed. 1985) and, co-author of *Understanding Central America* (1989).

Mark Falcoff. Resident fellow at the American Enterprise Institute for Public Policy Research, Inc., in Washington, D.C., where he specializes in Latin American issues. He received a Ph.D. from Princeton University and has taught at the Universities of Oregon, Illinois, California (Los Angeles), and the U.S. Foreign Service Institute. He is the author of *Small Countries, Large Issues* (1984) and *Modern Chile: A Critical History* (1989).

Ambler H. Moss, Jr. Director of the North-South Center and dean of the Graduate School of International Studies at the University of Miami, Florida. Former U.S. Ambassador to the Republic of Panama and member of the negotiating team for the Carter-Torrijos Treaty. He received a law degree from Yale University and is the author of various articles on U.S. relations with Central America and Panama.

James H. Michel. Assistant Administrator for Latin America and the Caribbean of the U.S. Agency for International Development (AID), where he oversees U.S. assistance programs in 18 countries throughout Central and South America and the Caribbean basin. Former U.S. Ambassador to Guatemala, he received a Juris Doctor degree from San Louis University Law School. He is a member of the American Society of International Law.

Ford Cooper. U.S. Special Coordinator for the Partnership for Democracy and Development in Central America. He received a master's degree in government from Cornell University. He entered the Foreign Service in 1960 and held several positions in the Department of State, including deputy director of Caribbean Affairs and director of the Office of Northern European Affairs. He was a senior advisor to the U.S. Mission to the United Nations during the forty-fifth General Assembly.

Renato Iturriaga. General Director for Technical and Scientific Cooperation at Mexico's Foreign Ministry. He received a doctorate in science from Carnegie Mellon University, Pittsburgh, and was the Director of the Consejo Nacional de Fomento Educativo (CONAFE). He was a professor at the National Autonomous University of Mexico (UNAM) and a visiting professor at the University of Illinois. Dr. Iturriaga is the author of various publications on scientific research and technological development.

Marko Voljc. Division Chief for Central America and Panama, Country Operations Division, The World Bank. A native of Yugoslavia, he studied at the University of Ljubljana and the University of Belgrade. He was the director of Yugoslavia Central Bank's Research Department. Since 1979, he has been with the World Bank, as a project officer for industrial projects in Latin America; senior economist at the Bank's Industrial Department, and resident representative to Mexico.